The Wisdom Within

The Wisdom Within

A Parashah Companion

Jonathan Shooter

TARGUM/FELDHEIM

First published 2002
Copyright © 2002 by Jonathan Shooter
ISBN 1-56871-223-5

Published by:
TARGUM PRESS, INC.
22700 W. Eleven Mile Rd.
Southfield, MI 48034
E-mail: targum@netvision.net.il
Fax: 888-298-9992
www.targum.com

Distributed by:
FELDHEIM PUBLISHERS
202 Airport Executive Park
Nanuet, NY 10954
www.feldheim.com

Printed in Israel

בס"ד

Talmudical College Institute
for Advanced Torah Studies
Rabbi Binyomin Moskovits
Rosh Yeshiva

Midrash Shmuel

ישיבה גדולה וכולל אברכים
הרב בנימין מושקוביץ שליט"א
ראש הישיבה

ו' אב תשס"ב

ידידי המחבר ר' יונתן שוטר נ"י, הלומד אצליני שלש שנים בשקידה, הראה לי מקצת ספרו על פרשת השבוע. המחבר מלקט ומסדר בעניני יראת שמים לפי השקפה נכונה על כל פרשה וגורם להקוראים להתעניין בדבריו.

ויה"ר שכשם שדברים אלו זכו להתפעלות כשיצאו לראשונה בכל שבועה, כן יזכה ספר זה להיות מקובל אצל הקוראים.

הכו"ח לכבוד התורה ולומדי'

הרב בנימין מושקוביץ
ראש הישיבה

YESHIVAS BAIS YISROEL
Neve Yakov Mizrach

Kollel Zichron Shlomo - Bais Yehudah Leib
Shlom Bonayich Graduate Institute, Inc.

Horav Doniel Lehrfield
Rosh Hayeshiva

חרב דניאל לרמלד
ראש הישיבה

בס"ד

18th day of Iyar 5762
Thirty-third day of the Omer

Our Sages tell us that the commandment of teaching one's son includes teaching one's students as well. In the same way one takes pride and satisfaction in the accomplishments of one's son, so does one take pride and satisfaction in the accomplishments of one's student.

Therefore, it is with great pride and satisfaction that I find that one of our *talmidim*, Rabbi Jonathan Shooter from London, who learned many years in our yeshivah and has grown to be an outstanding *talmid chacham*, is now publishing a collection of Torah essays on the weekly *parashos*.

Rabbi Shooter's essays are both informative and interesting and, above all, give us all a message by which we can enrich our lives. I wish him great success in all his efforts and may the Name of *Ribbono shel Olam* be sanctified by his hand.

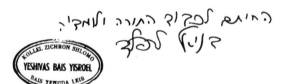

American Office:
MRS. HILDA CHILL - 212-388-0795
268 A East Broadway N.Y. N.Y. 10002
Suite 301

7/9 Rechov Harav Zevin
Neve Yakov Mizrach
Jerusalem, Israel

Phone: 02-5711343 **Rosh Yeshiva**
6562000, 835481 **Student Telephone**
6561959 **Office Telephone**
6561724 **Beis Medrash**

בס״ד

ראש חודש אייר תשס״ב לפ״ק

באתי בשורות אלו להגיד שבחו של תלמידי היקר האבר״ך כמדרשו ת״ח ויר״ש
מו״ה יונתן שוטר נרו יאיר, היושב באהלה של תורה בהתמדה גדולה, והוא עובד
ה' באמת ובתמים, והיות שהוא מוכשר בחכמת הכתיבה וכעת עלתה בידו ללקט
דברי תורה על התורה ושאר עניינים שונים, וראיתי דבריו שנכתב ונלקט בטוב
טעם ודעת ובהשכל, לכן אף ידי תכון עמו שיפיץ מעייונתיו החוצה ויהנו רבים
מאור תורתו, וחפץ ה' בידו להצליח בלימודיו ויזכה לעלות מעלה מעלה על במתי
התורה והיראה מתוך בריות גופא ונהורא מעילא עמו״ש

כעתירת הכו״ח לכבוד התורה ולומדיה

חיים היילפרין

Rabbi Elimelech Kornfeld
Rav Of Kehillas HaGra
16/9 Nachal Rivivim
Ramat Beit Shemesh

חרב אלימלך קורנפלד שליט"א
רב דקהילת חגר"א
נחל רביבים 16/9
רמת בית שמש
עמותה מס' 58-305-446-2

The Ramban writes in his introduction to his *perush* on *Chumash* that the term "Torah" is from the root *horaah*. The Torah is our *moreh derech*, our guide, to our proper approach to life. Our *emunah* and *bitachon* are built on our understanding of the creation of the world that is described in *Bereishis* and appreciating the constant *hashgachah pratis* that we witness throughout the Torah. Our striving for perfection and *middos tovos* is based on our appreciation of Hashem's great *chassadim*, which arouses within us a strong desire to follow in Hashem's great ways and the ways of our forefathers.

Even though the Torah is meant to be the source of our spiritual growth, one cannot properly take advantage of it without the deep insights and interpretations that were transmitted to us from the *gedolim* of the previous generations. Their deep understanding of the Torah and its values help reveal the powerful messages that are hidden in the Torah.

Rav Yonason Shooter, who is a *talmid chacham* and *yerei Shamayim*, has compiled a wonderful work that exposes us to many of these great insights and opens up our eyes to a deeper understanding of the Torah and its messages that can have a profound effect on our lives. I am sure that those who read this *sefer* will both enjoy it and grow from its wealth of *divrei Torah*.

יהי רצון שספר זה יהיה לזיכוי הרבים ושהמחבר יזכה להמשך לשבת באהלה של
תורה מתוך נחת והרחבה ויפוצו מעיינותיו חוצה לתועלת כלל ישראל ולכבוד שמים.

הכו"ח בכה"ית ובברכה,

Dedicated
in loving memory of

Abraham and Millie Lebetkin

Mark and Esther Shooter

Samuel Shooter

Hubert Shooter

Henry (David) Ewig

Chaim Shimon and Elizabeth Ewig

Dedication

Heinrich Rosenzweig
Chaim ben Aharon 1942

Paula Rosenzweig
Malka bas Alexander 1964

Oskar Rosenzweig
Meir ben Chaim 1964

Malwine Rosenzweig
Malka bas David Halevi 1993

David Feuerberg
David Zeinvel ben Eli Halevi 1920

Klara Feuerberg
Chaya bas Shimshon 1942

by
Alexander Rosenzweig

Dedicated in loving memory of

יוסף בן פסח אליעזר
Geoffrey Goldberg
by
Mrs. Michelle and Jonny Goldberg
and the Nassim family

Dedicated by
Sue and Alfred Birnbaum — London
in memory of their beloved parents

ר' דוד משה בן ר' שלום הלוי בירנבאום ע"ה
נפטר כ"א תשרי תשמ"ו
מרת חנה חדוה בת ר' צבי הירש ע"ה
נפטר כ"ג ניסן תשמ"ו
ר' שלום בן ר' יעקב אריה מינסקי ע"ה
נפטר י"ז מנחם אב תשנ"ח
יהי זכרם ברוך

לע"נ

אברהם בן אהרן יצחק

אלקסנדר בן דוד

פערל זיסל בת אברהם

לע"נ

רפאל ניסן בן יוסף

יוסף בן ניסן

נחמה פרומה בת פשע

Dedicated by
Edward Saleh

לעילוי נשמת

נתן יהודה בן אלעזר
חיה יהודית בת דוד
ברוך יוסף בן יהושע לב
רחל בת אשר יהודה

Dedicated by
Jonny and Henchy Kushner

לזכר נשמה

היבשא ראזנטאל ע"ה
ב"ר דוד ראטשילד
Mrs. Hedi Rosenthal

י"א אייר תרע"ו
14th May 1916 –
י"ג מנחם אב תשנ"ט
26 July 1999

Dedicated in loving memory of

ר' משה בן ר' יעקב ברוך ז"ל
Micheal Leigh
22nd Shevat 5754

and
מרת יעטא פריידא
בת ר' אברהם גוטמן ע"ה
Nettie Leigh
26th Shevat 5745

by their daughter Alison Riffkin
with Robert, Natasha, Joshua
and Zachary

לזכר נשמה

ר' מרדכי בן ר' שלמה ז"ל
אורמונד

נולד ר"ח לאלנות
שנת תרפ"ב לפ"ק
נפטר ביום הכפורים
שנת תשנ"ט לפ"ק

פעל הרבה בצדקה וחסד
באמונה שלמה בבורא עולם

Table of Contents

DEVARIM

Preface

In this preface I would like to answer two questions: firstly, how did this project start, and secondly, what is the purpose of this book. Oddly enough, you could say the writing of this book was inspired by a visit to the zoo. We were on an outing on *erev Shabbos, parashas Kedoshim*. While watching the monkeys, I couldn't help thinking how similar to humans they appeared to be. The following story came to mind. There were once some people traveling together on a train. Several hours into the journey, one of the gentiles asked an elderly Jewish man whom he had been observing, "Why is it that your grandchildren accompanying you on this trip are constantly helping you, bringing you drinks, making sure you're comfortable and all your needs are taken care of? Our grandchildren have no interest in us whatsoever." The elderly Jew responded, "This is the difference between our philosophy and yours. You teach your children that men are descended from monkeys. Therefore, elderly people are closer to monkeys, while the younger generation thinks of itself as more refined, more cultured and more educated than its predecessors, since it is further away from monkeys. We, on the other hand, have a teaching that the older generation is closer to the ultimate revelation at Sinai, where G-d spoke to the children of Israel and then taught His law to Moses, who in turn passed it on to others, in a process which has continued through the generations. Thus, the Torah previous generations learned is closer to the original source, making it purer and more authentic than our Torah is. When we hear a lecture from an elderly person, who in turn heard the teaching from his rabbi, we understand that the quality and authenticity of the teaching is greater than ours is, since it is closer to Sinai. That is why our offspring act as they do."

The next thought that came to my mind that day at the zoo was how the Ramban explains the opening verse of *parashas Kedoshim*, and how it tied in with the above story and the whole idea of human refinement. When I got home I began to put these ideas in writing. I then decided to expand on the concept and write about how several other commentators explained the same verse, each in his unique way. That week I e-mailed home to London what I had written for the benefit of all the family.

On the next Shabbos, as I was learning *parashas Emor*, I again focused on one particular issue and saw how different commentators dealt with it. I decided to send out an essay I had written on this topic to my shul in London, and I subsequently received very positive feedback on it. From there my writing continued and grew into a small e-mail list, and several of the people on this list began distributing the essays to other shuls. As the weeks went on, and I gained encouragement from the relatively small but loyal readership, I decided to go all the way and publish my work as a *sefer*.

What then is the need for another *parashah* book? I believe that these essays have remained consistent and have never diverged from their original purpose: to provide material that not only is readable, enjoyable and informative, but that can also be incorporated into one's everyday life as a Torah Jew. The essays were always meant to appeal to readers of all levels of knowledge, yet the concepts and ideas introduced in each chapter provide something for even the more advanced to think about. I have tried to pay particular attention to presenting the material clearly; as one reader put it, "You take difficult ideas and make them sound simple." Of course, there is room for further discussion and elaboration, but for the aims of this *sefer*, a balance had to be struck.

The train story above encapsulates a point about this book generally. The ideas within are gleaned from the words of a host of commentators, from many centuries ago up to the present day. The book does not contain *chiddushim* of the author; I have tried only to look to the words of our Sages and record how they answered the questions.

I would like to make one brief, final note on the structure of each essay, which tends to take one of two forms. One is to view a specific theme from the perspective of that particular *parashah*, and a second is to take one incident or question and examine several different explanations on it. I have tried to use stories wherever possible, for I believe they often bring out a point the best. It is my hope that these essays will be acceptable and pleasing to a wide audience, and may the Torah studied herein bring us closer to the final redemption speedily in our days.

Acknowledgements

First and foremost, I would like to publicly thank Hashem for the kindness He has shown my family in bringing us to this point, as well as for the publication of this *sefer*.

I would like to thank the staff at Targum Press for putting their experience and expertise into the production of this book. I thank in particular my proofreader, Mrs. Debbie Ismailoff, for her excellent and thorough job in bringing the manuscript up to scratch.

My profound appreciation goes to every one of the sponsors who contributed to this project, many of whom asked to remain anonymous or wished not to make dedications. Their desire to support the spreading of Torah and its commentaries is truly admirable. May they be blessed with all forms of blessing from "the One Who is the Source of all blessings."

I would also like to thank those who distribute my weekly *parashah* sheet, thereby helping to spread Torah to a wider audience — my father-in-law, Henry Ehreich, and Edward Saleh and Jonny Kushner.

Rav Binyomin Moskovits, rosh yeshivah of Yeshivas Midrash Shmuel, has created a *makom Torah* in which I have found the

drive for *emes* permeating every aspect of the learning, from ana-
lyzing a *gemara* to working on *middos*. I am grateful for Rav
Moskovits's personal guidance, as well as for the *chessed* that his
family always extends to us.

Rav Doniel Lehrfield of Yeshivas Bais Yisroel, together with
the *mashgiach*, Rav Avigdor Brazil and the other *rebbeim*, provided me with the foundations in Torah and *hashkafah* on
which I have tried to build.

I want to thank my parents, Alan and Susan Shooter, for all of
their help and support. While I worked on this project, their sug-
gestions were of great help, and in all matters concerning my
learning their encouragement has contributed significantly. Of
course, no words can express the profound *hakaros hatov* that I
have for the wonderful upbringing with which they have provided me. I pray that they continue to get much *Torah nachas*
from all of their children and grandchildren.

I thank my brother Mark for the help, support and advice
that he gave me while I was writing this book and that he gives
me at all times. I thank my brother Ben for faithfully fulfilling
his role as my older brother. May both of their families — Mark
and his wife Melissa, and their children Sam, Zack and David;
and Ben and his wife Katie, and their children Doron and Talia
— as well as my younger brother Simon and sister Sarah, be
blessed with much joy and success in all of their endeavors.

I also must thank my Uncle, Alex Rosenzweig, who has been
my *bein hazemanim chavrusa* for the last seven years. Learning
with Uncle Alex has certainly been one of the most happily an-
ticipated highlights of every trip I make to England. May we
merit learning together for many more years.

Acharonah acharonah chavivah, that which is dearest last: my
most heartfelt appreciation is for my wife Shoshana. Without her
support and encouragement, none of this would have been possible. She tirelessly edited the *parashah* sheets which formed the ba-

sis of this book. Her help, advice and intuition have been my *ezer* in all areas. May we merit to continue to have true *Torah nachas* and see our children, Yaakov Aaron, Ayala Malka and Shira Rivka, attain great heights in *ahavas Torah* and *yiras Shamayim*.

Bereishis

Shedding Light

The word "light" is mentioned five times in the opening verses of the Torah. Rabbeinu Bachaye comments that each one corresponds to one of the five books of the Torah. "Let there be light" symbolizes *Sefer Bereishis*, the book of creation. "And there was light" refers to *Sefer Shemos*, where *bnei Yisrael* were taken out from the darkness of slavery to the light of freedom. "Hashem saw the light" refers to *Sefer Vayikra*, as it contains the laws relating to sacrifices, representing *teshuvah*. "Hashem separated between the light and the darkness" corresponds to *Sefer Bemidbar*, where *bnei Yisrael* were divided into their various encampments. "Hashem called to the light" refers to *Sefer Devarim*, which contains many new mitzvos and a repetition of many earlier ones and is symbolic of the light of Torah and mitzvos.

What's the Point If Anyway...

Rashi on the verse "God saw that the light was good, and God separated between the light and the darkness" (*Bereishis* 1:6), says that when Hashem saw that the wicked did not deserve to benefit from the light in its full glory, He set much of it aside for the righteous to benefit from in the World to Come. If it was created just to be hidden away, what then was the purpose in creating it at such strength in the first place? Rav Dessler[1] compares this to a child who is taught Torah while in the womb, but is made to forget it before it is born. There we also ask, What is the purpose in the baby being taught Torah if he will subsequently forget it? The answer is that the child born will have greater ease in acquiring Torah, as he has already learned it once, even if it was forgotten, since he is just relearning what he once knew.

The same concept applies to the light that was created. Since it was once already in the world, it is easier for the righteous to obtain it in the future. We also see this concept in the very first line of the Yom Kippur service, when the *chazan* takes a Torah around the shul and everyone recites the verse "Light is sown for the righteous, and for the upright of heart gladness" (*Tehillim* 97:11). The message of the reward awaiting the righteous is a sobering thought with which to begin Yom Kippur.

Let us examine the exact nature of light, and then move on to see how we benefit from it. The verse says, "And the Lord saw that the light was good, and the Lord distinguished between the light and the darkness" (*Bereishis* 1:4). Rav Yonasan Eibeschutz[2] notes that good things can be recognized by contrasting them to their opposites. When one observes simultaneously a good person and an evil person, the good of the first is more easily recognizable when compared to the wickedness of the other. Similarly, the order of our verse should have been reversed; it should have first said that He distinguished between day and night, and only then would the light be seen as good. This line of thought, however, is relevant only to human beings. In contrast, Hashem sees the value of everything in absolute terms. He saw the light to be good even before the eventuality of darkness, as the verse in its real order indicates. However, in order for human beings to recognize its goodness, they have to contrast it with darkness; therefore, He then "distinguished between the light and the darkness."

What a Cave Dweller Knows

There is a great debate as to what is the exact nature of darkness. According to many philosophers, darkness is the mere absence of light, with no separate existence in and of itself. The Vilna Gaon[3] argues that darkness is in fact a creation in and of itself, as we say in *maariv*, "He forms light and creates darkness" (*Yeshayah* 45:7). Why is it that regarding day the word "forms" is used, but by night the word "create" is used? He answers that because Hashem gave light a form and perimeters to where it should spread, the word "form" is used. With darkness, He gave it no form, but simply instructed it to permeate any place where light does not rule. This is seen in our verse, "and the Lord distinguished between the light and the darkness." This is like air, which fills the entire world, but was created so that it moves away when an object or human being occupies its space and returns to that place when that person moves away. So too, whenever light moves from a place, darkness will fill the void.

The question could still be asked, Does it really make a difference whether or not darkness is a separate creation? Either way, in the absence of light there is darkness. The Netziv[4] explains that if one lights up a dark place, such as a dark cave, during the day, the flame will not light it up as it would during the night, which is the time when darkness rules. Apparently, people who dwell in caves know how to determine whether it is day or night using this principle. We find that the darkness that exists because of the absence of light is actually different from the darkness created to rule at night, and it therefore makes sense that it is a creation in its own right.

A Place in the Sun

The functions of light are next mentioned in the Torah's description of the creation of the sun and the moon and their setting in their rightful place. The Torah explains some of the purposes of their creation: "to distinguish between the day and the night, and they shall be for signs and for appointed times and for days and for years. And they shall be there for lights in the firmament..." (*Bereishis* 1:14–15). Rashi, on the words "for signs," says that when they are eclipsed, it is a bad omen for the world. Rashi then says, on the words "And they shall be there for lights," that they shall serve this function also. The Chofetz Chaim[5] says that we see from here that one would have thought that the primary purpose of their being created was to illuminate the world, and only then to have other uses. If one were to ask anyone what was the purpose of sunlight, he would reply that it was for the benefit of man, to lighten the way, to make plants grow, and so on. The order of the Torah tells us that the opposite is true. First it mentions that they are for signs and only then for illumination and other benefits. We see from this that the primary purpose of the sun and moon is to tell us about the situation of Yisrael and the nations of the world.

The sun's ability to create a distinction between day and night has important consequences. The resulting times determine, for example, when it is fitting to begin and end Shabbos. Likewise, when one davens *vasikin* one waits for the moment when the sun appears above the horizon to begin the *Amidah*. Similarly, the moon has many important functions. The Jewish calendar is based on the lunar cycle. This determines when Rosh Chodesh is, and as a result affects which particular day all the festivals will fall on. The interaction between the cycle of the sun and the moon tells us if a leap year should be observed, which has great ramifications for the determination of all the festivals. The Torah is telling us that the primary purpose was for this — to determine when day and night, Shabbos and the various festivals occur — and then the sun and moon have another, secondary function, to light up the land.

In a similar vein, the Alter of Slobodka[6] notes that of the twenty-six statements in the psalm *"Hodu...ki le'olam chasdo"* (*Tehillim* 136) three of them praise Hashem for the creation of light "to He Who made great lights...the sun for the reign of the day...the moon and the stars for the reign of the night." What is interesting is that the ending "for His kindness endures forever," applies equally to the verse praising Hashem for making the sun and moon, and the verses praising Him for setting them in their places. It follows that the correct placement of the sun and moon, with all its precision and ramifications, was equal in greatness to their actual creation.

A Hotel in Sun City?

Rav Yisrael Salanter[7] would express great joy and wonder during sunrise at the great benefits man derives from sunshine. He would say, "How fortunate are we, how thankful we must be to the Creator for His infinite kindness in bestowing such wonderful blessings on us." Rav Moshe Rosenstein asks, "What is the difference between Rav Yisrael and the rest of us? Why don't we also feel such joy at a sunrise?" He answers that there is a difference between our underlying attitude and that of Rav Yisrael. Human nature is such that one gets the most pleasure out of things that are exclusively ours. If one has an object in his possession that no one else has, he will derive great pleasure from it. If everyone else has it, one's pleasure is reduced. Similarly, we cannot have a full appreciation for the gifts of creation because everyone else also has access to them. Rav Yisrael was different. He overcame this flaw in the human character and so could derive the fullest joy from the gifts Hashem gave to mankind.

Once Rav Yisrael was in an expensive hotel in Paris and ordered a cup of coffee. When he looked at the bill he noticed the typically high price. He remarked, "Everyone knows the cost of a cup of coffee is very small, and yet they charged me many times the price it costs to produce. However, they are in the right. (Have you ever heard anyone say that when examining an expensive hotel bill?) Look at the magnificent building, luxurious garden and fountains, beautiful furniture and paintings...when I sit down to my cup, all these factors add to my enjoyment and pleasure at this moment, and that is why I am charged so much." He then continued, "So too, we are in the 'hotel' of Hashem. When sipping water one must think of all the surrounding benefits he enjoys — the ground he is standing on, the air he breathes, the blue sky over his head, the smell of flowers and the sounds of birds. By making a simple *berachah*, thanking Hashem for that water, he must acknowledge the enormous goodness involved in giving him this pleasure, and express gratitude for it."

What Noach Lived Through!

There is a famous dispute regarding the verse describing Noach as "a righteous man...in his generations" (*Bereishis* 6:9). Rashi comments that "some of our Rabbis interpret this as praise, that even in his generation he was righteous, despite the great evil going on around him. Others interpret the verse as somewhat derogatory; he was righteous only in his generation, but had he been around during the time of Avraham he would not have been anything special." We see that Rashi gives more credit to those who interpret it as praise, calling them "some of our Rabbis," while those who interpret it as a criticism are called merely "others."

There is a beautiful explanation from Rav Ilan Kodosh,[8] based on *Pirkei Avos*, that says that one should judge every person favorably. The explanation is that if one sees someone doing an action that could be interpreted in one of two ways, either that he is sinning, or that he's acting correctly, one should judge him favorably. Rashi is alluding to this idea, that when the Torah says Noach was righteous in his generations, one should choose the explanation that views him favorably. That is why he calls the people who interpret it this way "our Rabbis," while the ones who interpret it negatively are called "others."

Further on in the *parashah*, Hashem instructed Noach, "A light shall you make for the ark" (*Bereishis* 6:16). Rashi explains that according to one opinion this was a window, while a second opinion says it was made of a precious stone. The Pardes Yosef explains that the two arguments are really one. The opinion that says there was a window in the ark is also of the opinion that Noach was righteous by all standards; therefore, he was allowed to see the downfall of the wicked. The opinion that holds that the light was a precious stone is also of the opinion that the verse is limiting the praise of Noach; therefore, it was not appropriate for him to see the wicked perish. This is similar to what we find regarding the destruction of Sodom, where Lot was commanded not to look behind him as he escaped. Since he was saved only because of the merit of Avraham, it was inappropriate that he witness the destruction of others. In like manner, it was forbidden for Noach to see the downfall of the wicked, which is why he needed a precious stone to provide light.

Claim Not Upheld

Later on, Hashem instructed Noach to enter the ark, "for it is you that I have seen to be righteous before Me in this generation" (*Bereishis* 7:1). The Midrash says that the words "before Me" indicate that he was considered a tzaddik only before Hashem but not before the angels, as they all had accusations against him.

How can someone be righteous before Hashem but not before His angels? Furthermore, what sin did they accuse Noach of? Rav Zalman Sorotzkin[9] cites a Gemara (*Shabbos* 55a) that says that during the destruction of the First Temple, Hashem instructed that a letter be marked on the foreheads of the tzaddikim to symbolize that they should be spared the impending destruction. The *middas hadin* (attribute of strict justice) complained that surely they were also worthy of destruction, since they could have protested to the wicked but didn't. Hashem replied that their rebuke wouldn't have been effective. The *middas hadin* then claimed that while Hashem knew this, the tzaddikim didn't, and they should have protested anyway. Hashem accepted the argument and doomed them to destruction as well.

Similarly, Noach also didn't rebuke his generation, reasoning that he knew that his rebuke wouldn't be accepted. This claim would help only regarding Hashem. The angels, representing the *middas hadin*, would claim that although this was revealed to Hashem, it wasn't known to Noach, and he should have therefore protested anyway. Thus, Hashem said to Noach, "for it is you that I have seen to be righteous before Me." He was considered righteous only before Hashem, but the angels considered him guilty. However, since Hashem wanted to build a new world from Noach and his children, this time He didn't listen to the *middas hadin*. Additional proof that he didn't accept the claim of *middas hadin* is that this is the only verse in the entire passage that uses the name Hashem, indicating His attribute of mercy; in all other instances here the Torah uses the name Elokim, indicating His attribute of strict judgment.

Which One Was He?

Later on in the *parashah* we find the story of the Tower of Bavel, making this one of the most tragic *parashos*. What are the links between this and the episode with Noach, and what lessons can be derived from them? At the outset, Noach is described with a double praise, "a righteous man, flawless in his generations" (*Bereishis* 6:9). Why is it that later on, when Hashem instructs Noach to enter the ark, He says only one of the praises (*Bereishis* 7:1), "for it is you that I have seen to be righteous before Me in this generation"? In addition, why in the original narrative does the Torah use the plural "generations," while the later verse uses the singular "generation"?

The Beis Yosef[10] answers that Noach lived during two sinful eras. The main sins in the time of the flood were robbery and immorality, to name a few. By withstanding the temptations of his time, Noach earned the description "righteous," the same title given to Yosef for resisting the temptation of Potiphar's wife, following which he is referred to as Yosef Hatzaddik (Yosef the Righteous). By contrast, the sin of the Tower of Babel was an intellectual rebellion against Hashem, involving denial and idolatry. Noach remained loyal to Hashem, earning him the title "flawless," the same word used in the prohibition against idol worship, as the verse says, "You shall be flawless with Hashem your Lord" (*Devarim* 18:13).

Now we can understand the discrepancies. At the beginning of the *parashah* when we are introduced to Noach we are told of his overall qualities that sustained him throughout his life, referred to as his "generations," that he was both righteous and flawless. When he was about to enter the ark we are told only of the quality that saved him in that instance, being "righteous…in this generation."

Attention All Kabbalists

"In the year six hundred of Noach's life…the fountains of the great deep erupted and the windows of Heaven opened" (*Bereishis* 7:11). The Kotzker Rebbe[11] cites the *Zohar*, which says that this verse alludes to the six hundredth year of the sixth millennium (5600), which is 1840. Just like during the flood, the physical windows of Heaven opened, so too, in 1840 there was a great increase in human knowledge and scientific discoveries.

The industrial revolution began changing people's lives forever. In particular the steam engine was invented, which would change the world, opening it up to trade and travel. These events were already alluded to in the Torah thousands of years ago.

At the end of the *parashah*, during the story of the Tower of Bavel, the Torah describes members of that generation's conversation: "Come, let us make bricks and burn them in fire. And the brick served them as stone, and the lime served them as mortar" (*Bereishis* 11:3). Rashi tells us that since it was a valley and there were no stones, they made bricks instead. The next verse continues, "Come, let us build a city, and a tower...and let us make a name for ourselves."

What is the significance of this sequence of events, that we are specifically told that first they made bricks, and then a tower with which to challenge God? Rav Yosef Chaim Sonnenfeld[12] explains that the generation was obsessed with innovation and technology. Not having stone to build with didn't stop them; instead, someone invented bricks. The natural response to such discoveries is to think precisely as the Torah predicts: "My strength and the might of my hand made me all this wealth" (*Devarim* 8:17). Then one can go so far as to challenge Hashem. That is the lesson of this episode: the generation became so engrossed in their own technology that they forget their reliance on God. So too, we live in the most technologically advanced age; there is no end to the new discoveries and theories of science. Yet, every so often events occur that remind us of our limitations. The lesson from the *parashah* is that perhaps we are not as advanced as we would like to think.

The Best of a Bad Lot

Why was there such a great difference between the fate of the generation of the flood, which was wiped out physically, and as *Chazal* say, also lost its share in the World to Come, and that of the generation of the Tower of Bavel, which was only dispersed, and whose languages confounded? The Mikdash Mordechai[13] explains that the generation of the flood was corrupt in its morals, living depraved and base lives. This corruption would inevitably be passed on to future generations, who would grow up with the same values — or lack thereof — as their predecessors. By contrast, the generation of the Tower of Bavel was corrupt only in its ideology but not in its morals. The parents held erroneous beliefs, denying the existence of Hashem, but the children could still grow up having higher moral standards and values. They might also eventually reject the ideology of their parents. Therefore, the generation was allowed to survive.

With this in mind, we can understand Avraham's instructions to Eliezer, not to take a wife for Yitzchak from the daughters of Canaan, but to go only to the daughters of his birthplace, Aram. What was the difference between the daughters of the two places? Surely both nations were idol worshipers. The answer is that Canaan was the most morally corrupt of the nations. A wife from there would perpetuate this flaw in Yitzchak's offspring. On the other hand, the people of Aram were ideologically corrupt, which is a flaw that could be rectified in future generations; therefore, a wife from Aram was more suitable for Yitzchak.

On a War Footing

Most of what we hear about the life of Avraham regards his trials, *chessed* and other acts of piety, and yet in the middle of the *parashah* we find him in the midst of war. At first, there was an alliance of nine kings in and around Eretz Yisrael who all served Chadarla'omer, one of the kings. After nine years of such an arrangement, five of them rebelled against his authority. Finally, after thirteen years of putting up with the rebellion, the coalition of the remaining four kings went to crush it, once and for all. They went on a rampage across the land, and captured Lot, Avraham's nephew, in the process. Avraham took an army of three hundred and eighteen men and they defeated the four kings, rescued Lot, returned all the spoils and rid the world of this terror.

Doing the Right Thing

Why are we told of these events in such detail and what lessons do they come to teach us? To answer, we will look at a verse at the end of the episode, when the kings came out to greet Avraham following his victory. Particular mention is made of Malkitzedek, who brought out bread and wine to celebrate.

What is the significance of Malkitzedek's bringing bread and wine in particular? Rav Yehoshua Baumal[14] says that at the time following the war, the nations of the world were perplexed as to Avraham's conduct. He had always appeared as the pillar of *chessed*, and now it seemed as if he had undergone a change, becoming a man of war, on the same level as they were. Malkitzedek, by bringing out specifically bread and water, taught them that this was not the case.

We have a rule in *berachos*: any food which undergoes a change in appearance loses a level in *berachos*. For example, with oranges in their original form we make a more specific *berachah*, *ha'etz*, but when one squeezes them out for their juice, one makes the least specific *berachah*, *shehakol*. However, with bread and wine, undergoing change leads to an increase in the level of *berachah*. With grapes, for example, one makes *ha'etz*, but when one makes wine from them one says the more specific *berachah*, *hagafen*.

This idea is alluded to here. By bringing bread and wine, Malkitzedek was telling the world that the change in Avraham's behavior was not for the worse, but rather for the better. Avraham was not just another warlord terrorizing innocent people in order to be equal to the other kings in the region. Rather, he used the characteristic of strength and might to do battle against oppression and injustice. Rescuing Lot was his reason for going, proving that he did it all in the name of *chessed*.

What You've Got to Do, You've Got to Do

We still have to understand, why would Avraham put his life in danger to rescue Lot? Not only had he just banished Lot because of his wickedness, but Lot had chosen to live in Sodom of all places! The Be'er Yosef explains that before they separated, Avraham had given Lot his word that he would always come to his rescue, wherever he lived. Since Lot had been abducted, he felt bound to keep his word, even at great risk to himself, as failing to do so would cause a desecration of Hashem's Name.

With this idea we can also understand why this war was listed as one of Avraham's tests. With the other tests, such as Nimrod's throwing him into the furnace, or Sarah's being abducted, he was in a situation beyond his control. Similarly, with the *akeidah*, he was commanded by Hashem and fulfilled the commandment. With this test, however, he went of his own accord. The test was to see if he would risk his life for the honor of Hashem, and by keeping his word he sanctified the Name.

The Whole World Can't Be Wrong

When Avraham was informed of Lot's abduction the verse says, "And the refugee came and told Avram the Ivri" (*Bereishis* 14:13). The Midrash says that the word "Ivri" comes from the root *ever*, meaning "the other side." He was called this because while the whole world had their erroneous beliefs, he stood diametrically opposed to everyone else.

The Satmar Rav[15] asks, Why is it that throughout the rest of these *parashos* we find mention of Avraham's name, but never with the addition "Ivri"? The answer lies in the identity of the refugee. It was Og, king of Bashan, and we are told that he had an ulterior motive in his actions. Rashi says that he intended that Avraham should set out to rescue Lot and would get killed in battle, and that he would marry Sarah. Why did he imagine that Avraham would go out, against all the odds, to try and intervene? The answer is because Avraham was the Ivri, with the whole world on one side and he on the other, and yet he was not afraid. Of course he would set out to rescue Lot, which is why Og had hoped he would be killed.

Have Your Cake and Eat It Too

Og was ultimately rewarded with such an extremely long life that he was still around during the time of Moshe. We see from this an amazing concept. However wicked Og was, he was still rewarded for whatever good he did, but in time punishment ultimately came his way; he was eventually defeated at the hands of *bnei Yisrael* in the desert.

In addition, before the battle against Og Moshe was afraid that the merit of the mitzvah of informing Avraham would help Og defeat *bnei Yisrael*. Hashem had to specifically tell him not to fear Og, as that merit would not help him. Rav Yosef Zundel of Salant[16] remarks that from here we learn the value of a single mitzvah, and how Hashem rewards it even if done imperfectly. If Moshe, the greatest man who ever lived, who performed miracles and wonders to defeat the enemy, was worried about this corrupt Amorite who had done Avraham a favor even with such base intentions, how much more meritorious is a mitzvah done with pure intentions and lofty motives.

The following story[17] illustrates the power of a single mitzvah. In 1942 in Cracow, there lived a Jewish family with one child. As the situation deteriorated, they realized that the only way to save their son would be by having a non-Jewish family adopt him. They gave him to a gentile friend they thought they could trust and told her that if they survived the war she should return him to them, but if they should perish, she should contact their relatives in America, who would take him. Their only request was that he be raised a Jew.

Inevitably the couple were killed. The gentile friend raised him as her own, and being a devout Christian, began taking him to mass and taught him the hymns, so that the boy became a Christian in nature. In 1946, she decided it was time to have him baptised. She took him to the local church, where the priest inquired how it was that a ten-year-old boy had still not been baptised. The woman told the priest all the details of the story. The priest, for his part, told her she was acting improperly and that the wishes of his parents should be honored, following which she arranged for the boy to go to America.

The boy grew up and kept in touch with the lady, always feeling a great debt of gratitude to her. He grew up as a religious Jew and became very successful, always remembering the kindness done to him when he was a child. In 1978, the lady, who was getting on in years, wrote to him telling him of her faith-based dilemma as she raised him and her initial decision to have him baptised. She also revealed the name of the priest who convinced her otherwise: Karol Wojtyla, more commonly known as Pope John Paul II. The Bluzhever Rebbe remarked about this incident that although we cannot begin to fathom Hashem's ways, just maybe this young priest was rewarded for his actions by becoming the pope.

An Hour of Glory

There is another example in this *parashah* of how Hashem rewards good, even if later on punishment will come. Following the war of the kings, it says, "After these events the word of Hashem appeared to Avram, saying ...I am Hashem Who took you out...to give you this land to inherit it" (*Bereishis* 15:1,7). The words "after these events" usually indicate a connection between the previous and current events. What then is the connection between the war of the kings and Hashem's promise to give the land to Avraham's descendants?

The Meshech Chochmah explains that at the time this promise was given, the Canaanite people were in the process of conquering the land from the previous inhabitants. It was precisely at this time, with the Canaanites capturing city after city, seemingly unstoppable in their conquest, that Hashem chose to reveal this promise, to show how powerful His word is and that no army in the world can prevent His will being carried out. The Torah tells us that after the great war of the kings, Sodom emerged victorious, despite it eventually being doomed to destruction for the sins of its inhabitants. Its prisoners were returned, booty restored and its people subsequently lived in peace.

Why did Hashem arrange such miracles for a doomed city? We see that Hashem guides events according to His will. Once the city went beyond the point of no return it would receive its punishment, but until then it would remain in peace, even having miracles performed on its behalf. So too with the Canaanites. Eventually they would also be removed from the land, with Avraham's descendants inheriting it. Until then, however, they could still progress as conquerors. They would enjoy their hour of glory, but in the end it would all be to no avail. Hashem had promised it to His chosen one and his descendants.

Passed Down the Generations

Avraham Avinu is portrayed as the epitome of *chessed*, and in particular the Torah describes his involvement in *hachnasas orchim* (welcoming guests). We first find this in last week's *parashah*, when the Torah tells us the exact location where Avraham pitched his tent, between Beit El and Ai.

What is the reason for the place being mentioned in such detail? The Chofetz Chaim[18] answers that just as a person opening a business searches to find a location where he will be successful, so too, one must search for a place to live which will have a positive influence on his observance of mitzvos. The verse teaches us that Avraham searched to find a suitable place where he could practice *hachnasas orchim*, and publicize the Name of Hashem. He deliberately pitched his tent between these two great cities, as there would have been a great flow of traffic between them, with plenty of people passing whom he could welcome. This motivation of Avraham's is further proven in our *parashah* when he relocates following the destruction of nearby Sodom and its cities. Rashi tells us that because the cities were destroyed, there would be no more passersby, so it was time for him to move on.

Avraham's Agenda

On the third day following Avraham's bris, Hashem made it particularly hot so that visitors would not trouble him. The Gemara (*Bava Metzia* 86b) says that since Hashem saw that Avraham was troubled that no one was passing by, He sent three angels disguised as men to visit him.

Why was Avraham so troubled that he didn't have any visitors? Surely the mitzvah applies only when the opportunity presents itself; certainly he could not have been faulted for there not being any travelers. Furthermore, what was the purpose of his entertaining angels? Surely they don't count as human guests to fulfill this mitzvah.

Rav Shlomo Hymen,[19] the rosh yeshivah of Torah Vodaath, answers that Avraham had two intentions in his welcoming of guests. Firstly, he wanted to fulfill the essence of the mitzvah, which was to feed hungry travelers. Secondly, he wished to teach other people about the attribute of *chessed*, so that they should subsequently emulate his example. Even though in this instance he could not fulfill the mitzvah of welcoming guests, he still wanted to teach people about *chessed*. By welcoming these angels, although he couldn't feed them, he could still fulfill the other aspect: people would still learn from him about performing this mitzvah.

As a side point, since Avraham knew they were angels, why did he offer them bread and other foods? Surely angels don't eat, and yet the Torah writes that they ate. One answer is that Avraham was on such a high level that everything he did or made was permeated with holiness and purity. Therefore, even the bread he baked was transformed from a normal food into something which even spiritual beings such as angels could eat.

How Did He Know?

The *parashah* begins by saying that "Hashem appeared to him" (*Bereishis* 18:1) and yet the next verse says that upon seeing the three "men" he ran towards them. The Gemara (*Shabbos* 127a) says that Avraham asked Hashem to excuse him while he greeted the guests, from which it is inferred that *hachnasas orchim* is greater than an encounter with the Divine Presence. The question is asked, how did Avraham know this? The question is further strengthened when we consider that the Mesillas Yesharim says that the whole purpose of a mitzvah is to form a relationship with Hashem. Surely an encounter with Hashem is the ultimate in closeness, far surpassing any mitzvah. How then could Avraham justify his actions?

Rav Yaakov Shimshon of Shepitivke[20] says that when Avraham noticed the unusual intensity of the sun beating down, he realized that Hashem had made this happen so as to relieve him of the burden of welcoming guests while he was in pain from his bris. Since he also was in the Presence of Hashem, he surely would have been exempt anyway. When Hashem then sent guests, Avraham reasoned that it must be that hospitality takes precedence over a Divine encounter, and that he was meant to greet them and was therefore required to leave Hashem.

Rav Shach[21] says that in fact hospitality does take precedence over a meeting with the Divine Presence. With such an encounter he is standing before Hashem, while with welcoming guests he is doing even better than that, by actually emulating the attributes of Hashem. The Slonimer Rebbe[22] explains with a parable. A traveler once came to a town and his friend invited him into his home and gave him royal treatment. On a different occasion, another friend did the same to the son of his friend. Obviously, the second person was the more devoted, as his honoring of guests extended even to the friend's son. Although the first honored his friend, there is no indication that he would have done the same for his son, with whom he was not acquainted. So too, we can understand why hospitality would surpass a meeting with the Divine Presence. If the encounter with Hashem is an expression of devotion, then hospitality is even greater, as one's love for Hashem is so great that he even shows kindness to His children.

A Tale of Two Welcomings

When the angels went to destroy Sodom, they first had to rescue Lot. He took them into his house for the night, undeterred by the threat of punishment for this heinous crime. The Torah describes at great length Avraham's hospitality to the angels, while it gives no credit to Lot for his taking in guests. On the surface, Lot acted with considerable self-sacrifice, risking his life to bring in guests, much against the practice of his neighbors the Sodomites. Rav Yosef Shaul Nathanson[23] notes the difference between the two acts. The Torah describes that the travelers appeared to Lot as angels, and that was why he took them in. Therefore, this could not be remembered as one of the greatest acts ever; despite the inherent danger it was only because they were angels that Lot took the risk. With Avraham, the angels appeared to him simply as men, and he treated them with much honor, even while in considerable pain. Treating traveling Arabs this way on a boiling hot day certainly indicates something special.

Hurry... No, Don't Hurry

We find that when Avraham gave instructions regarding the preparation of the cakes he instructed Sarah to hurry, while he gave no such instruction regarding the preparation of the meat (although the lad did run of his own accord). Why didn't he order that the meat be prepared quickly as well? Rav Yisrael Salanter[24] explains that there are two situations when providing another with food is a mitzvah. The mitzvah of *tzedakah* is such that one is required to feed a hungry person under any circumstances. There is also the mitzvah of *hachnasas orchim*, which dictates that one must feed a person who is far from home, even if he has means of his own. If a traveler is both poor and hungry, one fulfills both mitzvos.

The hospitality one extends to a poor and hungry traveler will differ from that extended to a rich traveler. The poor man must be fed immediately, as he is desperate for food and delay could even endanger his life. On the other hand, the rich person must be given all the courtesies he is accustomed to. Therefore, to place food in front of him straight away, as one does with a poor person, could even be considered a slight to his honor.

The problem arises in the event of hosting a guest of an unknown background. One could give him his meal straight away but risk offending him, or withhold food and risk starving an impoverished man further. Rav Yisrael answers that one should give him something straight away to take the edge off his hunger, and serve him the full meal slightly later on. This is seen with the travelers who came to Avraham. He had no idea whether they were rich or poor, so he instructed that they be given cake straight away in case they were poor and starving. However, the main meal could be prepared in the usual manner, in the event that they were people of wealth.

Tales from Har Nof

We have a concept, *maaseh avos siman labanim*. In short, it means that whatever our forefathers went through was a sign for what their descendants would endure and become. This principle has effects on many character traits. We learn the trait of *chessed* from Avraham Avinu, and in particular its expression in the mitzvah of *hachnasas orchim*. One example I personally experienced was during one of my first Shabbasos in Israel. The yeshivah had set us up to spend a Shabbos in Har Nof, to sleep and eat at different families and experience life in a Jerusalem Torah-observant neighborhood. After we finished davening on Friday night my friend and I made our way to the address of the host family. Upon knocking on the door, we were a little surprised to find that no one answered. We thought maybe they had just stepped out for a minute, or were late back from shul, but as the minutes passed we realized they were not there and weren't going to come either. Before we could even begin thinking what to do next, a neighbor came along, in full chassidishe garb, and asked us in perfect English if we were waiting for that family. He then informed us that their child had had an accident and they were spending Shabbos with him in the hospital. Somehow the message had not been passed on to the right person. Without batting an eyelid, he proceeded to invite us into his home, and we gladly accepted.

It was only a while later that I really appreciated what that man had done for us. By taking the two of us in, he certainly helped us, but it was only at great sacrifice to himself. Because it was Shabbos his wife could not cook up more food; rather, there was less food for them, and they were a large family. Nevertheless, his only consideration was to fulfill the mitzvah, as well as to educate his children in it.

This is only one example of the many acts of *chessed* going on in Har Nof. As well as the open doors that exist, there are also the numerous *gemachim* which operate. Many of them are for the poor, such as the numerous free-loan funds, but many are for the benefit of the wider community. For example, if one has guests for Shabbos and needs a cot, instead of investing in a new one, one can borrow one for the duration. Once, our electric hotplate broke on a Friday afternoon, of all times. Within half an hour, we had located the nearest *gemach* and borrowed one. The trait of Avraham Avinu is alive and kicking in his descendants.

Shidduchim

This week's *parashah* is known as *parashas shidduchim* because it contains the guidelines, some specific, some more subtle, that our forefathers laid out for finding one's wife (or husband). Avraham sent his trusted servant Eliezer to find a wife for Yitzchak, from the place of his birth, Canaan. Eliezer prayed that Hashem would make his mission successful, with the request that the girl who would come to the well and offer him and his camels to drink would be the one sent for his master, with her acts of kindness proving that "her You will have chosen" (*Bereishis* 24:14). Rashi comments that she would be fitting for Yitzchak because she would perform acts of kindness, making her a worthy choice to marry into the house of Avraham.

Why is it that this attribute in particular would make her fitting for Yitzchak? Surely there are other worthy traits she could possess which would make her equally as fitting. The Chasam Sofer[25] answers by citing the comment of the Sages on the verse talking about the creation of the first woman: "I will make for him a helper against him" (*Bereishis* 2:18). Surely it is contradictory that one could be a helper, and yet be against him at the same time. The explanation is that if the nature of a woman is different from that of her husband, then she will be a helper to him. If they have exactly the same traits then they will both just maintain the same weaknesses, and their opportunities for growth will be limited. The optimal situation is joining two people with different characteristics, each complementing one another, building on each other's strengths, just like two pieces of a jigsaw puzzle, with the jagged edges of each as well as the main part of the pieces forming the full picture.

While Avraham Avinu was the epitome of *chessed*, Yitzchak had the characteristic of *din* (strict justice). This is where the term *pachad Yitzchak* (the fear of Yitzchak) comes from; his strength lay in Divine service and prayer. Therefore, it was appropriate that Yitzchak's wife should embody a different trait, *chessed*, which is why Eliezer said that by seeing these special acts, he would see that it is "her You will have chosen."

It's All in the "Eyes"

The Gemara (*Taanis* 24a) says that if a *kallah's* eyes are of good appearance, the rest of her does not need examination. Firstly, surely there are many people in the world whose eyes are nice, and yet the rest of them are ugly. Secondly, how can the saintly Rabbis of the Gemara, each capable of reviving the dead, give such shallow advice to look only at beauty? After all, the verse says, "False is grace and vain is beauty" (*Mishlei* 31:30).

The Kli Yakar answers that certainly the advice given here is to look at her actions, and especially to see whether she has an *ayin yafe* (a generous eye) and she does acts of kindness. The Gemara is telling us that if she is worthy in this area, one can be sure that all her other attributes are in order as well. This is learned from Eliezer, who saw fit to scrutinize Rivkah only in this aspect, from which he would know about her other attributes.

The Situation on the Ground

The verse relates that upon Eliezer's return "he told Yitzchak all the things that had happened to him" (*Bereishis* 24:66). Rashi comments that he told him of all the miracles that had happened to him on the way — the earth contracting for him, shortening his journey; then his praying and Rivkah appearing instantly. The very next verse relates that Yitzchak brought her into the tent of Sarah his mother and married her. The Targum explains that only when he saw that her actions were as worthy as those of his mother did he marry her.

Surely after hearing of all the miracles that had occurred, Yitzchak should have been sufficiently convinced that the match was *bashert*. Why did he have to wait to see her actions as well, since surely she was Heaven-sent? The Brisker Rav[26] answers with an important principle. Even in the face of all the signs in the world, Yitzchak was not impressed one bit. Only when he saw that Rivkah's actions mirrored those of his mother did he marry her. Very often people see what they think is a sign from Heaven, and they interpret it to mean it "has to be." However, the important lesson here is that only the facts on the ground should impress one. Keeping one's feet on the ground, being intellectually honest and just plain thinking straight are what is required in these situations.

Once there was a *yeshivah bachur* who went to stay in Tzefat for a Shabbos. As he went for a walk Shabbos afternoon a young seminary girl caught his eye. It was truly love at first sight. He wanted to go up to her and ask her name, but knowing it was inappropriate he resisted. The next morning on his way back to Jerusalem he made a stop in Amuka, the legendary place to daven for a *shidduch*. As he arrived he saw the same girl he had seen on Shabbos also praying for her *shidduch*. By the time he had finished, she seemed to have already left, but on the wall outside he found the siddur that she had been holding. He opened it up and saw that it had her name and phone number inside. He couldn't believe his find, for he realized that this was a perfect way to make his introduction.

When he arrived back in his apartment he found on his answering machine two messages from two different people, both suggesting a *shidduch* for him with the same girl, whose name was in the siddur! Not believing his luck, he eagerly pursued the marriage made in Heaven, and soon enough they were married. Four months later they were divorced. (So the story goes. Please draw your own conclusions.)

How to Ask

The Midrash says that four individuals in *Tanach* made improper requests. Three were answered favorably despite the improper request, while one was answered unfavorably. First, Eliezer requested that the girl who would offer him and his camels to drink should be the intended match for Yitzchak. The Midrash calls this an inappropriate request because it could have been a simple maidservant who would have come out, but fortunately Hashem sent Rivkah. Second, Kalev promised to give his daughter in marriage to whoever would capture Kiryat Sefer. He didn't know who it would be — it could have been a slave — and yet he was answered favorably when Osniel ben Kenaz captured it. Next, Shaul promised his daughter to whoever would kill Goliath; again Hashem answered positively by sending David. The fourth incident, however, ended in tragedy. Yiftach was in battle against Ammon and made a promise to Hashem that should they be successful in battle, he would sacrifice the first thing that would greet him on returning home, assuming it would be an animal. Tragically, his daughter was the first to emerge. The commentators suggest that either he actually sacrificed her, or he sent her away for the rest of her life, but either way this was a punishment for the inappropriate request.

Why is it that the first three people made improper requests, and yet were answered favorably, while the fourth request resulted in tragedy? The Beis Av[27] explains that all of the favorably answered requests involved *shidduchim*. This is one area of endeavor where one can ask Hashem to take care of him and rely on His intervention. One way or the other he will end up with his or her intended mate. On the other hand, Yiftach's request had nothing to do with *shidduchim*, and in that case, anything can happen.

Divine Promises or Not, Just Do It

Why do we find that when Eliezer went out to find a wife for Yitzchak, he first stopped to pray? Surely all marriages are in the hands of Hashem, for we have a principle that forty days before a child is born, a Heavenly voice announces who his or her intended is. Furthermore, Avraham was Hashem's chosen one in the world; in his hand were placed all the *berachos* in the world. He was explicitly promised that "through Yitzchak seed shall be called after you" (*Bereishis* 21:12), so why was it necessary to pray?

Rav Reuven Dessler[28] says that despite all of this, at the appropriate time — even before then — one still needs to pray. Similarly, we find that when Yitzchak was childless after many years of marriage, he still prayed, despite being promised by Hashem that he would have children. He might not have bothered; with a Divine promise perhaps he could have been complacent. From here we learn that every matter still needs prayer.

Weapons of War

Parashas *Toldos* contains the issue of the birthright, in which the spiritual role of Yaakov and the material role of Esav are clarified. Let us examine some of the critical events of the *parashah*. Esav came home completely exhausted, as Rashi says, from a hard day of murdering. Seeing that Yaakov had prepared a lentil stew, he requested some in order to revive himself. Yaakov seized the moment and demanded in return that Esav sell him his birthright, to which Esav readily agreed.

The commentators ask, why was it appropriate that Yaakov lured Esav into this trap? Surely it was not moral to prey on a hungry man and take advantage of him. The Beis Halevi answers that certainly it wasn't the issue of finances that was at stake here (especially since the law that a firstborn inherits a double portion may not have been applicable before Har Sinai). Rather, the matter of the firstborn was a purely spiritual one, indicating who would carry on his father's name, with its spiritual ramifications.

Hashem had told Avraham that only one of Yitzchak's children would carry on his name, and on that particular day Esav began to do evil, deviating from his father's ways so much that he could no longer be called a son to Yitzchak, never mind a firstborn. Only the one whose actions resembled Avraham's would be considered the firstborn. Therefore, the issue of actually carrying out the duties and spiritual responsibilities expected of the firstborn were irrelevant to him, as Esav said, "of what use to me is a birthright?" (*Bereishis* 25:32). His only interest was to deprive Yaakov of it. Therefore, Yaakov sought to buy it from him, since it was a case of one person with everything to gain, and the other with nothing to lose. This is also seen when Hashem says, "My son, My firstborn Yisrael" (*Shemos* 4:22). The question is, surely if one is the firstborn, isn't he also a son? Rather, the verse tells us of this extra quality of Yisrael: they are considered Hashem's firstborn, while the children of Esav are not only not the firstborn, but not even called His children.

Leave Me Out of It

The Beis Halevi explains another aspect of the sale. The Midrash relates that when Esav returned from the fields he asked Yaakov why he had prepared the stew, to which Yaakov replied that it was for the mourners, as Avraham had died that day. Esav then replied by denying Hashem: "If the attribute of judgment struck even the elder, then there is no justice and no judge."

Why did the death of Avraham drive Esav to heresy? Had he really expected him to live forever? Since Avraham himself had been promised that he would "come to your ancestors in peace," in "a good old age," surely his death at such an age confirmed Hashem's existence and how He fulfills His word.

The Beis Halevi explains that Hashem had informed Avraham that his descendants would be "strangers in a land not theirs" and that they would be afflicted. Upon hearing this, Avraham asked if he would also be enslaved, to which Hashem told him he would be buried "in peace." In other words, as long as Avraham was alive, the slavery would not begin. However, only part of Yitzchak's offspring were to endure this fate, the burden of exile falling on only one of them, as the verse says. "for within Yitzchak your seed will be called" (*Bereishis* 21:12) — only someone "within" them and not through all of them. When Esav heard of Avraham's death, he sought to avoid bondage. He got involved in evil and became a heretic so that he would not be considered the firstborn.

The Beis Halevi adds that this ties in with the Zera Beirach's explanation of the verse "Sell me this day your birthright" (*Bereishis* 25:31). Yaakov was telling him, "On this day, that the enslavement has become possible, sell it to me, whether the privileges of the firstborn, or the burden of exile, and this way you do not have to resort to heresy."

Sticking to One's Guns

Yaakov used a special ploy to receive the blessing of the firstborn from his father. He dressed up in the clothes of Esav and placed hairy skins over his arms, so that Yitzchak, who was blind, would feel him and think it was Esav. Yitzchak sensed things were not normal and made the famous declaration "The voice is the voice of Yaakov, but the hands are the hands of Esav" (*Bereishis* 27:22). The Midrash interprets the verse to allude to the fact that when the voice of Yaakov is heard in the shuls and in the *battei midrash*, then the hands are not the hands of Esav; there is no power in them. If the voices are not heard, then the hands of Esav have the power to do as they please.

Rav Zalman Sorotzkin[29] explains the Midrash as follows. When the sound of Torah and *tefillah* emanates from Yaakov, then the hands of Esav will be hands only to Esav, not affecting or harming Yaakov. If Yaakov forsakes Torah, and *tefillah* is also not heard, then the hands of Esav will have the power to act forcefully against Yaakov. In such a situation, it will be as if Hashem doesn't recognize His people as the chosen, treasured ones. This is alluded to in the very next verse: "But he did not recognize him because his hands were hairy like the hands of Esav his brother." This refers to the fact that under such circumstances, when Yaakov's acts are devoid of spirituality like Esav's, then Hashem won't recognize him, and Esav's hands will have permission to be upon him.

Rav Yoel Shurin[30] asks an interesting question on the above Midrash. Surely in this very incident we find that simultaneously "the voice is the voice of Yaakov," and yet the hands involved are those of Esav (even if not literally, yet Yaakov did place goatskins on his arms to have this effect). How could this be, considering the above Midrash that says only one of these forces has power at any one time? The answer lies in the conduct of Yitzchak. He was seeking to channel blessing to Esav, but Yaakov came before him with his own voice, and yet with hands like Esav's. Surely in light of this confusing state of affairs he should have waited to clarify the matter before giving the blessing. Why then did he give it straight away? From here we see that Yitzchak knew that since the voice was Yaakov's, the hands of Esav would have no effect, and he could give the blessings immediately. Since the voice was Yaakov's, it didn't matter that the hands of Esav's were also lurking there.

Annulling Tears

The verse relates that when Esav returned from hunting and discovered what Yaakov had done, "He cried out an exceedingly great and bitter cry" (*Bereishis* 27:34). The Midrash relates that he cried three tears, each alluded to in the phrases "he cried out," "exceedingly great" and "bitter." The Midrash continues that Mashiach will not come until the tears of Esav have ended.

The question is, why does Hashem care about Esav's tears? Myriads of Yaakov's descendants have been crying for nearly two thousand years and Mashiach has not yet come. Rav Shmelke of Nikolsburg[31] explains using a halachic principle, that a species mixed in with its own type is not considered annulled even by a ratio of one to a thousand. The tears of Esav are shed only because of *olam hazeh*, materialistic matters relating to this world. If the decendants of Yaakov come on the Days of Awe and also shed tears only about matters of this world, without a thought for the Kingship of Heaven, then their tears are of the same type as Esav's and do not annul Esav's tears. If, on the other hand, the tears are only for matters relating to Hashem's sovereignty and His ruling over us, then they can annul the tears of Esav, as they are a species mixed within a different species, which can become annulled. He continues by saying that many tzaddikim certainly pray for the sake of Heaven, but their love for the rest of Yisrael is such that they pray for the materialistic welfare of Yisrael as well. With all the prayers joined together, since they are of a species different from Esav's, they are able to annul Esav's tears, with both aspects of prayer being answered.

Tomahawks and Tehillim

In *parashas Chukas*, *bnei Yisrael* made a request to pass through the land of Edom (the land of Esav's decendants), who gave the response "lest I go forth against you with the sword" (*Bemidbar* 20:18). Rashi comments that they were saying, "You pride yourselves on the voice your forefather bequeathed you: 'We cried out to Hashem and He heard our voices.' I shall go against you with that which my forefather bequeathed me: 'By your sword you shall live.' " Reb Chaim of Volozhin[32] says that the very nature of Yaakov is the power of his voice, while Esav has the power of the force of his hands. Therefore, if Yisrael try to exchange their weapon, the power of prayer, and rely on weapons of war, they will not succeed. All attempts to win by physical might will fail, when "the hands are the hands of Esav" and they try to imitate Esav. On the other hand, if the nations try to use Yisrael's weapon of prayer, they will not succeed, as the verse continues, "and any tongue that will rise against you, in judgment, you will condemn." The reason for all of this is as the verse continues, "This is the inheritance of the servants of Hashem"; in other words, this is the Divinely ordained way that *bnei Yisrael* are to rely on.

License to Kill

Finally, Rav Shach[33] comments that if we look into the blessings given to Esav, we do not find any mention of them coming from Hashem; rather, they all come from Esav himself. So much so, that included in the blessing "by your sword you shall live" (*Bereishis* 27:40) is their ability to pick up the sword and smite to their heart's content whenever a desire to do so is aroused in them. On the other hand, with the blessing given to Yaakov, all the blessings were from Hashem directly, as it says, "may Hashem give you of the dew of the heavens..." (*Bereishis* 27:28). Therefore, even when Yisrael did go out to war with the sword, they couldn't do so of their own accord and at any time they chose. Rather, they had to ask the Sanhedrin, who would inquire of the word of Hashem on the matter, and only by His word would they go out to war. All of this proves that the attribute of physical power alone is something alien to the thinking of the descendants of Yaakov. Only through the power of the "voice of Yaakov" have *klal Yisrael* prevailed, and will they prevail in the future.

Visiting the Wall

One *motza'ei Shabbos* we went to the Kosel. As I paid the taxi driver and stepped out into the pouring rain, the driver handed me back some of the money and said something in Hebrew which of course I didn't understand. Following further clarification, it emerged that he wanted me to give the money to *tzedakah* to the poor at the Wall. I was struck by his eagerness to perform the mitzvah, and then I asked myself the following question: What is it about the Kosel, the site of the Beis Hamikdash, that inspires people and causes such religious feelings?

An Early Night

As I entered the forecourt, and ran into the covered area because of the rain, I realized that this meant I was getting closer to the site mentioned in the opening portion of this week's *parashah*. Yaakov was on the run from Esav and realized that he had failed to pray at the site where his fathers had prayed, so he backtracked. The verse says, "He encountered the place and spent the night there" (*Bereishis* 28:11). This place was Har Hamoriah. The Midrash relates that he prophetically saw the Beis Hamikdash in its destroyed state.

Rav Nosson Adler[34] relates that originally the site of the Temple was on flat land, and it was referred to simply as a place. This is seen in the verse describing Avraham and Yitzchak's approach to the site of the *akeidah*: "and he [Avraham] saw the place from a distance" (*Bereishis* 22:4). Following the *akeidah*, Avraham suggested that it was not fitting that the Divine Presence rest on flat land, following which the "place" became a mountain, as Avraham said, "on the mountain Hashem will be seen." When the Beis Hamikash was destroyed, the enemy said, "Destroy, destroy, to its very foundation" (*Tehillim* 137:7), and it subsequently became flattened and turned into a "place" once again.

Therefore when the verse says about Yaakov, "He encountered the place" and not that he encountered the mountain, *Chazal* derive that he saw it in its destroyed form. This is also alluded to when the verse continues, "for the sun had set." *Chazal* say that it was the sun setting early that day which caused him to spend the night there. This unnatural setting of the sun alluded to the destruction of the Temple, which also occurred earlier than it should have, two years before its scheduled time. This was so that the measure of sin would not have been even greater, condemning the Jews to complete destruction. Hashem in His mercy brought forward the time of the destruction so as to save *klal Yisrael*.

The premature setting of the sun was felt all over the world. When the shepherds gathered at the well, Yaakov told them that they had gathered too early: "Look, the day is still long; it is not yet time to bring the livestock in; water the flock and go on grazing" (*Bereishis* 29:7). Why did Yaakov have to inform them of this? Surely they knew that it was still early. The Sefer Torah Ladaas[35] answers that this was precisely because of the miraculous setting of the sun the previous day. Because it was unexpected, the shepherds were forced to water their flocks in the dark. Therefore, on the next day, they gathered earlier than usual because they were worried it would happen again. Yaakov, on the other hand, knew the reason why it set earlier, and reassured them that on this day it would set normally and they could carry on their grazing without fear.

A Look into the Future

Subsequently, Yaakov met Rachel at the well, and the verse says, "He raised his voice and wept" (*Bereishis* 29:11). Rashi explains that this was because he saw through Divine inspiration that he wouldn't be buried with her. The Be'er Yosef explains that he wasn't crying merely for their separation in death, but for the reason for it.

Rashi, in a comment later on in *Sefer Bereishis*, explains that following the destruction of the First Temple, the Jews would be led away in captivity to Babylon. On this most tragic, depressing of journeys they would pass Rachel's grave in Bethlehem, and her spirit would come out and bemoan what had befallen them and plead with Hashem for mercy. This is seen in the verse "A voice is heard in the heights, lamentations and bitter weeping; Rachel weeps for her children" (*Yirmeyahu* 31:14). The Be'er Yosef cites the Ramban, who comments that this alludes to the intensity and bitterness of her weeping, which would be heard even on the heights of the mountaintop where the Temple had stood, in the portion of her son Binyamin.

The prophet continues with Hashem's reply: "there is reward for your efforts...and your children will return to their borders" (ibid., 15–16). Rachel was buried outside the Cave of Machpeilah to enable her to cry at their plight in their hour of need and despair, when mercy was needed most. Thus, when Yaakov saw that Rachel would not be buried with him, he heard her loud and bitter weeping and then saw the causes of it. For this, he raised his own voice and wept at their fate.

Light at the End of the Tunnel

Returning to our original verse, Rashi derives from the phrase "he encountered" that Yaakov prayed at the site of the Beis Hamikdash, and instituted the *maariv* prayer. There is a *midrash* that cites the verse "Give praise to the Lord our strength; blow a *teruah* to the G-d of Yaakov" (*Tehillim* 81:2). This *midrash* asks why Yaakov is singled out here, and answers with a parable. Once a king had three friends to whom he showed a site where he intended to build a palace. The first looked and said, "You mean on that hill," and the king left him. The second said, "You mean in that field," and the king also left him. The third friend looked and said, "There's going to be a palace over there." The *midrash* says that Avraham called the Beis Hamikdash a mountain, as quoted above. Yitzchak called it a field. Yaakov, on the other hand, called it a house, as when he awoke he declared, "This is none other than the House of Hashem." The *midrash* then relates that Hashem said that because Yaakov called it a house even before it was built, it would be called by his name.

To understand this *midrash* we have to look at the significance of the prayers the forefathers institutued. *Shacharis* is prayed in the morning, a time of brightness and hope for the new day ahead. So too, Avraham's life was one of daylight, full of peace, security and plenty, and he was admired by all. He instituted the prayer to be said at a time when things are good. Rav Shlomo Breuer[36] notes that the first time the Torah mentions that Avraham prayed was when he gazed at the destruction of Sodom and Gomorrah. This teaches us that when things are good one must pray to and thank Hashem, but one must also look at what happened to Sodom and see what too much abundance can do to a person.

Yaakov, on the other hand, instituted *maariv*, which is recited at night. This is appropriate, as his whole life was one of darkness and troubles — running away from Esav, dealing with the deceitful Lavan, suffering through the episode with Dinah, and enduring the loss of Yosef. This teaches us that one must also pray at night when things are going badly. Yaakov first prayed *maariv* at the site of the Beis Hamikdash. At that moment, all he could see was night and desolation. However, he could still stand there and see the light at the end of the tunnel, at what would be there in the future.

Chazal say that one must mention the attribute of night during the day, as we say in the blessings before the Shema at *shacharis*, "He creates light and darkness." So too, one must mention the attribute of day during the night, as we say, "He rolls away the light from darkness, and the darkness from light." The lesson from here is exactly as mentioned before. During the day, when things are going well and there is great hope, one must remember how quickly it can change. Similarly, at night, when we seem at the peak of despair, the darkest of moments, we must remember the light that will soon come.

Now we can understand the *midrash*. Avraham looked at the site of the future Beis Hamikdash and saw a mountain. Yitzchak looked and saw a field. Yaakov looked, and despite the darkness and desolation saw that this would be the site of the future Beis Hamikdash, which is why it was called after his name. By extention, although the *midrash* says that it was his foreseeing the future destruction of the Temple which caused him to weep, nevertheless, seeing that the tearful prayers of his wife Rachel would be answered and that his children would again return to the land gave him the positive outlook to pray even at night. With this idea we can understand why the site of the Beis Hamikdash evokes such powerful emotions. Not only does it represent the glorious past of the Jewish people, but it also is the hope of the future, that we will be redeemed.

And When They Were Down They Were Up

Let us conclude with the following idea. While Yaakov slept at the site of the Beis Hamikdash, he dreamt of a ladder which the verse describes as having "angels...going up and coming down" (*Bereishis* 28:12). Surely the order should be reversed, with the angels first descending from Heaven and then ascending. Rav Chaim Berlin[37] answers that whether one is rising or descending depends on the location of his destination. Since in this instance, the Divine Presence was on earth, at the site of the Beis Hamikdash, the angels' drawing close was considered as rising, and their moving away was descending. This point also conceptualizes another aspect of the Beis Hamikdash — that it is called the resting place for the Shechinah (the Divine Presence) on earth. This was more openly felt when the Beis Hamikdash stood, with the many miracles that occurred there. Even nowadays, we still pray in the direction of the Beis Hamikdash, as from there our prayers go up to Shamayim. This explains why every year hundreds of thousands of people follow the footsteps of Yaakov Avinu and return there to pray and be inspired.

A "Love"-Hate Relationship

A s was mentioned earlier, in *parashas Vayeira*, we have a principle, *maaseh avos siman labanim*, which means that everything that happened to our forefathers is a sign for what would occur to their descendants. In this week's *parashah* we find Yaakov returning from the house of Lavan, about to face a confrontation with Esav. We learn from this encounter how to act in exile and in particular how to handle the hostile elements around us. This lesson is so important that before Rabbi Yanai would go to plead on behalf of his people in Rome he would study *parashas Vayishlach*, with its account of how Yaakov dealt with Esav, and would see how he could apply it. Let us examine some of the key events that give us these guidelines.

In 1933 the Nazi Party was already announcing its plans for the Jewish people. Seeing the situation deteriorating around them, one of the roshei yeshivah asked the Chofetz Chaim[38] what the fate of the Jews would be. He replied that the Germans would not be successful in destroying the Jews, as the verse says, "If Esav comes to the one camp and smites it then the remaining camp will be a refuge" (*Bereishis* 32:9). (In his preparations to face Esav, Yaakov divided the camp into two so that should one be struck, the other would survive.) The questioner was terrified at this answer and asked the Chofetz Chaim about the nature of the "remaining camp," to which he answered with the verse "And Mount Zion will be a refuge" (*Ovadiah* 1:17). Indeed, his prophetic words came to pass. Within ten years, European Jewry was decimated, but the enemy's efforts floundered at the gateway to Eretz Yisrael.

Brothers with Arms

The next instruction Yaakov gave us was to daven for help from Hashem: "Rescue me, please, from the hand of my brother, from the hand of Esav" (*Bereishis* 32:12). Why did he use this double expression, first asking to be saved from the hand of his brother and then also from the hand of Esav? The Beis Halevi answers that there are two ways Esav tries to destroy the Jewish people. First they try physical might, which began with Esav's descendants, the Romans, and continues throughout "civilized" history, involving cultured and enlightened nations acting as only Esav knows how. This is what Yaakov prayed to be saved from — "the hand of Esav."

Hashem protects His people, and eventually Esav realizes his efforts to completely destroy them are in vain, so he tries a different approach. By acting like a brother, Esav seeks to destroy Yaakov with his friendship and brotherhood. Esav accepts Yaakov into mainstream society, knowing this will weaken his allegiance to Torah and mitzvos. Because it is a more subtle approach, disguising itself as friendship, it is therefore more dangerous, which is why Yaakov prayed to be saved from "the hand of my brother." This also explains why he first prayed to be saved from Esav in the guise of a brother, and only then in the guise of Esav the wicked, indicating that he was more worried about the former.

A Frightening Thought

This fear of Esav's friendship also manifested itself during the lifetime of Yitzchak. We see that Yitzchak trembled twice during his lifetime. The first was when he was upon the altar about to be sacrificed, and the second was when he realized he had given the blessings to Yaakov instead of Esav: "And Yitzchak trembled a great trembling" (*Bereishis* 27:33). The commentators say that Yitzchak trembled upon the altar because he saw the future suffering his descendants would endure. The altar itself was symbolic of the countless Jews willing to give up their lives rather than abandon their faith for one moment. On the other hand, he trembled at the incident of the blessings because he saw the spiritual harm the sons of Esav would do to Yaakov through their befriending him. When Esav went out to hunt for his father, it was symbolic of his descendants befriending Yaakov by offering that they join him as partners in worldly pursuits, and offering him gifts in the process. It is interesting that the second type of persecution, the spiritual one, caused in Yitzchak "a great trembling," indicating that he was more worried about that type and the harm that would ensue because of it.

What Day Brings

Another incident that illustrates this point is Yaakov's battle with the angel of Esav. The Torah tells us that when the angel saw he could not prevail, he touched Yaakov on the upper joint of the thigh, and his hip joint became dislocated. At that point the verse doesn't mention any consequences of this action. It is only later on, when the Torah says the sun rose, that it describes that Yaakov was limping on his thigh.

Why does the Torah wait to tell us this? Rav Shlomo Breuer[40] answers that the battle during the night represents the darkness of physical persecution. Esav tries to damage Yaakov through pogroms, inquisitions and holocausts, which tragically cause much loss. However, because the "remaining camp" is a "refuge," all is not lost. With the sunrise, things appear to be much better; after all, it represents an age of enlightenment and "friendship" with Esav. That is when Yaakov is actually reported as "limping on his thigh." The damage is done when Esav takes Yaakov into society and accepts him as an equal. Millions of Jews were tragically lost physically through Esav's persecutions, but who can estimate the spiritual damage done by the friendly side of Esav? According to statistics, Esav the brother has done more harm than the worst of our physical enemies could ever do.

Real Enemies

Why is it that the angel of Esav fought only with Yaakov and not with either of his predecessors? The answer lies in what each of them represented. Avraham was the pillar of *chessed*. The angel, whose task was to destroy all vestiges of *kedushah*, could deal with that. Yitzchak represented Divine worship, which the angel also didn't have a problem with. Yaakov, on the other hand, represented Torah, characterized by the fourteen years he spent in the yeshivah of Shem and Ever.

Rav Elchanan Wasserman[41] explains, citing a *midrash* that says Hashem is prepared to overlook the three cardinal sins of idolatry, adultery and murder, but He does not overlook the abandonment of His Torah. This can be explained by the following comparison. If there are two sides at war, and one side has seemingly emerged victorious, the war is not over while the enemy still has weapons in its hands. The defeated side could make a counterattack and turn the tables. If the defeated party has its weapons taken away, the battle is over.

So it is with the battle against the evil inclination. Hashem has given us a weapon, as the Gemara (*Kiddushin* 30b) says, "I have created the evil inclination, but I have created Torah as its antidote." As long as *klal Yisrael* is involved in Torah study, even if they commit the most severe of sins, there is still a chance they will repent, since the weapon is in their hands. If they abandon Torah, the weapon is out of their hands and the evil inclination will emerge victorious. That is why the angel fought against Yaakov, who represented the power of Torah. The aspects of the other patriarchs he could deal with, but in order to defeat Yisrael he knew he had to "disarm" them.

A Bad Loser

Eventually the angel was defeated and Yaakov demanded that he bless him before he would send him away, to which he replied by changing Yaakov's name to Yisrael, "for you have fought with lords and people and have prevailed" (*Bereishis* 32:29). How could this be called prevailing, when he ended up with a wound on his thigh and a limp? The Rachmistrivka Rebbe[42] answers that the physical wound was in itself the greatest sign of victory. Yaakov had fought with the angel on a spiritual level, with the angel trying to destroy him spiritually, a battle that would manifest itself again and again with his descendants, as mentioned. When the angel saw he could not prevail, only then did he wound him on his thigh. This proves that the spiritual defenses of Yaakov are impenetrable. The angel could harm him physically but not spiritually.

One and Only

Finally, let us return to the beginning of the battle. *Chazal* say that just like Yaakov was alone, as the verse says, "Yaakov was left alone" (*Bereishis* 32:25), so too, Hashem is alone "and Hashem alone will be exalted on that day" (*Yeshayah* 2:11). The

Yalkut Hamelitzos[43] says that the intention of *Chazal* is as follows. Yaakov is held in low esteem, downtrodden and persecuted by the other nations. However, to this day Yisrael remain the only survivors of all the ancient nations and cultures, whose names have long ago vanished. This attests to the greatness of Hashem, that "Yaakov was left alone," having survived all the terrible suffering inflicted on him by Esav, and this proves that "Hashem alone will be exalted." This also answers the question of the philosophers who ask, "How can you prove God exists?" The proof lies in the survival of His chosen nation, Yisrael. If such a small nation can survive two thousand years of bitter exile, this is the greatest proof of Hashem's existence.

At the climax of the *shirah* read during *shacharis* it says, "The saviors will ascend Mount Zion to judge Esav's mountain, and the kingship will be Hashem's (*Ovadiah* 1:21). Then Hashem will be King over the entire world; on that day Hashem will be One and His Name will be One" (*Zechariah* 14:9). The Radak comments that in the future Mashiach will come and mete out retribution on Esav for his cruelty to the Jewish people, and then Hashem will be recognized by all as the true, only Ruler.

Flowers, Fruits and Snakes

This week's *parashah* contains the famous incident of the sale of Yosef. The Sages say that the brothers convened a *beis din* and ruled that Yosef was deserving of death. Reuven, upon hearing their plan, suggested that they throw Yosef into a pit instead, with the intention that he would return and save him. His plan was foiled while he was away, as the brothers sold Yosef in the meantime.

There is a famous *midrash* on this incident, which quotes a verse from *Shir Hashirim* (7:14), with the following interpretation: "The mandrakes emit a fragrance..." refers to Reuven, who tried to save Yosef from the pit; "at our doorway are all precious fruits," refers to Chanukah lights, which are lit at the doorway. This *midrash* needs an explanation. Exactly what is the connection between Reuven's actions and Chanukah, and why are they compared to flowers and fruits?

Good Publicity

Why is it that on Chanukah we have the unique obligation to publicize the mitzvah, which we fulfill by placing the lights at the entrance to our homes? This is in great contrast to the megillah

reading on Purim, which may be done even in the most se-
cluded of places. The difference is that the Purim miracle happened with great publicity. Everyone knew of the "relief and
salvation for the Jews" (*Esther* 4:14); therefore, it didn't need any
further publicity, since it was already well-known. The megillah
is read only to commemorate the event. On the other hand, the
Chanukah miracle of the flask of oil being discovered was known
only to the small number of individuals who were in the Beis
Hamikdash at the time. Therefore, it needed to be publicized.

This idea can be further understood with a story. Someone
once asked the Rashba[44] the following: A man had donated his
money for part of a shul, and he wanted to place his own name
there as a remembrance, but the community objected to his
wishes. The Rashba answered that indeed it was permitted for
him to do so, as we must publicize the names of those who do
mitzvos, even privately.

We see this in our *parashah* when it says, "Reuven heard and
he rescued him from their hand" (*Bereishis* 37:21). His intentions were known only in the recesses of his heart, and yet the
Torah publicized it for all generations to see. It is derived from
here that a mitzvah done even in secret is publicized. This is also
the source for the decree that we light Chanukah candles where
they are visible, in order to publicize what came about because
of the heroic efforts of the Chashmona'im.

This is what the Midrash refers to when it says, "The mandrakes emit a fragrance"; this is Reuven, who tried to save Yosef
from the pit, and the Torah chose to publicize his good intentions. His deed is just like a fragrance, which spreads beyond the
physical limitations of its source, and from which we learn the
idea of publicizing the names of people who do mitzvos. So too,
"at our doorway are all precious fruits," refers to Chanukah,
where the miracle was performed in secret, and yet the mitzvah
is to light outside so that it should be publicized.

Smell versus Taste

The Pardes Yosef comments on the placement of these two events together, and the choice of comparison the Midrash uses. Reuven had wanted to save Yosef, and similarly, the Chashmona'im saved the Jews through great self-sacrifice, which is why they are mentioned together in the same *midrash*. However, there is a significant difference between the two. Reuven wanted to save Yosef, but he couldn't put his thoughts into action. On the contrary, Yosef still ended up being thrown into a pit full of snakes and scorpions. This can be compared to the mandrakes, which have a good smell but no taste; Reuven had good intentions but no ultimate benefit came to Yosef because of them. On the other hand, the Chashmona'im were successful in their plans and their actions bore fruit. They were successful in driving out the enemy and are compared to "precious fruits" that have both a good scent and good taste.

Rav Shimon Schwab[45] elaborates on this idea. He asks, What is the difference between a pleasant smelling flower and a good tasting fruit? The answer is that the flower may smell nice but doesn't leave anything lasting behind it; one enjoys it momentarily and then it is gone. With a fruit, one eats and enjoys it, and the pleasure and satisfaction in alleviating one's hunger last much longer.

With this we can understand the Midrash. Reuven's action was compared to a sweet smelling flower that we enjoy for the moment but has no lasting benefit. He had good intentions but stopped short of delivering. What was really needed was for him to take a firm stand and to state loud and clear that his brothers' actions were unacceptable. On the other hand, the Chashmona'im acted with tremendous *mesirus nefesh* (self-sacrifice). A small band of people stood up against all the odds to battle the mighty

Greek army and was victorious. This resulted in "at our doorway are all precious fruits," which is more everlasting.

Could You Use a Slave...

Let us now examine a completely different explanation of the Midrash. The Kol Yehudah[46] asks, Why was it that Reuven was praised? Surely he still suggested that Yosef be thrown into a dangerous pit full of snakes and scorpions. Even though Reuven didn't know it contained these, surely the credit should have been given to Yehudah, who suggested selling Yosef, thereby removing him from the dangerous pit. It is even more of a wonder that not only does the Torah not praise Yehudah, but later on writes "and Yehudah went down" (*Bereishis* 38:1), which the commentators explain to mean that following this incident he descended from his greatness as a result of it.

The Kol Yehudah goes on to explain that the difference between the advice of Reuven and that of Yehudah was that Reuven's advice was not dangerous spiritually. In the pit, Yosef was in no spiritual danger (for that purpose it was probably one of the safest places on earth). While he may have been in physical peril in the pit, this was doubtful at the time of his being placed in it; there may not even have been any dangerous creatures there, and furthermore, this was a danger which would pass, as Reuven intended to rescue him from the pit. However, the advice of Yehudah, to sell him to the passing traders, would certainly place him in spiritual danger. He was sold to a band of Yishmaelites on their way down to Egypt, which was described as the most immoral of places in its day. Therefore, the Torah ascribes the saving of Yosef to Reuven, who wanted to save him spiritually.

Now we can also understand the connection between the Chanukah lights and Reuven's intentions. Chanukah was really about the spiritual victory of the people. The Greeks had decreed numerous edicts, making a war on religion in an attempt to wipe out Judaism. The flame of a candle represents spiritual victory, as a flame represents Torah. Therefore, the Midrash connects Reuven, who tried to save Yosef spiritually, to Chanukah, which was also a spiritual battle.

One or the Other

The results of the dedication and spiritual victory of the Chashmona'im can be seen in the verse describing the pit Yosef was thrown into as "empty; it contained no water" (*Bereishis* 37:24). The Gemara (*Shabbos* 22a) explains that although there was no water in the pit, there were snakes and scorpions. The Vilna Gaon[47] explains that water is an allusion to Torah, as the verse says, "everyone who is thirsty, go to the water" (*Yeshayah* 55:1). Therefore, when the verse says, "the pit was empty" it refers to one who is without Torah; that there were snakes and scorpions refers to the darker, lower side of human nature which he will otherwise possess. The Gemara is telling us that just like the pit contains one of two things, either water or snakes, so too, a person either has an attachment to Torah, or his actions are compared to snakes and scorpions.

The Greeks tried to sever our attachment to the Torah, and in particular to the oral law. This is not surprising, as it is the main source for our delving into Hashem's law, and without it one cannot understand the written law. This assault repeated itself throughout the previous millennia, when the nations continuously tried to destroy our link to the Talmud. The Greeks tried to replace Torah with their own culture and laws, which were so vain and vulgar that Greek culture is called darkness, a mixture of snakes and scorpions. On the other hand, the Torah is called light, as it says, "for a candle is a mitzvah, and the Torah is light"

(*Mishlei* 6:23). Indeed, the Chashmona'im should be remembered publicly for the way they cast away the dark spiritual clouds hovering over the Jewish people and replaced them with the Torah's light.

In G-d We Trust

D uring the First World War, the Brisker Rav[48] was living in Warsaw when it came under serious aerial attack. The Rav went into a bomb shelter with the rest of the people. Suddenly the explosions intensified and even the ground in the strong bomb shelter shook. The Brisker Rav got up, left the shelter and returned to his top-floor apartment. The rest of the people in the shelter were amazed. Later on he told them, "A person is required to have perfect faith that Hashem will save him. However, the Rambam writes that despite this, a person shouldn't put himself into a situation which will require a miracle to save him. When the bombardment was light I stayed in the shelter that was built to withstand this sort of attack. Once it intensified I realized it would also take a miracle to survive even in the shelter, and I was just as safe outside as inside."

Thanks for Nothing!

During the Israeli War of Independence, the Brisker Rav was in Jerusalem when it came under heavy gunfire and mortar attack. Regardless of the explosions around him at the time he would always stay in his top-floor apartment. During one particular attack, his students managed to persuade him to come down to the ground floor where it was safer. In this instance he reluctantly agreed. When there was a break in the gunfire he went up to his apartment and found a shell had ripped through it, causing great damage. He then turned to the student who had persuaded him to leave and said, "You are indirectly responsible for the damage to my apartment. Had I stayed there none of this would have happened." It never occurred to him that he might have been killed. The same God Who could save him on the lower floor could just as easily have saved him on the upper floor as well. The shell would never have ripped through his apartment and it would have remained intact.

The Pits

We find a similar concept at the beginning of our *parashah*. "And it happened at the end of two years that Pharaoh dreamt..." (*Bereishis* 41:1). The Midrash explains that because Yosef placed his trust in the butler, he was punished with two more years in jail. This refers to an incident in last week's *parashah*, where Yosef was in prison with the butler and baker, who both had dreams. Yosef interpreted the butler's dream as signaling that he would be freed. Yosef then requested that upon his release the butler should remind Pharaoh that he was still in jail, hoping he would free him. The Midrash says, " 'Happy is the man who puts his trust in Hashem' — this refers to Yosef. 'And turns not to the arrogant' (*Tehillim* 40:5); because he told the butler to mention him to Pharaoh, he was sentenced to another two years in jail."

There is an apparent contradiction within this *midrash*. First it describes Yosef as an example of one who trusts in Hashem, but then it turns around and says that he was punished for placing his trust in the butler. The approach of the Beis HaLevi and

Rav Eliyahu Lopian[49] is that *bitachon* (trust in Hashem) is a relative concept. Yosef was on such a high level that he placed all his hope only in Hashem and not in human beings. While his actions would not have been sinful for any other person, Yosef was on such a level that his depending on the butler was considered a sin. The Midrash is saying that Yosef is the man who "puts his trust in Hashem" — in every other instance. Because that time he failed to do so, he was punished.

How to Win the Jackpot

The concept of leaving everything to Hashem works only if one has complete trust in Him. Once someone came to Rav Yisrael Salanter[50] and said, "Rabbi, you say that perfect faith is always rewarded. Well, I bought a lottery ticket with perfect faith that I would win, and I didn't!" The Rav told him, "Well, try again and go and buy another ticket with the same perfect faith." On the day before the draw the Rav arranged that one of his followers would go and try to buy the ticket from the man. He refused to sell it, but the emissary persisted until finally he offered him half the jackpot. The man accepted as long as he would pay in cash on the spot. Because this was not forthcoming the deal broke off. The draw came and went and his ticket did not win. He ran to the Rav and complained, "I lost even though I had perfect faith." Rav Yisrael replied, "Have you ever seen someone swap ten thousand gold coins for five thousand? Had you had perfect faith, you would have seen the ticket as cash in hand and would not have swapped it for even one coin less than the full amount." Only then did he realize that the prospective buyer had been sent by Rav Yisrael to teach him what perfect faith really is.

Cause and Effect

There is another approach brought down by the Beis HaLevi, based on an interpretation of the theory of cause and effect. If one buys some produce and sells it at a higher price, thereby making a profit, most people think of the buying of the produce as the cause, and the profits as the effect. In truth, this is a mistake. Really, it was decreed from Heaven that he should profit, and circumstances arose such that he would buy the goods. Therefore, the profit is the cause, and his original purchase the effect.

The verse says, "And it happened at the end of two years that Pharaoh dreamt." The Midrash quotes the verse "He put an end to darkness" (*Iyov* 28:3), and comments that Hashem put a limit on Yosef's time in prison. Once the time for him to leave arrived, Pharaoh dreamt his dream. Most people think that the verse is saying that it was the dreams that subsequently caused Yosef to be called upon to interpret them, following which he was released. The Midrash is telling us that rather, it was because the time had come for Yosef to be released, and this is what caused Pharaoh to dream. Therefore, the release of Yosef was the cause, and the dream of Pharaoh the effect. The verse can thus be read as follows: "And it happened at the end of two years" that the time in prison decreed on Yosef had ended, which caused Pharaoh to dream. This is what the Midrash teaches us when it quotes, "He put an end to darkness"; since the time had arrived, it was time for Pharaoh to dream.

In the Shadow

There is another principle regarding the consequences of one's actions. It says that the way one conducts himself with Hashem, Hashem acts towards him. The Baal Shem Tov[51] compares this to a shadow. If one raises his hand, the shadow also raises its hand. If one jumps, the shadow jumps with him. Similarly, if one places all his trust in Hashem, He will respond to him appropriately. If, on the other hand, one wishes to live a life governed only by the laws of nature, with no Divine assistance, then Hashem will leave him to the elements, and "natural" things will happen. The extra years Yosef spent in jail were not necessarily a punishment but the natural consequences of his actions. Since he went through the channel of relying on human beings, Hashem allowed nature to take its course. As human nature would have it, the butler forgot the favor done for him, only remembering two years later.

In a Rush

The Torah then describes how following the butler's recommendation of Yosef as an interpreter of dreams, "Pharaoh sent, and he called Yosef, and they rushed him from the pit" (*Bereishis* 41:14). The Chofetz Chaim[52] explains that since the time had come for Yosef to leave the prison, Hashem didn't delay it for one moment longer than necessary, which is why "they rushed him." Similarly, when the time for redemption comes, it will not be delayed even for one moment, as the verse says, "suddenly He will come" (*Malachi* 3:1). Indeed, says the Chofetz Chaim, He will rush us out of exile, full speed ahead, to our land.

Elsewhere, the Chofetz Chaim[53] comments on the verse "Behold, I send you Eliyahu the Prophet" (*Malachi* 3:23), that instead of the future tense, "will send," it uses the present tense, "send." He explains that Eliyahu Hanavi is literally always ready to be sent by Hashem and announce the redemption to *klal Yisrael*. However, the matter is dependent on us; we have to be ready and desire his coming. Not surprising coming from a man who kept a bag packed ready for the arrival of Mashiach!

A Shoulder to Cry On

L ast week's *parashah* ended dramatically with Binyamin being accused of stealing Yosef's silver goblet, and with the
threat of his being taken as a slave. This was the worst possible punishment, as the brothers feared causing their father any
more anguish than he had already suffered. Our *parashah* opens
with Yehudah stepping forward with an emotional plea on his
youngest brother's behalf: "If you please, my lord, may your servant speak a word in my lord's ear" (*Bereishis* 44:18). Rashi comments that Yehudah wanted his words to enter directly into his
ears. What does this comment add to our understanding of the
text?

Rav Yitzchak Ze'ev Soloveitchik[54] explains that prior to this,
they had been using Yosef's son Menasheh as an interpreter.
This was to conceal Yosef's identity as one familiar with the holy
tongue. In this instance, Yehudah requested to speak directly to
the viceroy himself, in order for his words to have maximum
impact. This is because it was a plea for mercy. If you examine
the entire speech, there is no reference to the logistics of the case
itself, but instead to emotional matters, such as the sorrow it
would cause his father, the brother who had already died, and so

forth. Yehudah wanted his request to go directly to the viceroy, since he was "like Pharaoh" and could grant clemency for any reason, regardless of the facts of the case. And because it was a purely emotional appeal for mercy, he wanted it to be heard directly.

One difficulty remains: If the brothers spoke only Hebrew, which the viceroy supposedly didn't understand, surely disposing of the interpreter would be counterproductive. This can be resolved by the following story. Before the war, the Polish government had decided to remove the independent status of the Jewish schools, placing them under the authority of the ministry of education. This would have resulted in the destruction of Torah education in Poland, and therefore efforts were made to have this law repealed. An arrangement was made for a meeting between the Chofetz Chaim and the Polish president. In the presence of an interpreter, the Chofetz Chaim delivered a great plea straight from his pure and holy heart. Although he spoke in Yiddish, the president listened carefully throughout. At one point, when the Chofetz Chaim became particularly emotional, the president actually burst into tears. When he had finished, the interpreter was about to start his translation, when the president waved him off. "Although I don't speak the language," he said, "certain things don't need translation; these are words straight from the heart." Similarly, this was the language Yehudah wanted to use — straight from his heart, to enter Yosef's heart.

Key to Greatness

The emotional theme continues throughout the *parashah*, as we find many examples of Yosef being reduced to tears. During the meetings with the brothers he had to turn to a side room as emotion overcame him. When he revealed his identity, he was crying. He cried again, on the neck of his brother Binyamin, amongst other instances. Rav Zalman Sorotzkin[55] asks, what does all this come to teach us? He explains that one who has many burdens and troubles in his life cries frequently even when he is dwelling in serenity and harmony. This is because he will be sensitive to and pained by others' problems. On the other hand, the brothers of Yosef didn't shoulder this type of burden, and therefore even when tears were appropriate, they were not forthcoming. Yosef, however, was used to crying, and it was precisely because he was concerned and emotional about others' problems that he merited greatness.

Shouldering the Burden

We find several examples of people showing concern for others in our *parashah*. The verse (*Bereishis* 45:14) tells us that Yosef cried on the neck of Binyamin, and Binyamin cried on Yosef's neck. Rashi says that Yosef cried because he saw with Divine inspiration that the two Battei Mikdash would be destroyed in the portion allocated to Binyamin, and Binyamin cried because he saw that the Mishkan in Shilo (in the portion of Yosef's son) would be lost. We see that each was crying over the losses of the other, rather than over his own losses. This becomes even more significant when we consider that the reason for the destruction of the Second Temple was *sinas chinam* (baseless hatred). When Yosef and Binyamin cried for each other, it indicated that they rose above the selfish feelings people usually have, of being concerned only for oneself, to the polar opposite of shouldering the other's burden. By crying, they were countering the reason for the Beis Hamikdash's future destruction.

Taking a Step Back

The Torah tells us that when Yaakov and Yosef were reunited, Yosef "appeared to him" (*Bereishis* 46:29). Rashi comments that "Yosef appeared to his father." Again we ask the question, what does Rashi's comment add to our understanding of the verse? Rav Leib Chasman[56] answers with a profound insight. This meeting was one of the most emotional ever. Yaakov had mourned over his favorite son for twenty-two years. Yosef also wanted desperately to see his father. Each obviously had their own feelings and agenda during this reunion. The verse is telling us that part of Yosef's greatness was that he managed at this emotional time to let his father's needs override his own. He was able to step back and give his father the chance to view him and get the maximum satisfaction and pleasure from the meeting. Thus Rashi is emphasizing that Yosef was passive. He allowed himself to be seen by his father, which was his father's primary interest.

There in Spirit

Later on in the *parashah* we are told the names of Binyamin's sons. In lasts week's *parashah*, Rashi tells us that Binyamin called all his children after aspects relating to his missing brother. For example, one was called Bela, which means "swallowed," a reference to the fact that Yosef was swallowed up amongst the nations. Another was called Achi, referring to the fact that he was his brother, while another was called Rosh, because Binyamin considered Yosef as his leader. Another name was Chuppim. This comes from the word *chuppah*, and the Midrash tells us that this refers to the fact that Yosef hadn't attended Binyamin's wedding, and he wasn't at Yosef's. Rav Chaim Shmuelevitz[57] comments that we see that being unable to participate in a brother's wedding was a tragedy worthy of naming a son after.

Once, Rav Avraham Grodzensky[58] was paying a visit to a family in Warsaw. In the middle of the meeting he looked at his watch, and suddenly he began to sing. Soon enough, he got up and started dancing. This went on for an hour, while the family watched in amazement. Eventually, he sat down and explained, "At this time, one of my students is getting married in Slobodka. Unfortunately I can't be there to participate with him, but I can certainly celebrate myself. After all, his celebration is my celebration."

I heard the following story from Rabbi Pesach Krohn that illustrates the effects of placing other's needs above one's own. He is a *mohel*, and was once at a bris when he saw a woman crying in the corner. He went to ask her what was wrong, and at first she was unwilling to talk, but after he persisted, she told him how much pain she felt attending these sorts of celebrations when she had no children of her own. He told her that she should give charity, and also about the *gemara* that says that if one prays for someone else who has the same need as oneself, that person praying will be answered first. A year later Rabbi Krohn got a phone call from that woman. She reminded him of their conversation, and told him that she had prayed for a friend of hers, and that just yesterday she herself had given birth to a baby boy. She then asked if he would be the *mohel*!

I'm Leaving

Rav Aryeh Kaplan[59] was not from a Torah-observant home, but decided to spend a few weeks in a yeshivah to try out Judaism. After four weeks of assessing it, he decided it was not for him. He informed his roommates and the yeshivah that he would be leaving the next day. He woke up at five the next morning, and much to his surprise, found his roommates awake and dressed. He asked them what they were doing, and they explained, "We're going to come with you to the station." He replied, "Don't you understand? I'm leaving yeshivah and

Judaism. It's not for me. Why do you want to come?" His room-mates answered, "It's sad you're leaving yeshivah, but you're still a Jew and should be accompanied." To this he replied, "If you're willing to do all this for me, despite my plans to leave, then there must be more to Judaism than I thought, and I need to investigate it some more." He stayed in yeshivah and became the great Rav Aryeh Kaplan. What brought him back was this trait of Yosef and Binyamin. Each put aside his own needs in order to care and be concerned for the other. As we have seen, this trait has been passed down through the generations. Indeed, placing ourselves in others' shoes, sharing in their burdens and in their joy, should bring the *geulah, bimheira veyameinu.*

Father to Son

I n this week's *parashah,* Yaakov gave over his blessings first to Yosef's children, Ephraim and Menasheh, and then to the remaining brothers. From these episodes we can gain tremendous insights into relationships between the generations.

Let us examine some of the crucial issues of the *parashah.* Yaakov blessed Yosef's children with what would become the standard blessing that all parents give their sons: "Through you shall Israel bless, saying, "May God make you like Ephraim and Menasheh" (*Bereishis* 48:20). Why did Yaakov introduce them with "Through you," referring to Yosef? Instead the verse should have said, "Through your children."

Rav Zalman Sorotzkin[60] explains with a thought-provoking principle. A person is viewed by his *chinnuch,* the teachings and examples he gives over to his children. If one wants to know about a person, and about his inner self, one should look at the *chinnuch* he gives over to his children. There was a particular reason that Yaakov wanted the *chinnuch* Yosef gave to his children to be remembered for future generations. Egypt was on the lowest level spiritually, a place full of *tumah,* with witchcraft, sorcery, lewdness and immorality running rampant. One can also imagine the house of Yosef being frequented by many Egyptian princes and leaders of the day. This environment was a far cry from that of the other brothers, who grew up and studied Torah in the house of Yaakov. That Yosef could raise his children in such an environment, and yet have them remain faithful to Hashem and to His Torah despite the surroundings, was a fact worthy of everlasting memorial. They were so great that they even merited to be counted as two of the twelve tribes, despite only being grandchildren of Yaakov.

"Through you shall Israel bless" tells us that should such a challenge arise in the future, people should learn from how Yosef raised his children even under the worst of circumstances. The Vayakhel Moshe adds that since Yaakov knew that in the future his descendants would be scattered amongst the nations, even in places far-removed from the centers of Judaism, they should still have the strength to stand the test as did Ephraim and Menasheh.

Not an Identity Crisis

When Yosef brought in his children to be blessed, Yaakov asked a rather unusual question, "Who are these?" The Chofetz Chaim[61] explains that obviously Yaakov knew they were Yosef's sons, but that reason alone was insufficient to bless them. He wanted to know what it was that they stood for. When Yosef replied, "They are my sons" (*Bereishis* 48:9), he was not merely pointing out their relationship to him, but was confirming his sons' righteousness, that they followed in his footsteps. Only after hearing that was Yaakov satisfied and did he call them forward to be blessed.

Once someone came to the Chofetz Chaim for a blessing that his children should all remain observant. The Chofetz Chaim answered, "You expect to accomplish this by means of a blessing alone? In this day and age it requires tremendous self-sacrifice!"

The Advantage of Fish

Yaakov blessed Yosef's sons, "...may they reproduce abundantly like fish in the land" (*Bereishis* 48:16). Why did he bless them to be specifically like fish, and not like any other type of living creature? The *Sefer Hadra shel Torah* explains that there is a great difference between animals and birds in comparison to fish. While with all these species, there are types which are kosher and types which are not, with animals and birds, even the kosher species first need to be slaughtered in the required way. Then they need internal examination, following which their flesh is salted, rinsed, and so on. During all these processes there is always the fear that somewhere along the line they will become *treif*. On the other hand, kosher fish remain kosher from the beginning of the process until the end, without all the potential problems that can arise with other animals.

This is what Yaakov intended with his blessing, that Yosef's sons should be like fish, which remain in their kosher state from beginning to end. So too, their children should be conceived in holiness and purity from beginning to end, and should remain attached to their heritage throughout all generations.

Taking the Credit...and the Blame

I'm sure many people will be able to relate to the following. Why is it that a distraught mother, discovering the latest havoc her darling two year old has wrought in the house, will turn to her husband and ask, "Have you seen what your son has done?" However, only hours later, when that same child has done something good, she will say, "You see, that's my son." Perhaps the answer lies in this:[62] Yaakov blessed Epharim and Menasheh, "and may my name be called upon them, and the names of my forefathers Avraham and Yitzchak" (*Bereishis* 48:16). The commentators say that should a son tragically turn to evil ways, the parents will be embarrassed of their offspring. Therefore, Yaakov blessed them that it should always be fitting that their ancestors' names could be called upon them, and it should not be embarrassing to say, "These are the descendants of Avraham, Yitzchak and Yaakov."

The Weakest Link

The Gemara (*Bava Metzia* 85a) says that if three consecutive generations of a family are Torah scholars, Torah will subsequently remain with their future descendants. If so, since all Jews are descendants of Avraham, Yitzchak and Yaakov, surely everyone should be learned, with no weak links in the chain. The Chofetz Chaim[63] answers that the Gemara does not guarantee that Torah will be acquired by the fourth generation regardless of the efforts (or lack thereof) made. It applies only to a situation where Torah is welcome, so to speak. This can be compared to a guest. As long as the guest is welcome in his host's house he will return on his next trip. As soon as the host acts coldly towards him, he will seek alternative accommodations. The same applies with Torah. It returns to the same place only when it is welcome there; otherwise it seeks alternative dwellings.

First Things First

Yaakov blessed Yosef's sons: "May the angel who redeems me from all evil bless the lads, and may my name be called upon them, and the name of my forefathers Avraham and Yitzchak." Why did Yaakov place his own name before that of his fathers? The Kol Yehudah answers by examining what each of the forefathers stood for. Avraham was the epitome of *chessed*, Yitzchak embodied Divine worship, and Yaakov was the pillar of Torah. This is why Yaakov began with his own name. First Ephraim and Menasheh should acquire the attribute of Torah, and from there it is possible to reach higher levels of *chessed* and Divine service. However, from *chessed* and Divine service it is not possible to acquire Torah.

You Can't Make Something from Nothing

At the moment before Yaakov gave the blessings, he placed his right hand on Ephraim and his left hand on Menasheh, much to the horror of Yosef, as Menasheh was the firstborn and the right hand should have been placed upon him. Yosef pointed this out to his father, who replied, "I know, my son, I know; he too will become a people and he too will become great; however, his younger brother will become greater than he will" (*Bereishis* 48:19).

Rav Yerucham Levovitz[64] asks, How does this answer the question? Surely Yosef made his request because Menasheh should have been blessed as the firstborn, regardless of other considerations. He answers that these blessings were to be given not to whoever would request to be blessed, but rather to the one upon whom it was fitting for the blessings to rest. Regarding the blessings given to the rest of the brothers, even Yaakov did not have the power to change the order and structure; rather, each was blessed according to his existing strengths and nature. This is seen when the verse says, "each according to his blessing he blessed them" (*Bereishis* 49:28).

The Torah describes an episode with the prophet Elisha, where he told a poor woman to find as many vessels as she could, and from one jarful of oil she miraculously filled up them all. In that instance, the miracle needed a receptacle within which to occur, without which its realization would not have been possible. Similarly, with the blessings of Yaakov there needed to be a receptacle for the blessings. The receptacles were the existing features that the brothers already had: their *middos*, their natures and their characteristics. It was only through these existing features that each merited the blessing that was appropriate to him. It is like saying each blessing has an address on it, and that the blessing which is fitting for one is totally unsuitable for another.

Now we can understand why Yaakov replied, "I know, my son, I know…however, his younger brother will become greater than he will." Yaakov was telling Yosef that this was the only *berachah* suitable for Menasheh; even though he was the firstborn, it was the one from which he stood to gain the most. On the other hand, Ephraim's potential could best be reached by his receiving the blessing due to the firstborn.

We see a similar idea in the verse "each according to his blessing he blessed them." On examining the blessings, we find that they describe in full each of the brother's strengths and weaknesses, but where are the actual blessings? The commentators explain that the greatest blessing one can give a person is to tell him of his strengths and weaknesses. If he will take this information to heart then he will turn into someone great. He will know in what direction to channel his energies, and he can use this knowledge to be productive for *klal Yisrael* and reach his potential.

Shemos

The Home Stretch

S efer *Shemos* begins with the story of *bnei Yisrael*'s slavery and their subsequent redemption. These events are so crucial that we have a mitzvah to remember the Exodus daily. They are also mentioned many times throughout davening, as well as in Kiddush. Let us examine some of the key elements of their slavery, and their subsequent road to freedom.

The first verse says, "These are the names of *bnei Yisrael* who came (*haba'im*) to Egypt with Yaakov (*Shemos* 1:1). The generation that came with Yaakov was popular with the Egyptians. Yosef had been in command preparing the country for the crisis ahead. Subsequently, the famine actually stopped with the arrival of Yaakov.

Several verses later the Torah writes, "A new king arose who did not know Yosef" (*Shemos* 1:8). According to one interpretation it was literally a new king, while according to another it was the same king, but his attitude towards the Jews had changed. This king made many decrees against the Jews and eventually forced them into slavery.

What caused this change in attitude? The commentators say that the first verse mentioned above should have stated *ba'u* (who came), in the past tense. The word *haba'im* actually means "coming," in the present tense. The verse is telling us that the initial seventy people who came to Egypt viewed themselves as "coming." They never saw themselves as permanent residents of Egypt, but as just visiting. As we shall see, the next generation was different.

Being in the Right Place

The verse says, "the land was filled with them" (*Shemos* 1:7). The commentators explain that the Jews spread out throughout the land and participated in all the Egyptian events of culture and entertainment. Rav Yehoshua Leib Diskin[1] says that many years earlier, Hashem had promised Avraham that his descendants would be "strangers in a land not theirs" (*Bereishis* 15:13). The difficulty is, surely the verse is stating something superfluous; obviously strangers are in a land not belonging to them. Rather, the verse is teaching us that the Jewish people living in a land not theirs was a factor contributing to their slavery. The implication is that as long as they were in a land that was theirs they would not be enslaved.

The Jews had lived in the land of Goshen. Pharaoh had given this to Sarah many years before and it was an inheritance to her descendants. Had *bnei Yisrael* remained in Goshen, doing what they were supposed to be doing, they would not have been enslaved; that was a land that was theirs. However, once the first generation died out, the next generation began to integrate into Egyptian culture, beyond the confines of Goshen. Then it was time for Pharaoh to act; the slavery began.

Mixing with the "Upper Class"

The verse also describes that "they became very, very mighty (*beme'od me'od*)." The Kli Yakar says that the word *me'od* also refers to wealth, as in the verse (*Devarim* 6:5) "and you shall love Hashem…with all your wealth (*me'odecha*)." The second generation became wealthy and affluent. They felt they had made it and wanted to mix with the top brass of Egyptian society and culture.

With this we can now understand the verse "a new king arose who did not know Yosef." Pharaoh said to himself, "These aren't the same people I knew. They are different; therefore, I will act differently towards them as well." As long as the Jews viewed themselves as still "coming," passing through, they were respected. Pharaoh had respect for the differences between them. Only when they tried to become fully integrated into Egyptian culture did he turn against them.

It's Good to Get Fed Up

With this in mind, we can see some clues as to the cause of the Jewish people's eventual redemption. In next week's *parashah* the verse says, "and you will know that I am the Lord Who takes you out from under the sufferings (*sivlos*) of Egypt" (*Shemos* 6:7). The Chiddushei Harim[2] says that the word *sivlos* doesn't only mean "suffering," but it also has the same meaning as that well-known Israeli word *savlanut*, which means to have patience and be able to bear a burden.

The Sages say that no slave ever escaped from Egypt. The simple meaning is that the nation had such great security that no one could break free. Rav Gedaliah Schorr[3] explains that "no slave ever escaped" means that Egypt had such a great propaganda machine that the people felt a life of bondage was good. They had no desire to break free; they thought that being a slave was the be-all and end-all of life.

The Chiddushei Harim explains that as long as the Jews had no desire to be freed, redemption could not occur. Being taken out "from under the sufferings (*sivlos*) of Egypt" means that Hashem implanted in *bnei Yisrael* the desire to be freed. Until then, they were *sovel* the exile, the slavery. Getting fed up with the exile was the first stage of redemption.

Once, Reb Nachum Chernobler[4] was staying at an inn. He arose at midnight, as was his custom, to say *tikkun chatzos*, the plea for Hashem to bring Mashiach and end the exile. The innkeeper heard him praying and went to inquire as to what he was doing. Reb Nachum replied, "I'm saying *tikkun chatzos*, that Hashem should end our bitter exile and that we should all go to Eretz Yisrael." The innkeeper liked the idea and ran upstairs to tell his wife. "There is a Jew downstairs who is praying that the exile should end and that we should all go to Eretz Yisrael," he said. His wife turned over in bed and said, "Go there? Who is going to look after the farm? Who'll feed the cows and the horses?" This bothered the innkeeper. He went back to Reb Nachum and asked, "But Rabbi, what will be with the farm, the cows and the horses?" Reb Nachum replied, "You're worried about that? When the Cossacks and the Tartars come and plunder it all then will you be happy? Hashem will take us all to Eretz Yisrael; no more Cossacks, no more Tartars." Again the innkeeper excitedly ran up and related it all to his wife. His wife replied, "Go and tell the rabbi that Hashem should take all the Cossacks and the Tartars to Eretz Yisrael. We'll stay here with the farm, the cows and the horses."

This is what "the *sivlos* of Egypt" means. As long as we can bear the exile, and as long as we tolerate and enjoy it, then redemption is far away. Once we desire it, and say "Enough!" then it can be hastened.

A Good Stretch

One of Pharaoh's decrees was that all Jewish baby boys be

thrown into the Nile. The daughter of Pharaoh was bathing there one day when she noticed a basket in the reeds by the side of the river. The verse says, "and she sent her maidservant (*amatah*) and she took it" (*Shemos* 2:5). This was the basket that contained Moshe, who would lead *bnei Yisrael* out of Egypt.

Rashi explains that *amatah* actually refers to her arm, which extended by many *amos* so that she could reach the basket. Surely she knew how far her arm could reach, so why did she bother trying in the first place? Furthermore, why did her arm extend so much to enable her to reach it? The Chofetz Chaim[5] explains that although it appeared as an impossible task, nevertheless, she didn't refrain from making the effort. Hashem then helped her so that her arm extended and she could reach the basket. This teaches us that one should not refrain from helping those who need help, or from performing a particular mitzvah, even if initially it appears that he will be unable to follow the act through to its conclusion through natural means alone. Instead he should exert himself as far as his hand will reach and then he will be helped.

The verse tells us that Miriam, Moshe's sister, stood watching by the river "to determine what would be done with him" (*Shemos* 2:4). The Chofetz Chaim[6] comments that she never had any doubts that he would be saved; she just wanted to know through which method salvation would come.

After the Second World War, the remaining roshei yeshivah met in Eretz Yisrael to discuss how Torah would be rebuilt. The Ponovezher Rav got up and spoke. "What is it we are gathered here for?" he asked. "If it is to save Torah, we already have a promise that Torah will not be forgotten without any extra effort from us. The only question we can deal with is how we can participate in the renewal of Torah that we will witness soon. How can we have a share in it?" The Rav was telling them that they should stretch out their hands and do what they could. With help from Heaven, they would be successful.

No Ordinary Lottery

During the Second World War,[7] Rav Aharon Kotler received a letter from America. It was from Rav Moshe Feinstein, who invited him to move to the United States. All the arrangements had been made including obtaining the all-important visa. He was undecided whether to accept the invitation, or whether to attempt to reach Eretz Yisrael. He resorted to the *goral haGra*, a mystical method of seeking Divine assistance through the verses of Scripture. The verse he was led to is from our *parashah*: "And Hashem said to Aharon, 'Go towards Moshe in the desert' " (*Shemos* 4:27). He took this as a sign that he was meant to join Rav Moshe in America, which at the time was a spiritual desert. Together they would try and stretch out their arms as far as they could reach, and have their share in spreading Hashem's Torah.

To Believe or Not to Believe

R ecently the Israelis intercepted a boat containing huge amounts of weapons heading into the wrong hands. As with everything, there are two ways we can view this event. We can see it either as due to successful intelligence efforts and a great performance by the military, or as a great miracle in which Hashem prevented our enemies from amassing even more weaponry against us.

The story of the ten plagues gives us tremendous insight into the difference between these two ways of thinking and their ramifications. First let us begin with an amazing principle of the Chazon Ish.[8] He asks, What is the purpose of the Torah listing the miracles and wonders of Hashem in such great detail? He answers that it is not to establish the truth of the Jewish faith in the eyes of nonbelievers; rather, it is for the benefit of those who already believe. He continues that nonbelievers will continue to disbelieve even after seeing what the Torah has to say. Just as they deny the Divine origin of the Torah, so too, they will deny the miracles recounted in it. No amount of proof or codes will satisfy them. On the other hand, one who believes doesn't need any further proof. Rather, the purpose is just to relate the story so that they should know of what took place and observe the commandment of remembering the Exodus daily, as well as commemorate these events in more detail at the Seder.

Tanks and Tehillim

During the War of Independence,[9] the Jews of Eretz Yisrael would gather frequently to pray that they should be saved from the enemy. The Brisker Rav related that during the plague of frogs, Pharaoh asked that Moshe pray that the frogs be removed from him and his people. Moshe agreed, but he asked Pharaoh at what particular time he should remove them. This was so that people should know that it was only through Hashem that the frogs were removed and not through any other means. Pharaoh tried to call Moshe's bluff by choosing the next day. This was because he suspected Moshe of being an astrologer who had prior information about the appearance of frogs and when they would subsequently be removed. By choosing the next day, he hoped this would be beyond Moshe's means, thus exposing Moshe as a liar once and for all. However, despite being proved wrong at the end of all this, the Torah relates "Pharaoh, hardened his heart." The Brisker Rav continued, "It is the same with us. There is no doubt that it is our prayers and *tehillim* that will make us victorious. However, there will certainly also be those who wish to deny Hashem and say, 'The strength and might of my hand made me this wealth,' that it is our power that won this battle and not the hand of Hashem."

Now That's Magic

Using these principles, let us see how the miraculous events in the *parashah* follow this course. Moshe and Aharon stood in front of Pharaoh and Aharon threw down his staff, causing it to turn into a snake. Pharaoh's magicians did the same, but

Aharon's snake then ate all their snakes, proving that it was the truly miraculous staff. Rav Yosef Dov Soloveitchik[10] points out that surely there was a much easier way of proving that Aharon's was the only miraculous staff. The Gemara (*Sanhedrin* 67b) says that the effects of sorcery can be undone by pouring water over the affected object. If Moshe and Aharon would have poured water over the snakes, all the others would have reverted to a rod, while Aharon's would have remained a real snake, as his was created from the will of Hashem rather than from sorcery.

The reason they didn't use this approach is that this would not have been enough for the Egyptians. They would have argued that Aharon's staff was not a staff, but a snake to begin with. They would have contended that Aharon had made a snake turn into a staff before entering the palace. He then turned it into a snake once again using sorcery, while alleging that he had turned a true staff into a snake. If so, then using the water test would be worthless; the Egyptians would argue that of course nothing happened because it was really a snake all along. That is why the only way to show Aharon's authority was for his staff to swallow the others. We see how the miracle occurred in such a way so as not to give anyone an excuse for not believing, and yet we find this was not enough for the Egyptians.

How Not to Deal with a Crisis

The Torah describes that during the first plague, all the water in Egypt turned into blood. The verse describes Pharaoh's reaction, that he "turned and entered his house; he did not take this to heart either" (*Shemos* 7:23). Rashi comments that he ignored not only the snake episode, but also the water turning to blood.

The Netziv[11] explains that the Torah is telling us more about Pharaoh's misguided attitude. Here we have the leader of a large nation. One would have thought that under these circumstances he would have gone into crisis mode, setting up an emergency center to deal with the problem causing so much suffering for his people. Yet what did he do? He just turned and went home! He was so sure of his belief that Moshe had caused the plague by witchcraft and that it would shortly pass that he acted as if nothing had happened. In his efforts to distort the truth, he became completely irrational.

Itching for War

Why did the plague of lice follow that of blood and frogs? *Chazal* say that after Titus destroyed the Beis Hamikdash, he set out to return to his homeland by boat. A great storm arose which threatened to kill him. Arrogantly he said, "It seems that His power is only in water. That is how He wiped out the generation of the flood, and the Egyptians were also destroyed through water." Hashem said, "Wicked one! I have a small creature in the world called a flea. See if you can do battle with it." When Titus ascended dry land the flea entered his nose, ultimately killing him. Similarly, Pharaoh saw the first plague involving water, and then the plague of frogs, which also came from the water. He then said to himself, "You see, His power is only through water." Hashem then sent the smallest of creatures, the lice, to teach him how wrong he was.

Hail Forecast

Before the plague of hail, Moshe gave the Egyptians an additional chance to change. He warned them it was coming, and promised that by taking their animals indoors they would be spared further loss. It is unbelievable that some of Pharaoh's servants, intelligent, intellectual people, would choose, after suffering so much already, to ignore the warning and leave their animals in the fields. Even if they didn't wish to accept the warning as coming from Hashem, surely the laws of probability would suggest that just maybe Moshe had a point? The Birkas Peretz explains that denial of Hashem is caused not by a lack of understanding or intellect, but rather by a lack of will, and a desire to continue going after the dictates of one's heart. One who wants to deny Hashem will deliberately suppress any thoughts that could cause him to believe. This is why we find people who reject Hashem in the strongest possible terms, but yet cling to all sorts of crazy ideologies, beliefs and "isms." The same was true in Egypt. The servants of Pharaoh didn't wish to believe and therefore managed to suppress all rational thoughts that could have saved them and their property.

Down-to-Earth

The Midrash says that when Moshe told Pharaoh, "Behold, I will make it rain tomorrow" (*Shemos* 9:18), he drew a sign on the wall to indicate that when the sun's shadow would reach it, the plague would start. The absurdity of the Egyptians' requiring this was that if the hail would come a moment earlier or later, then they would reject Moshe's credibility.

The Malbim explains using a basic scientific fact. There were three elements in this hailstorm — hail, thunder and lightning — which all travel to earth at different speeds. Although they all may originate simultaneously, the lightning would reach the ground much more quickly than the hail or thunder, since it travels at the speed of light. Therefore, it follows that Moshe's sign would have been problematic. The Egyptians would argue that all three elements were part of the plague and that Moshe was therefore a false prophet.

To deal with this problem, Hashem made the thunder, lightning and hail all arrive on earth at exactly the same moment that the sunlight reached the mark on the wall. We see how

Hashem deliberately orchestrated events, even changing the properties of the elements, so that the Egyptians could not possibly deny the truth of Moshe's prophecy, and yet we all know how it ended.

About Midnight

If we look for a moment at next week's *parashah*, we see that before the plague of the firstborn, Moshe said, "At about midnight (*ka'chatzos*) I shall go out in the midst of Egypt" (*Shemos* 11:4). Rashi explains that the word *ka'chatzos* means "at approximately midnight." Moshe said this because he thought that perhaps the Egyptian astrologers would err in their calculations and say that Moshe is a liar. To preempt this, Moshe gave only an approximate time, so that no one could have any claims against him or Hashem.

This is a most unbelievable Rashi. The Egyptians, having just suffered nine devastating plagues, their country in ruins, experience the hardest-hitting plague of them all, and yet there would still be those amongst them who would look at their watches and say, "You see? That Moshe, he's a liar." This ties in with the comment of the Chazon Ish that we started with. One who does not want to be open to the possibility of believing will do everything he can to disprove the facts that stand before him. There are people who spend their whole lives conducting "scientific projects," such as showing how the ten plagues were the result of natural occurrences at the time. They can likewise provide "proof" that the splitting of the sea was also a natural occurrence. No amount of Torah codes or lectures will help them.

With this in mind we can reassess events around us. By recognizing that the hand of Hashem is operating around us, we will be better able to do His will, being servants of Hashem rather than like the servants and countrymen of Pharaoh.

The Past Meets the Future

An interior ministry is never a happy place to be even at the best of times, all the more so in Egypt, where Pharaoh ran it. Moshe had been "negotiating," using a bit of "gentle" persuasion that *bnei Yisrael* be released. After many devastating plagues it had reached a point where Pharaoh was willing to let all the adult males leave. Moshe replied, "With our youngsters and with our elders...with our sons and our daughters, with our flock and with our cattle shall we go, because it is a festival of Hashem for us" (*Shemos* 10:9). Subsequently, Pharaoh refused, only allowing the males to go.

The Chasam Sofer[12] writes that the early philosophers used to flee to remote caves, a forest or a wilderness, thinking that there they could find spirituality. Our Torah tells us that in fact the opposite is true. We have a principle that a mitzvah performed by many is greater than that done by few. An example is the halachah that if one has a choice of two shuls, then, all other things being equal, one should daven in the shul with more people. We also have a concept of *kiddush Hashem* (sanctifying Hashem's Name), which is done specifically in public.

With this in mind we can understand the claim of Pharaoh: "let the men go now; serve Hashem, for that is what you request" (*Shemos* 10:11). Pharaoh felt that surely the service would be better performed if only the males would go, without the interference of the women, or the children running around. Moshe told Pharaoh that he was wrong and that *bnei Yisrael* needed everyone there — men, women, boys, girls, both the elderly and the young, and even the animals for sacrifices. Only with all the parts of the whole can we serve Hashem properly and be involved in the building of the Jewish people.

A Nightmare Journey

There is another aspect to Pharaoh's reversal of his previous decision to free the Jewish people. He said, "see that evil faces you. Not so, let the men go now" (*Shemos* 10:10, 11). Rav Moshe Yehudah Leib of Kutnah[13] explains that one of the considerations one must bear in mind when undertaking a long journey is that it is certainly not conducive to Divine service and spiritual matters. One needs a certain amount of serenity and peace of mind to serve Hashem. Everyone knows that if one takes children on a long trip (or even a short one) he will be constantly occupied with them, because this one needs food, this one is bored, these two are fighting — the list is endless. The elderly also need caring for. Pharaoh was asking Moshe and Aharon if he would send them out with their children, would Hashem really still be with them and interested in their service? Surely the journey would be far too tedious, preventing *bnei Yisrael* from performing proper Divine service. That is why he said, "see that evil faces you" — if you take the children. He then advised them, "let the men go now" — and then you will be able to serve Hashem properly — "for that is what you request." Pharaoh then concluded that if they were to reject this offer, it must be a sign that they had motives other than serving Hashem in their request to leave. Since Moshe did reject it, Pharaoh drove them away.

Who Gets the Benefit?

Appropriately, the one time of the year that we place particular emphasis on the involvement of the children is Seder night. This is accomplished by the obligation to tell over the story of the Exodus. The importance of relating the story to the younger generation is obvious, but there is also great significance in the telling by the older generation. "And in order that you shall speak it into the ears of your son and your grandson...that you will know that I am Hashem" (*Shemos* 10:2). Rav Shalom of Belz[14] explains that from the verse it sounds like the intention of the telling is purely to make the children wiser. However, the end of the verse informs us that "you will know that I am Hashem." The Torah is teaching us that by relating the story to the children, the adults will increase their own level of faith and love of Hashem. This idea is also proven from the fact that the halachah states that if one is alone with no one else to relate the story to, he has to relate it over to himself.

The Chida gives another interpretation of the verse. The Gemara (*Bava Metzia* 85b) says that if three consecutive generations of a family are Torah scholars, then Torah will never leave their descendants. The *Tosafos* says that this applies only if the three generations actually knew each other. This *gemara* is telling us that the bond with Torah will survive only if the generations were linked, that the fathers tell it to their sons and grandsons. With such a solid link, the chain of Torah will not be broken.

Pyramids and Pentium

What is the significance of the emphasis on relationships between the generations, as well as on past events such as the Exodus? In a zoo, one of the most popular exhibits is always that of the monkeys. Perhaps this is because the nations of the world believe they came from monkeys. They look at these animals and think about how clever they act while at the same time are still so primitive. They comfort themselves by saying that they are the more advanced, refined beings. Their philosophy is that every generation is an improvement on the previous one. "Look at our technology," they think to themselves. "We have 2000 MHz computers, while only a few years ago we ran on 1 MHz. (I'm sure that by the time this goes to press this will also be out of date.) Look at how we can travel into outer space, and look at our weapons of mass destruction."

The Torah view is somewhat different from this. We look at previous generations as having been on a higher level than we are. When *bnei Yisrael* received the Torah at Sinai, they were on the highest level ever, having experienced Divine revelation. Moshe received the Torah directly from Hashem, with the full complexity of the oral law. This was handed down from one generation to the next. This means that previous generations are closer to the original source; the Torah they learned was purer, less diluted.

On the other hand, the wisdom of the nations is different. No one can say that one particular theory is correct, because inevitably a new theory will take its place. The mathematical proofs of years gone by were refuted by later mathematicians. Economic models are out of date even before they have been publicized. However, with our Torah, we look to earlier generations. We examine how they unraveled the complexities in the Talmud, precisely because each older generation is closer to the source. While the nations' ancestors were apes, we have the glorious past of Rabbi Yehudah HaNasi, Rashi and the Ritva, to name a few. This idea is seen in the verse "ask your father and he will tell you, your elder and he will say to you" (*Devarim* 32:7).

Coining the Future

Now we can understand Pharaoh's problem. Although he was wicked, he understood the key to Jewish survival. Apparently, Pharaoh was willing to let those between the ages of twenty and sixty leave, but he could not allow those above or below that age to go. Pharaoh knew of the concept of the tradition that we receive from our fathers and grandfathers. He also knew that without someone to give it over to, there is no future.

The Midrash[15] says that Avraham was one of four people who minted coins. On one side was a picture of an elderly man and woman. This represents that the Jewish people need an older generation for guidance and to transmit important teachings to us. On the other side of the coin was a young boy and girl, representing that there must also be a future. This is what Pharaoh wanted to take away, but Moshe insisted that "with our youngsters and with our elders shall be go."

Coming Out of Retirement

Once[16] there was a Palestinian terrorist called Salah Tamari who was incarcerated in an Israeli prison. He related that while there, he underwent a great transformation. He had given up hope that his movement would ever reach its goals. Israel was simply too strong, and he was ready to give up the struggle. One Pesach, he saw his jailer eating a pita sandwich. He was shocked at how a Jew could do such a thing and asked the jailer why he was doing it. The jailer replied, "I feel no connection with events that took place over two thousand years ago; they have nothing to do with me." That night, Tamari couldn't sleep. He thought to himself, "A nation with no connection to its past, openly transgressing its most important laws, has cut off its roots to the land." He concluded that his people could indeed achieve their goals and should not give up on any of their aspirations, for the opposition was a nation that has no connection to its roots and could therefore be defeated.

The importance of the Exodus is that it is central to our beings as Jews. It was what led to the giving of the Torah, and we are commanded to remember it daily. The Torah gives as the reason for many of the mitzvos that they are a remembrance of the Exodus. We are remembering we are a nation with a past, and a destiny for the future. In fact, there are many connections between the Exodus from Egypt and the future redemption. While the text of the part of the Haggadah that is read before the meal commemorates the past Exodus, a close examination of the part of the text read after the meal shows that it is referring to the future redemption. By understanding the significance of our past, and knowing how strong our attachment to these events must be and what they represent, we should merit the redemption speedily in our days.

PARASHAS BESHALACH

Who's Running the Show?

The splitting of the Yam Suf (the Red Sea) was one of the greatest open revelations of Hashem's might. It is so central to our belief that we recite *Shiras Hayam* daily in the climax of *pesukei dezimra*, the buildup of our prayers before the reading of the Shema and *Amidah*. There is a noticeable change in the sequence of the verses in this *parashah*. "And *bnei Yisrael* came within the sea on dry land, and the water was a wall (*chomah*) for them" (*Shemos* 14:22). First the verse informs us that they came into the sea, and then it became dry land. This is in contrast to seven verses later: "*Bnei Yisrael* went on dry land in the midst of the sea; the water was a wall for them." Here the order is that first they were on dry land, and only then in the midst of the sea. How can we account for the change? Another question is, Why is the word *chomah* (wall) written with a *vav* in the first verse, while in the second verse it is shortened and spelled without a *vav*?

The Vilna Gaon[17] resolves these problems. There were two groups at the splitting of the sea. The first had great trust in Hashem, while the second was of much lesser faith. The first group was led by Nachshon ben Aminadav and walked straight into the sea. As soon as it reached up to their mouths, threatening to drown them, the sea split. The first verse is referring to this group, as it says that they "came within the sea on dry land." First they walked into the sea, and in the merit of their faith it became dry land. When the verse says that the water became a *chomah* it is spelled in the full way, with a *vav*, meaning that the water became literally a wall for them on either side.

In contrast, there was a second group that was of little faith. They would not hear of such actions and chose to remain on the shore to see what would happen. While the other tribes were deliberating over who would go in first, they were happy to give a typically English "After you...no please, you first."

The Midrash says that at the time of the splitting of the sea an accusing voice in Heaven said to Hashem, "What is the difference between this group (*bnei Yisrael*), who served idols in Egypt and who will be saved, and the Egyptians, who are also idolaters and are destined to perish?" Hashem replied that it was in the merit of the group that did believe that the others would also be saved.

It is described that this second group "went on dry land in the midst of the sea." They waited until it became dry land, and only then did they go into the sea. The word *chomah* is spelled there without a *vav*. If you take away the vowels, the word can also be read as *chemah*, which means anger, indicating the accusation against this group, and Hashem's anger towards them.

Jump In

There was a famous stuntman called Buffer the Great. Once, with great publicity, he announced what his next feat would be: to walk over Niagara Falls on a tightrope. The day arrived and a huge crowd gathered to see this daring act. As he was about to put his foot on the rope he shouted to the crowd, "Do you believe that I, Buffer the Great, can walk over this tightrope to the other side?" The crowd responded with great cheering and in one voice shouted, "Yes, we believe!" He reached the other side amidst great applause and cheering. Several weeks later an announcement was made. Buffer the Great would perform an even greater feat. The day arrived and an even larger crowd than before attended. He stood by the rope and shouted to the crowd, "Do you believe that I, Buffer the Great, can walk over this tightrope to the other side?" The crowd shouted with one voice, "Yes, we believe."

"Do you believe I can walk over this tightrope blindfolded wheeling a wheelbarrow?" he asked. The crowd shouted unanimously, "Yes, we believe!" Again he reached the other side, causing the crowd to go wild from excitement. A few weeks later, he announced he would be doing his most daring stunt. The day arrived and he stood up by his tightrope. He called to the crowd, "Do you believe I can walk over this tightrope blindfolded?" They all shouted, "Yes, we believe!" "Do you believe I can walk over this tightrope blindfolded wheeling a wheelbarrow?" he asked. To which they shouted "Yes, we believe!" "Do you believe I can walk over this tightrope, blindfolded with a wheelbarrow, with a person in it?" They all shouted, "Yes, we believe!" "Who wants to volunteer to go in the wheelbarrow?" There was silence.

The First Move

As the Egyptians were fast approaching, *bnei Yisrael* cried out to Moshe that Hashem should save them. Hashem responded to Moshe, "Why do you cry out to me? Speak to *bnei Yisrael* and let them journey." Reb Chaim of Volozhin[18] asks, "Surely it was the natural thing to do, to cry out to Hashem in their distress, so why did Hashem instruct them otherwise? He answers that

Hashem was telling Moshe that their salvation depended on them alone. If they would have perfect faith and trust that Hashem would save them, so much so that they would venture into the sea, then this would cause a response from above and Hashem would perform the miracle for them.

From this we learn an important principle. The way that we place our trust in Hashem will affect the way He deals with us. If we take the first step, showing that we are dependant on Him, rather than thinking we can live without any Heavenly assistance, then Hashem will surely respond in kind. The question is, can we jump into Hashem's wheelbarrow?

Who Really Fights the War?

Why were the Jews so afraid of the Egyptian army? *Bnei Yisrael* numbered in the millions, and since they went out armed (as is the literal translation), surely they could have fought against them. Furthermore, why in this instance was a miracle performed for them with the sea splitting, while in the attack by Amalek they actually went to war?

Rav Yaakov Neimann[19] answers that Hashem didn't want the Jewish people to win through a physical war, as they would have thought, "The strength and might of my hands made me this wealth" (*Devarim* 8:17), that it was their might that had won them the battle. At this point, in the mother of all wars, their very first battle, Hashem wanted to implant within them that it is Hashem Who fights their battles. Although the camera will tell you that it is the soldiers, the tanks and the airplanes that win, nevertheless, in reality it is Hashem Who causes the victory. This is why Hashem is described as "the Master of war" (*Shemos* 15:3).

This is exactly what happened at the sea; Hashem fought the battle while *bnei Yisrael* traveled over dry land. This is what

Moshe told them: "Stand fast and see the salvation of Hashem that He will perform for you today...Hashem will do battle for you, and you shall remain silent" (*Shemos* 14:13). The effect of all this was that "the people feared Hashem, and they believed in Hashem and in Moshe His servant" (*Shemos* 14:31). Having had this experience, they were subsequently allowed to go to battle against Amalek. The experience from the sea would certainly cause them to acknowledge Hashem's power rather than attributing victory to their own might.

Some Things Always Remain the Same

The war against Amalek could certainly be described as nonconventional. The Torah relates that Moshe stood on a mountain overlooking the battle and held his hands aloft. When they were raised *bnei Yisrael* had the upper hand, but when they were lowered, Amalek appeared stronger.

The Mishnah (*Rosh Hashanah* 3:8) asks, was it really the hands of Moshe that made them stronger or weaker? It answers that this act was symbolic of the fact that as long as *bnei Yisrael* would focus their hearts on their Father in Heaven they would emerge victorious, while if they would lower their sights, they would suffer defeat. This also tells us that as long as they relied on Hashem, He would do battle for them, but as soon as they placed their trust in themselves and their own ability, they would lose.

Vision

One might be tempted to say that it was easy to believe in Hashem then, when so many open miracles happened, but nowadays it's much harder to believe, since we don't have open miracles. I would like to suggest two factors that could help refute this, one from the verses and then a parable. On their journeys *bnei Yisrael* stopped in two places. The first was called Marah. There they complained bitterly to Moshe that there was no water. However, only a day later they reached Eilim, where there were twelve springs of water and seventy date palms. It was so pleasant there that they stayed for twenty days. Regarding these travels, the Chofetz Chaim[20] comments on the short-sightedness of man. Had they known what was waiting for them only around the corner they would never had complained in the first place. This is the weakness of man, that he knows neither what is in front of him nor what is behind him. This is why he is full of complaints about his lot. In contrast, only Hashem has perspective, the ability to see all things from beginning to end.

A Work of Art

Once[21] there was a tour group looking around an art gallery. All the people were expressing wonderment at the beauty of the art, except for one man who seemed unimpressed. Someone came over to him and asked him what he thought of all the works, and he replied that they were awful. He complained that all he could see was a lot of lines mixed in with the paintings and all the colors were so gloomy. The other member of the group could hardly believe his ears and asked to see his glasses. He saw that they were smudged and covered with scratches. No wonder he couldn't appreciate anything! It is the same with us. Hashem runs the world in a way that miracles are constantly happening; it's just that we don't always realize it. He orchestrates events that are seemingly beyond the comprehension of man. If we had the right glasses on, what we would observe would be far different.

It's Good to Listen

This week's *parashah* is named after the most famous father-in-law: Yisro. After hearing of all the great miracles that Hashem had performed for *bnei Yisrael*, he came to join them in the desert. The verse tells us that after he was informed of all the great happenings, he declared, "Now I know that Hashem is greater than all the gods" (*Shemos* 18:11). Rashi derives from the words "now I know" that he had tried out every single form of idolatry in the world. He was a successful priest, admired and respected by the masses. What was it that caused him to change?

Who Will Jump In First?

The *parashah* begins, "And Yisro heard...all that Hashem did to Moshe and to Yisrael" (*Shemos* 18:1). Rashi cites a question from the Gemara (*Zevachim* 116a) that asks, What was the specific event that he heard of that caused him to change? He answers that it was the splitting of the sea, and the war against Amalek. We can understand why the splitting of the sea caused Yisro to change, since it was a great open revelation for everyone to see, but why did the war against Amalek inspire him so?

Rav Moshe Leib Yehudah of Kutnah[22] answers that the whole world, including Amalek, had seen the splitting of the sea. This was because not only the Yam Suf, but also all the waters in the world split. If someone were drinking a Coke in Australia, it would part in front of his very eyes. Nevertheless, even after experiencing this miracle, Amalek still had the brazenness to attack the beneficiaries of the miracle. Yisro saw from this that if one only follows his own feelings, the dictates and emotions of his heart, how wrong he could be. This is because a person has biases that corrupt his vision and straight thinking.

The Midrash relates that after the splitting of the sea, no one dared approach *bnei Yisrael* to wage war. What Amalek did is compared to a boiling hot bath which no one dares touch, until one fool jumps in, cooling it for the benefit of everyone else. Yisro realized the dangers of following one's own biases and agenda. He thought that perhaps he too was wrong, and thought that it was time to be subservient to something else. Seeing all the miracles that had occurred, he concluded, "Now I know that Hashem is greater than all the gods" and understood it was time for him to be subservient to the Torah and convert to Judaism.

What Did You Say?

We still need to ask, Surely the rest of the world also heard about the miracles. Why was it that only Yisro converted? Rav Yosef Leib Nendick of Kelm[23] answers that the nature of the world is such that when a few people all hear the same thing, they all will come away as if having heard something else, each drawing different conclusions. For example, if it is heard in the city that a certain person suddenly became rich, many people will take different things away from that information. His relatives will hear and rejoice for him, merchants will think that they should now approach him to do business. On the downside, thieves will think they should try and rob him.

It was the same with the splitting of the sea. We see this in the *Shiras Hayam*: "Peoples heard, they trembled; terror gripped the inhabitants of Philistia" (*Shemos* 15:14). They thought their fate would be the same as the Egyptians. "Then the chieftains of Edom were confounded; trembling gripped the mighty of Moav; all the dwellers of Canaan melted" (*Shemos* 15:15). Each nation in its own unique way feared the hand of Hashem. Amalek was also afraid, and yet how did it react? They arose and went to war with *bnei Yisrael*. Yisro also heard; however, he took the initiative and ventured into the desert to join them.

Rav Zalman Sorotzkin[24] adds that the fact that all these groups drew different conclusions after the splitting of the sea is a refutation to those that claim, "If only Hashem would perform open miracles, then we would all believe." This is because to accept the miracle for what it is needs a certain amount of preparation and frame of mind. Only one who is actually searching for the truth will recognize the miracle and be affected. He then goes on to say that one who truly believes will have no need for miracles, but if one does not want to believe, no miracle in the world can change him.

Bringing Up the Past

Let us examine this issue with a slightly different approach. The Alshich comments on the title given to Yisro: "the priest of Midian" (*Shemos* 18:1). He asks, Surely this priest business was all in the past. We aren't allowed to remind a *baal teshuvah* of his past, and yet the Torah seems to be doing so. The Alshich answers that the key to Yisro's success was that "he heard." He was able to listen, learn and take the message to heart. That was how he went from being "the priest," to having a whole passage in the Torah added because of him.

With this understanding we can answer our question. While everyone heard about the splitting of the sea, they all merely heard in the passive sense of the word — in one ear and out the other. Yisro heard in the active sense; he got out of the hearing what no one else did. Because he was open to change, intellectually honest and with a desire to learn, he converted while no one else did.

If It's Not Beneath Your Dignity

There is another type of listening mentioned in the *parashah*. Yisro advised Moshe that he should set up a system of judges and leaders below him. This would alleviate the burden on Moshe, and the people would also not have to wait in line all day for a *pesak din*. The Torah says, "And Moshe listened to the voice of his father-in-law" (*Shemos* 18:24).

It is interesting to note that the same Hebrew word for "listened," *vayishma*, is used in this instance as when describing earlier that Yisro heard (*Shemos* 18:1). Rav Yehudah Ze'ev Segal[25] derives from here the importance of listening to the advice of any person, regardless of his status. The situation here was that Moshe, the leader and prophet, was being advised by a former idol worshiper and convert, and yet he still listened to him. This is most unbelievable. Moshe could have turned around and said, "I'm the big *macher* around here. I'm the president of this congregation. Who are you to tell me what to do?" Yet we see that Moshe listened and took Yisro's advice, so much so that a whole portion of our *parashah* is taken up with this incident. Rav Segal goes on to note that this occurrence preceded the giving of the Torah, showing us that the willingness to give up one's pride, and the ability to listen and take the advice of others, whatever their situation in life, is in fact a prerequisite for success in To-rah.

Somewhat Partners

There is another way to answer our question of why these two miracles in particular inspired Yisro to come, since surely there were other great miracles in Egypt as well. Rav Tzvi Padida[26] explains that while the plagues of Egypt were indeed great miracles, all of these came about solely through Hashem, involving no partnership with Yisrael. The same God Who could make water could also make it turn into blood. Because of this Yisro saw no reason to join Yisrael in particular. With the splitting of the sea however, Hashem had a slight partnership with Yisrael; in addition, there was an element of *mesirus nefesh* (self-sacrifice) on their part. This was because Nachshon ben Aminadav first entered the water until his neck and only then did it split. So too, in the war with Amalek, Hashem provided the means for *bnei Yisrael* to emerge victorious, but they still risked their lives to fight the battle. Since Yisro saw this element of self-sacrifice on the part of Yisrael, he decided he would like to be a part of such a nation.

Family Fortunes

There was also *mesirus nefesh* on Yisro's part. Rav Shlomo Ganzfried[27] relates that there is a *gemara* (*Yevamos* 24b) that says that in the times of Mashiach, converts will no longer be ac-cepted. There was a precedent for this during the reigns of David and Shlomo when converts were also not accepted. This was be-cause during these times the fortunes of the Jewish people were at their greatest, and it could therefore be that people would have wanted to convert for the wrong reasons.

If this is the case, how could it be that the Jewish people accepted Yisro when they were on such a high level that the whole world feared them? The Gemara (*Yevamos* 76a) relates that there was a similar problem when Shlomo married the king of Egypt's daughter. She was able to convert despite the fact that this was one of the golden ages of the Jewish people. This was because she lived a good life prior to this, as she was of the Egyptian royalty. Therefore, the reason she converted could not have been because she wanted to enhance her quality of life; she already had that. She could be accepted even at a time when others would be turned away.

The same applies with Yisro. Being the "priest of Midian," he was honored and respected. He certainly wouldn't have wanted to convert for potential gain; instead, it must have been out of conviction, and he could therefore be accepted. The verse says, "And Yisro...came...to the wilderness" (*Shemos* 18:5). Rashi comments, Surely we already know that the Jews were in the desert. Why then does the Torah need to inform us that Yisro came to the wilderness? He answers that the Torah is telling us something praiseworthy about Yisro. He was living in a place where he had great honor, and yet his heart moved him to go out into the wilderness to hear the words of the Torah. We see that he also underwent self-sacrifice to convert, leaving his pulpit of honor to venture into the desert.

The High Court

Once Rav Leib Chasman[28] was sitting at home when a student came to visit him. "What improvements can I make in my service of Hashem?" asked the student. They discussed this for a while until the Rav pointed to an empty cup on the table and asked, "Could you do me a favor? Take the cup to the kitchen and ask my wife for a cup of tea." The young *bachur* jumped up, excited at the opportunity to serve his Rav. Suddenly the Rav grabbed his arm and said, "Tell me, why are you so eager to do as I ask?" The student didn't have the courage to answer. The Rav pressed him until finally he answered, "Because I want to fulfill the mitzvah of serving Torah scholars." The Rav replied, "It is exactly as I thought. A young man is presented with the chance to do a true kindness by bringing a feeble old man a cup of tea. Instead of focusing on doing kindness for its own sake, he chooses to focus on other considerations like serving Torah scholars, which is anyway questionable in this case." The words of Rav Leib Chasman left a great impact on the student and on his whole approach to serving Hashem.

The True Judge

Parashas Mishpatim focuses on mitzvos *bein adam lachaveiro* (between man and his fellow). The *parashah* begins, "These are the judgments that you shall place before them" (*Shemos* 21:1). Let us examine a comment of the Vilna Maggid.[29] One would think that there should be a difference between the law regarding a rich man who steals to fulfill his lusts, and a poor man who steals because he is hungry. Similarly, there should be a difference between one who eats *treif* to anger Hashem, and one who does so because he can't control his lusts. If this is so, how could the Torah fix one rule for everyone? Surely everyone's individual circumstances are not taken into account. He answers that the judgment from Heaven on a matter does take everyone's different circumstances into account. However, the Torah couldn't differ for every individual. Human judges do not know how to determine one's intentions, whether someone did something because he was rich, poor, lustful or hungry. Because of our lack of knowledge, we only have laws that apply equally to everyone. This is what the verse refers to. "These are the judgments that you shall place before them." The laws in the Torah are for placing "before them" — only in front of our earthly judges. However, Hashem understands all actions and knows what's in the recesses of one's heart; He judges it to its full depth, which no human can fathom.

On one hand, when one is liable for Heavenly judgment he may be acquitted because of circumstances. On the other hand, for other offenses, where the judges didn't have all the available evidence or the crime even went undetected, one cannot escape Heavenly judgment. A case mentioned in the Gemara comes to mind (*Makkos* 10b), where two people both killed a man, one deliberately, one accidentally. There were no witnesses to either, preventing the deliberate killer from being killed and the second from going into exile. Hashem arranged it so that they both were at an inn at the same time. The one who killed accidentally was at the top of a ladder, and the deliberate killer was underneath the ladder. The one on top fell on the other and killed him. Justice was done, with the accidental killer having to go into exile, and the deliberate murderer meeting his fate.

Take It, It's Yours

There is an interesting *midrash* on the above verse. It says, " 'You founded fairness' (*Tehillim* 99:4). You founded fairness for Your loved ones. By the judgments You gave them they make strife with one another; they come for judgment and make peace." Why does this *midrash* talk of the judgments making arguments? Surely the whole purpose of them is to make peace. Rav Yaakov Neiman[30] answers that the difference between Yisrael and the other nations is that in laws between man and his fellow Yisrael are as precise and exact in the relatively minor cases as they are in the big cases. When Hashem gave these *mishpatim* to Yisrael, they became involved in them and worried about even the slightest amount of money in their hands that was not rightfully theirs. Because of this they came to a new form of strife. Instead of each litigant claiming, "This money is all mine," there are now cases where each claims, "It is all his," because no one wants money which is not rightfully his.

With this we can understand a difficulty in last week's *parashah*. Yisro asked Moshe, "Why do you sit alone and all the people standing by you, from morning until evening?" (*Shemos* 18:14). Moshe answered, "Because the people will come to me to seek God. When they have a matter, one comes to me and I judge between a man and his fellow" (*Shemos* 18:15-16). The question is, What kind of response is this that Moshe was offering? Surely Yisro knew of this matter that Moshe was telling him about. Secondly, why hadn't Moshe placed a helper with him? Thirdly, why does Moshe state, "one comes to me" in the singular form?

We can answer all these questions as follows. Moshe was explaining to Yisro that when *bnei Yisrael* come to be judged, people are concerned about potentially unjust gains that may be in their hands. It is for this that they come to seek out the word of God, just as they do in matters of kashrus. The proof of this is that the Torah states, "When they have a matter, one comes to me"; in other words, one comes without his fellow. This is because the case is not about one claiming against the other, but about one person claiming that he may have an unjust gain in his possession. Finally, Moshe was telling Yisro that these cases are much easier than others to judge, but the only one who would bear the burden of the judgments and have the patience to deal with so many cases was him.

I Can't Be Wrong

The Imrei Emes[31] gives a different answer to our question. Once one of his chassidim complained, "I was sued by one of my fellow businessmen. Before we went to the *beis din* I reviewed all the necessary parts of the *Shulchan Aruch* and I was sure without a doubt that I would win. Yet the judges ruled against me. How can this be?" The Rebbe replied, "The *midrash* at the beginning of *parashas Mishpatim*, about how laws lead to disputes, had always bothered me. Now I understand. In making the laws accessible to all, Hashem enabled everyone to prepare his own case. However, everyone will inevitably conclude that he is right, because one isn't objective enough when it comes to oneself. Therefore, this familiarity with the laws leads to greater disputes. However, the power of the Torah is such that after the judges rule, the litigants accept it and make peace amongst themselves."

Get It Together

The Beis Halevi[32] comments on the juxtaposition of *parashas Mishpatim* and *parashas Terumah*, which deals with the construction of the vessels of the Mishkan. It comes to teach us that before one fulfills the commandment in *Terumah* to "take for Me a portion," towards building a house for Hashem, one's own house has to be in order, in that it should contain no unjust gain. The Beis Halevi compares this to a stolen *lulav*. When one takes such a *lulav*, it looks like one is performing the mitzvah, but the action is actually worthless. This is seen in the verse "Justice has been set back, and charity stands afar" (*Yeshayah* 59:14). First comes justice, and then charity. If one sets back justice, then his charity will have no positive effect. So too, first comes our *parashah*, the laws of justice, and then the building fund for the Mishkan, but only in that order.

Chained to the Kitchen Sink

In his *Iggeres Hamussar*, Rav Yisrael Salanter writes that it is ingrained into everyone not to eat *treif* meat, and that if a butcher finds something questionable he will take it to a rabbi even if it could involve financial loss. No one would dare eat such meat without asking a *shailah*. However, with business matters the opposite is the case. People do not scrutinize their own affairs to root out any unjust gain. He goes on to say that people must understand that all the Torah's prohibitions must be treated with the same severity. He emphasizes that one should study these laws so that he will know how to act and when to ask a question in this area also; otherwise, one could be stealing, albeit inadvertently, on a daily basis. Regarding this idea, I once heard a rabbi say that all people ask about is kitchen-sink *shailos*, but virtually no one asks about the laws of correct business practice, whose transgression could have far more damaging consequences.

No Cop-out

Once, a *shochet*[33] came to Rav Yisrael Salanter. "I want to resign my position," he told him. "I can't take the responsibility." Rav Yisrael asked him what he planned to do instead. "I was thinking of opening a store and starting a business." The Rav replied, "Amazing! You're worried about ritual slaughter, which involves only one Torah prohibition. Surely you should be worried about business activity, where many prohibitions are at stake!" On another occasion, someone once came to Rav Yisrael and asked, "What is better, someone who learns day and night, or someone who runs a store with absolute integrity?" He answered, "The second is the greater, but if such a person exists, why is he wasting his time in business?"

One and the Same

Rashi comments that when our *parashah* begins, "And these are the judgments..." the "and" is telling us that these laws are connected to that which came before, namely, the Ten Commandments. What is Rashi adding here? Surely we know that all the laws were given at Sinai.

The Ramban says that both *parashas Mishpatim* and the Ten Commandments were said at the initial meeting at Sinai between Hashem and Moshe. This was before the forty-day period during which Moshe received the rest of the Torah. It follows from this that the laws dealing with man and one's fellow, the details of the interactions in daily life, have the same status as the Ten Commandments, since they were given at the same time.

How can it be that the laws dealing with damages to one's

borrowed car were said in the same session with the most fundamental commandment, "I am the Lord your God"? (*Shemos*
20:2). Rav Moshe Feinstein[34] says that this teaches us that one
who doesn't keep the *mishpatim* doesn't believe in "I am the
Lord your God" either. He goes on to say that a person must believe that his livelihood is fixed on Rosh Hashanah. It is only because he doesn't believe this that he will come to cheat. If he
believes that Hashem anyway determines all he earns then he
will have no reason to cheat. That is why the laws of *parashas
Mishpatim* were stated at the same session as the first commandment about believing in Hashem.

PARASHAS TERUMAH

A Bit of Give and Take

P arashas *Terumah* contains the commandment to collect contributions of precious metals and other commodities to be used in the Mishkan. The verse says, "take for Me a portion" (*Shemos* 25:2). Why is the word "take" used here; surely "give" would be more appropriate. On a simple level, the whole world belongs to Hashem; "to Hashem is the earth and all that it contains" (*Tehillim* 24:1). Therefore, what can one give Hashem when it is all His anyway?

The Chasam Sofer[35] answers that when one gives charity, what he is giving is indeed Hashem's, as the verse says, "for Mine is the silver and Mine is the gold, says Hashem" (*Chaggai* 2:8). Therefore, the only thing he is giving of his own is the good intentions of his heart, the spirit within him that caused him to donate. He then goes on to say that if one doesn't give with a generous spirit, it's as if he is not giving at all, since anyway the money is Hashem's. This is seen in the continuation of the above mentioned verse in our *parashah*, "from every man whose heart will motivate him you shall take My portion." The portion should be taken only if it's going to be given with a full heart, with generous feelings and wholeheartedly. However, about one who gives begrudgingly, the verse instructs us not to take anything more from him than the compulsory minimum, since his offering is lacking the most important element.

A Different Giving

Rashi comments that the words "for Me" indicate that this mitzvah should be done *lishmah* (specifically dedicated for the sake of Heaven). The Kehillas Yitzchak explains the intention of Rashi. If one gives a poor person charity, even if he gives it not *lishmah,* but for some ulterior motive, it is still considered a mitzvah, as either way the poor person benefits from the charity. However, giving for the sake of the Mishkan was different. It was meritorious only if given purely for the sake of Heaven. The reason for this is the verse "for Mine is the silver and Mine is the gold." When one gives to Hashem, there is nothing physical he can give Him, since everything is His. It is only one's intentions which count; hence, the additional requirement of *lishmah.*

Best Out of Three

Rav Bunim MiPeshischa[36] explains that there are three types of givers referred to in our verse. The first is one who gives purely for the sake of the mitzvah of giving *tzedakah.* This is not necessarily out of compassion for the poor, but to fulfill Hashem's commandment. The second type is one who gives out of a good spirit; he cannot bear to see the poor suffering. The third type is one who doesn't really want to give, but yet under pressure succumbs. He goes on to say that all three types are alluded to in our verse. The first is alluded to when it says, "Take for Me a portion," with "for Me" indicating it is done exclusively *lishmah;* the donor's intentions are purely to fulfill Hashem's commandment. The second type is alluded to as the verse continues, "from every man whose heart will motivate him"; he gives when his heart uplifts him, as he can't bear to see the suffering of the poor. The third type is alluded to as the verse continues, "you shall take My portion." From him you literally have to take a portion, as he has no desire to do it on his own. Perhaps that part of the verse is alluding to such a person giving one of the compulsory donations and that it has to be forced out of him before he will part with it.

Who Gets the Better Deal?

This brings us to the next point. Rav Shlomo Breuer[37] comments on why the word "take" is used as opposed to "give." He says that whenever we give something, whether with our bodies or with our money, we are in fact taking something for ourselves.

The Midrash says that the poor do more for the *baal habayis* than the *baal habayis* does for the poor. How can that be? If someone provides a person with a meal, the physical gift is a rather temporary thing. However, when one looks at it with perspective, viewing the whole picture from beginning to end, he sees that there is a whole lot more to it. He is in fact gaining a share in Olam Habah (the World to Come). Therefore, his act causes a long-term effect as well.

That is why the Midrash says that by giving to a person, he is taking far more than he is giving. He then goes on to point out, regarding the first act of *chessed* mentioned in the Torah, that the same expression is used: "Let water be taken...I will take bread" (*Bereishis* 18:4-5). Shouldn't Avraham have said that he will give water or bread? The answer is that Avraham was teaching us an eternal lesson, that when you help someone else, you are in fact not giving, but taking.

Taking a Ride

This idea is further seen regarding the holy ark. It was to be carried on two poles, inserted through hoops, one pole on each side. The Gemara (*Sotah* 35a) tells us that to the human eye, it appeared that the people transporting the ark were bearing the weight. However in actuality, the ark transported its bearers. The ark wasn't so heavy that they would have been unable to carry it, but rather a miracle occurred whereby the ark carried its own weight, easing the load of its bearers.

Rav Nosson Adler[38] suggests that the same is true in a Yissachar-Zevulun relationship. To the casual observer it seems that the Zevulun is supporting the Yissachar, but in fact the opposite is the case. In reality, the ark is supporting its bearers. The Torah that the Yissachar learns is in fact supporting the Zevulun, who is its bearer.

Shulchan or Just Wood?

Another item to be constructed was the *shulchan* (table). On it were placed twelve loaves of bread that would miraculously stay fresh from one *erev Shabbos* to the next. Rabbeinu Bachaye explains the symbolism of the bread and the table. The table was to be made of *atzei shittim* (acacia wood). He says that the word *shittim* is an acronym for *shalom, tovah, yeshua* and *mechilah* (peace, good, salvation and forgiveness). The ark and altar were all made of this wood. It is as if to say that the Jewish people received all four of these gifts during the time of the Beis Hamikdash as a result of the vessels of the Temple.

Rabbeinu Bachaye then goes on to ask, surely this was fine when the Temple was standing, but now that it has been destroyed for over two thousand years, what is it that has kept us going? He quotes a *gemara* (*Chagigah* 27a) that says that now that the Temple is no longer standing, a person receives atonement through his table. This is an amazing *gemara*. One would think that perhaps fasting, prayer, and service of that nature would provide atonement, and yet one's table is what provides it. This is because of what takes place at the table. One feeds the poor, welcomes the bride and performs other acts of kindness that are his own altar of atonement. He then relates that the custom of the righteous of France was to be buried in a coffin made of the wood of one's dining-room table. Can you imagine what an impression that would make on a person? This was to teach that when one goes to the Olam Ha'emes, he has nothing to take with him except for the charity he gave in his life and the goodness performed at his table.

The Beis Halevi explains that there is a way this mitzvah must be performed. When a person gives charity, the recipient acquires a special status, similar to an object with which a mitzvah has been performed. An example is an *esrog* taken on Sukkos. Although after it is taken it has no sanctity, while it is being used it has sanctity and it is forbidden to derive any benefit from it. Similarly, it is forbidden to treat objects of mitzvos with disrespect. For example, the Gemara (*Shabbos* 22a) derives from the Torah that one is forbidden to perform the mitzvah of covering the blood of a slaughtered animal with one's foot because it is disrespectful, a disgrace to the mitzvah. Similarly, when one gives charity to the poor, it is a biblical prohibition to give it in a way that could cause the recipient embarrassment.

Not for the Fainthearted

The following story[39] illustrates the last two points. There was once a Marrano couple who escaped from Portugal and settled in Tzefat. One Shabbos the husband was in shul and heard the rabbi speaking about the showbread that would be brought to the Temple. The rabbi concluded with a sigh, "And today, we have nothing to put before Hashem."

The words of the rabbi made a great impression on the man, who ran home and told his wife that every Friday she should make with the purest intentions two beautiful loaves of bread, and that he would place them before Hashem and perhaps they would be accepted. The next Friday he took two loaves of bread to the shul and placed them in front of the ark, praying fervently that Hashem would accept them. Then he left. Minutes later, the shammash came in. Seeing the delicious loaves, he didn't wait to find out what their purpose was; he just took them to eat himself.

That night the Marrano came to the shul to see what had happened with the bread. When he saw it was gone, he was overjoyed. He ran and told his wife, "He ate them while they were still warm. We don't have much with which to honor God, but if He accepted them we must do this every week." This routine continued for many months. The Marrano would place the loaves of bread in front of the ark, the shammash would take them, and the former would return and see they were gone and be overjoyed.

One Friday, the Marrano came to shul. The rabbi was sitting at the back preparing his speech for that Shabbos. He watched as the man lay down the loaves and prayed. Suddenly it dawned on the rabbi what was happening. "Fool!" he shouted. "Do you think God eats and drinks? Who do you think ate them? Obviously it was the shammash. How could you commit such a sin, to suggest that God has a physical side to Him and eats bread?" The rabbi continued his diatribe until the shammash walked in. "You should thank this man for the bread. You are the one who has been taking it, right?" the rabbi asked. "Indeed, I have," replied the shammash. These words caused the Marrano's face to pale even further. In tears, he begged the rabbi for forgiveness, saying that he had only acted on his speech and he didn't mean to anger God.

As they all stood there, a messenger sent from the Arizal came in. Addressing the rabbi, he said, "In the name of the holy Arizal, you are to go home and inform your family that tomorrow, at the time you normally give your speech, you will die. The announcement in Heaven has been issued." Instead of going home, however, the rabbi ran to the house of the Arizal. "What have I done to deserve this? How could I have sinned?" he cried out. "According to what I have heard from above," replied the Arizal, "you put a stop to Hashem's greatest pleasure. From the time the Temple was destroyed, Hashem enjoyed no greater satisfaction than from the Marrano bringing the loaves of bread with perfect sincerity and purity. Since you put an end to it, it has been decreed that you are to die." The rabbi went to his house and told his family the sad news. The next day, the message of the Arizal came to pass.

Moshe's Disappointment

The *parashah* begins with the command for *bnei Yisrael* to "take for you clear olive oil, crushed for illumination, to light a lamp continually" (*Shemos* 27:20). Reb Chaim Shmuelevitz[40] asks, Why does it say that they should take "for you," referring to Moshe? The Ramban says that they would bring the oil to Moshe, who would inspect it to determine whether it was pure and crushed as was necessary. The question remains: Surely there was someone else in the whole of *bnei Yisrael* who could check it. Why did it have to be done specifically by Moshe?

One and the Same

It says in *Tehillim* (133:1–2), "how good and how pleasant is the dwelling of brothers, moreover, in unity. Like the precious oil upon the head, running down upon the beard, the beard of Aharon, running down over his garments." We see that the word "beard" is used twice. This refers to the fact that when the anointing oil was placed upon Aharon, it was as if it was also placed upon Moshe; hence, "the dwelling of brothers, moreover, in unity." This is telling us that the bond and unity between the two brothers was so great that it was as if the anointing oil flowed off the beard of Aharon onto Moshe's beard.

We see this earlier on in *Sefer Shemos*. The commentators say that when Moshe was sent to take *bnei Yisrael* out of Egypt, he refrained from going for seven days, as he was worried about the honor of Aharon. Moshe thought that perhaps Aharon was a more fitting leader. On the other hand, Hashem said to Moshe about Aharon, "behold, he is going out to meet you and he will see you and he will rejoice in his heart" (*Shemos* 4:14). The effects of this unity were such that if one would do an action, it would be considered as if the other were also doing it. That is why the verse instructs, "they shall take for you" — for Moshe. Just like the olive oil was taken for Aharon and checked by him, so too it could be taken to Moshe to be checked. Their togetherness was so strong that even though it was really Aharon who would actually light the menorah, nevertheless, because the oil could be brought to Moshe to check, it was considered as if Moshe had lit it. Because they exemplified the "dwelling of brothers," Moshe gets as much mention as Aharon despite his limited role.

How Good

The Gemara[41] (*Kerisos* 5b) says that when Moshe poured the anointing oil on Aharon's head, Aharon trembled, fearing he was not worthy of being anointed and was therefore guilty of *me'ilah* (misusing that which was dedicated for the service of Hashem). The chapter of *Tehillim* quoted above continues saying that, "Like the dew of Hermon on the mountains of Zion." The Gemara continues, saying that just like the dew of the Hermon is not subject to the laws of *me'ilah*, neither was the oil on Aharon's beard. We have to understand, what does the first section of the verses, about brothers dwelling together, have to do with the second half, that the laws of *me'ilah* don't apply with regard to the oil on Aharon's beard?

The answer is that we are being taught a lesson about how to create peace between brothers. Brothers are not considered to be dwelling together when each is saying, "I deserve more," that when one receives something, the other has to ask, "What about me?" Instead, the attitude of Aharon was: Maybe I don't deserve all this. Maybe Moshe deserves to be *kohen* and I am guilty of *me'ilah.* So too, as mentioned, Moshe originally thought that Aharon should be the leader. As long as each is concerned for the honor and needs of the other, then there is peace. Not having the "I" syndrome, then one can say, "How good and how pleasant is the dwelling of brothers...in unity."

I heard an interesting observation, that the difference between the words "united" and "untied" is where you put the *I.* As long as the *I* is in the right place, being concerned about the other, then unity and togetherness will exist.

Is It Me?

The verse says, "And you, bring near to yourself Aharon your brother, and his sons with him, from among the children of Israel, so that he shall be a *kohen* to Me" (*Shemos* 28:1). The Midrash says that at the time of this instruction to Moshe, it seemed bad in Moshe's eyes that Aharon would become the *kohen gadol.* Hashem then said to him, "The Torah is Mine and I gave it to you." This Midrash is particularly difficult to understand, especially in light of the previous idea, that if Moshe and Aharon were so united, why did it trouble Moshe that Aharon was being made high priest?

The Vilna Maggid,[42] Rebbi Yaakov Yosef, explains that if one wants to know the state of a generation, or know the nature of a town or country, one should look at its leaders. This is because the people and its leaders are intertwined. For example, after the sin of the golden calf, Hashem told Moshe to "Go, descend from the mountain" (*Shemos* 32:7). He was telling Moshe to descend from his greatness, as Rashi explains that Hashem said, "I gave you greatness only on their account."

Similarly, when Hashem told Moshe to appoint Aharon and not him as the *kohen*, Moshe wondered why he had been disqualified from the priesthood, what shortcoming had prevented it. He didn't know whether it was the state of the generation or his own status that prevented him from attaining the priesthood. To this, Hashem replied, "The Torah is Mine and I gave it to you." Hashem was telling him that when He needed to give the Torah to Yisrael, they were on the highest spiritual level, and the Torah was given through Moshe's hands. This was because there was no one more fitting than he was to receive it on behalf of Yisrael. Therefore, his not becoming high priest was not due to any lack within Moshe; instead, it was just because there were to be different roles for each of them.

Levels

The Dubno Maggid[43] uses a parable to answer the same question of how Hashem's answer appeased Moshe. There was once a Torah scholar who hired a teacher to come to his house to teach his son Gemara. Shortly afterwards another of his children reached the age to learn aleph-beis and he hired another teacher for that purpose. When the first teacher saw this he asked the father, "Why did you choose a new teacher? I could have taught your other son aleph-beis." The father answered, "According to what you are saying, you could also ask why I don't teach my son myself. Why do I hire you to teach my son?" The answer the father was giving was that he had reached a very high level in his own learning, and he wanted to hire someone who was closer to the level of each of his children. Since the level of the first teacher was too advanced for the younger son, he needed to hire a second teacher more on that child's level.

Similarly, Hashem said to Moshe that he shouldn't be troubled about his not being chosen as high priest. When Hashem said, "The Torah is Mine and I gave it to you," He meant that He too could have taught the Torah Himself to *bnei Yisrael*, but instead He appointed Moshe. Hashem's level was too high for the people, as they themselves said, "You [Moshe] speak to us and we shall hear; let God not speak to us lest we die" (*Shemos* 20:16). It was the same regarding Moshe and the priesthood; he was above that level, as the Torah itself was given through his hands.

Another comment of the Dubno Maggid[44] explains how Moshe was above the level of the *kohen gadol*. He was allowed to enter the Mishkan in regular white clothes, while the *kohanim* had to wear the priestly garments. Similarly, he was allowed to enter at any time, and perform the duties when necessary. The Dubno Maggid compares it to an earthly king, who has many ministers that wear special clothes and appear before him at appointed times. However, most kings have one minister who is closer to him than all the others, who may enter at any time, even in regular clothing. The same was true of Moshe; because of his special status, he was above the priesthood.

Pass It On

The Ridbaz[45] gives a different answer to our questions as to why Moshe was so upset when he heard Aharon was to be appointed high priest, and how to understand the response of Hashem, "The Torah is Mine and I gave it to you." He answers that the main thing that bothered Moshe wasn't the appointment of Aharon, but the appointment of "his sons with him."

Moshe did not merit that his sons would subsequently inherit his position! To this Hashem replied that the laws of inheritance apply only to what is left over from the departed after his death, but the *niftar* himself is not to be inherited. This is seen in the verse, "But his desire is in the Torah of Hashem, and in his Torah he meditates" (*Tehillim* 1:2).

First the Torah is called by Hashem's Name. Once it is learned by a person, it is ascribed to his name. Aharon performed the Divine service, which is attributed to Hashem's Name: *avodas Hashem*. Therefore, the one performing it is an outside factor. When that person passes on, the *avodas Hashem* is left in the world and can be inherited by his children to perform. The Torah of Moshe was ascribed to his name, since it became a true part of him. Therefore, upon his death he would take it with him. His Torah was an inseparable part of him, not something that others could inherit. This is what was meant when Hashem responded to Moshe, "The Torah is Mine and I gave it to you." Hashem was saying that originally the Torah was His — "the Torah of Hashem" — but since it was given to Moshe, it became a part of him and would go with him upon his death. Therefore, he could not pass it on to his children.

Once[46] the rabbi of a city passed away and the leaders of the community appointed another rabbi to replace him. The sons of the deceased rabbi were upset, as they thought the position should be theirs by right of inheritance. They came to the Chofetz Chaim to hear what he would say on the matter. He responded to their claims as follows. The question here is if the right of inheritance applies to this position as it does in other positions. While the position of *kohen gadol* was hereditary, the position of the priest appointed for war was not. The difference was that the priest who led the people to war had to have been a warrior in his own right; the position therefore could not have been hereditary, as a particular priest may not have been cut out for battle. So too, there was a time when the vast majority of Jews were Torah observant and the role of rabbi was relatively straightforward. His main duties were to rule on Jewish law and arbitrate litigation. This type of office could have been hereditary. Now, times have changed. Fires are burning in every quarter, and a rabbi must be a warrior to stand in the breach and deter the forces that threaten to destroy his community. Therefore, the position is no longer hereditary; whoever is most suitable to fight the battle is the one who must be chosen.

Mysteries

Following the sin of the golden calf, Moshe prayed fervently that Hashem forgive *bnei Yisrael*. When Hashem accepted his prayers, Moshe sensed that this was an opportune time to request, "make Your ways known to me, so that I may know You" (*Shemos* 33:13). This is a very difficult request to understand. What was it that Moshe was asking to know?

The Gemara (*Berachos* 7a) says that Moshe asked Hashem, "Why is it that one finds a righteous person suffering, and an evil person living in tranquility? The Bialystocker Rebbe[47] explains this discussion using a verse from *Hoshea* (14:10): "for the ways of Hashem are straight; the righteous walk in them and sinners will stumble over them." The prophet is telling us that "the ways of Hashem are straight"; it is just that not everyone merits understanding them. One type of person sees the righteous suffer and the wicked prosper, and gains strength from what he sees. He thinks to himself, "How can it be that Hashem, Who created everything in the world, would do it purely for the wicked to enjoy?" Rather, he concludes that it must be that there is a higher purpose to one's existence, the World to Come. What takes place in this world is in order to facilitate one's place in the World to Come. It is a person with this understanding who is referred to when the verse says, "the righteous walk in them." On the other hand, other people stumble through what they see. They call it injustice and say that Hashem doesn't see what's going on and that's why things are as they are. They are described as "sinners will stumble over them." In truth we must realize that the ways of Hashem are just; it is only that we do not always have the capability to understand them.

Later Understanding

The Chasam Sofer[48] says that there are many things in life that at the time seem totally incomprehensible and only later on do they become clear. The Purim story, which is relevant to our *parashah*, since Purim often occurs during the week when we read it, is a classic example of this. Many strange events took place — the execution of Vashti, the rise of Haman, Esther being taken as queen. It is only when all these occurrences had taken place and the story was played out in full that it became clear how events were orchestrated. So too, we have to believe that there is a plan and purpose to everything in life. Even though we don't always understand what happens and events don't appear to be Divinely sent, in the course of time things become clear. This is seen in the verse "and you will see My back" (*Shemos* 33:23), meaning that at a later stage one will understand why things happened as they did, "but My face may not be seen" — at the time one will not understand.

I heard the following two stories from Rabbi Pesach Krohn:

No AC — What a Shame

One boiling hot summer day outside a shul in America, the regulars turned up for *minchah* to find the door to the shul locked. After waiting five, then ten minutes for someone to unlock the door, the men decided to daven outside. As they finished *Ashrei*, another car pulled into the parking lot. The man stepped out, and as he went around to the other side of the car he suddenly fell to the ground. At first, the others thought he had slipped, but when he failed to move they realized he had suffered a heart attack.

Within minutes, Hatzalah was on the scene. They tried to resuscitate the ill man, and were about to take him to the hospital for further treatment, when someone asked, "Did anyone check the car?" They went to inspect it and found a very dehydrated baby inside. *Baruch Hashem*, they managed to save the baby as well. What everyone realized later was that the only reason the two were given such quick attention was because the shul door was locked, forcing those men to daven outside. What at first was cause for much complaint, davening in the sweltering heat without the comfort of air conditioning, saved those two lives.

A Restless Night

There was once a rabbi in Gateshead who had a *bachur* staying with him over Shabbos. As the rabbi was on his way to shul with his son on Friday night, he asked him, "Where is your Shabbos *kippah*?" The boy replied that he had left it at home. They went the short distance back to get it. The boy went up the stairs and found it in his parents' room.

Later that night, following the meal, the rabbi went up to bed. Much to his distress, he found that his bedroom light had been left on, on Shabbos. He quickly realized that his son had gone into his room to get his *kippah* and had left the light on. He tried to get to sleep, but of course the light was bothering him, so he went downstairs to learn for a while. After some time passed he thought, "Now I'll definitely fall asleep," and he went upstairs again. Again he couldn't sleep, so as a last resort, he went upstairs to the attic, to a room next to his guest's. Try as he might, however, he still couldn't fall asleep; the feel of a different bed was bothering him.

Not long after, the rabbi heard a crackling noise coming from the room next to his. He ran in to see his guest lying asleep with a huge fire burning next to him. He had left a lamp on to enable him to read in his room over Shabbos, but he had tilted it towards the floor and fallen asleep. The rabbi woke the *bachur* and his entire family, and they all fled the house. By the time the fire brigade arrived, the whole attic was burnt out. The *hashgachah pratis* was such that by his child leaving the light on in his bedroom, the rabbi slept in the attic, which caused him to notice the fire before it was too late.

Switching On a Light

There is an amazing conclusion to the story of Yosef. The brothers were in Egypt. Unusual things had been happening to them for the last twenty years. There was a famine in Canaan. The viceroy of Pharaoh had treated them strangely, seeming to know a lot about them. Then one of them was taken prisoner. Following that was the incident with Yosef's cup. The brothers were desperately asking, "What is happening to us?" Finally Yosef said, *Ani Yosef*, "I am Yosef" (*Bereishis* 45:3). With those words all the mysteries became clear, all their questions were answered.

A similar turn of events happened with the incident of the golden calf. The people thought that Moshe was dead and sought an intermediary. The Satan was able to confuse everyone; when Aharon threw the gold into the fire, a golden calf emerged. The people were dancing and sacrificing to this entity, when Moshe suddenly appeared. He raised his hands and the party came to an end.

How could it be that the entire train of events was stopped so fast in its tracks? The Beis Av[49] says that *bnei Yisrael*'s whole sin was based on falsehood, a well-orchestrated scheme of the Satan. The power of truth is such that as soon as it emerges, the falsehood is immediately dispelled. This is like turning on a light in a dark room; immediately the darkness disappears. So too, when Mashiach comes, all the falsehood in the world will immediately disappear.

A similar idea occurs in the haftarah of that *parashah* (*Yechezkel* 37:27–28): "And My dwelling place shall be upon them and I shall be a G-d unto them, and they shall be unto Me for a people. Then the nations shall know that I am the L-rd (*Ani Hashem*)." The verses are talking about the future redemption, when Hashem will reveal Himself — *Ani Hashem*. This is exactly the same language used when Yosef revealed his identity. For two thousand years the Jewish people have been suffering all types of persecutions, to an extent entirely beyond rational comprehension. All we have had is questions about why these events have happened. Yet with two words, when Hashem reveals His Name, all the answers will become clear.

On the verse "you will see My back" (*Shemos* 33:23), Rashi comments that Hashem showed Moshe the knot of His tefillin. As mentioned earlier, Moshe was seeking an answer as to why the righteous suffer and why the wicked prosper. The Gemara (*Berachos* 6a) says that in Hashem's tefillin is a praise of Yisrael, the verse "Who is like Your people Yisrael, one people in the land?" How did Hashem's showing Moshe His tefillin answer Moshe's question?

Rav Chezkiyahu Eliezer Kahan[50] answers that Hashem wanted to show that if one has questions about Providence and the way it works, he should know what is written on Hashem's tefillin: "Who is like Your people Yisrael?" This shows how Hashem holds His chosen people dear to Him, and that all that is done for them is for their benefit, even if at the time they do not understand it.

A Great Turnaround

This brings us back to Purim. Rav Shimshon Pinkus[51] comments that Hashem runs the world with *hester panim*; He hides His face from us so that we cannot see His hand operating openly. This is so much so, that we also have no understanding why one person is rich, another poor, this one healthy, this one sick. It is comparable to a father who sends his three-year-old child to a cheder. If you ask the child why he goes to cheder, he will answer, "Because my father told me they play nice games and give out sweets." What the child has no idea of is that his Torah learning has ramifications which are far beyond what he sees.

Similarly, how are we supposed to understand the way Hashem runs the world? We have to know that certain actions of ours do affect the way Hashem deals with us, as we say in Shema, "And behold, if you will surely listen to My commandments...and I will give rain" (*Devarim* 11:13-14). This, however, did not apply to the Purim miracle. The Jews had sinned and the decree had been sealed in Heaven; they deserved destruction. It was only out of Hashem's love for Yisrael and His mercy that He ultimately changed the decree.

The sealing of this decree was a result of the way Hashem usually runs the world, based on what Hashem had deemed *bnei Yisrael* deserving of. Yet Hashem could change the decree for no apparent reason other than the fact that He wanted to have mercy. This idea is symbolized in the requirement on Purim to drink until drunk. When one is so intoxicated that one doesn't know the difference between "cursed is Haman and blessed is Mordechai," he also comes to realize that someone else has to take care of everything for him, and that if he were on his own, without any Heavenly assistance, his situation would be hopeless.

The Yerushalmi says that in the future all the books of *Tanach* will be annulled except for the Five Books of Moses and *Megillas Esther*. This is because all the books of the prophets anyway follow the rules of how Hashem runs the world, as set out in the Torah. Many of the prophets urged the people to repent, the origin of which comes from the Torah. With *Megillas Esther*, however, Hashem used an extended hand of mercy, over and above that which is normally done.

The whole story of Purim is about great turnabouts — Esther being made queen, the rise of Mordechai, Haman being hanged on the same gallows he had prepared for Mordechai. The lesson is that Hashem can turn around events in a single moment. This is seen when it says, *venahafoch hu*, "and it was turned about" (*Esther* 9:1). The word *hu* also means "He," that it was Hashem Who turned it around. One moment the situation looked like *bnei Yisrael* were doomed and then the next moment they were saved.

Let us conclude with one final idea about Purim. The decree was made against the Jews. Mordechai said to Esther, "if you persist in keeping silent at a time like this, relief and deliverance will come to the Jews from another place" (*Esther* 4:14). Mordechai was telling her that either way, the Jews will be saved. If it doesn't come about through one particular channel, it will come about through another. So too, there are times in life when one is sure something will happen through a particular means, yet it instead occurs through a completely different pathway. We have to understand that the ways of Hashem are completely beyond us. He causes events to happen that are fully beyond our comprehension and He performs miracles in the blink of an eye. The most important thing to understand is that we are entirely in His hands.

Making Shabbos

There is a great discrepancy between this week's and last week's *parashah.* In *Ki Sisa,* the mitzvah of Shabbos follows the detailed account of the construction of the Mishkan, while in *Vayakhel,* first comes the commandment to observe Shabbos and then come the details of the building of the Mishkan. The Beis Halevi cites a parable to explain the difference in order: A wealthy man about to marry off a son will buy him not only his essential clothing, but also jewelry and ornaments, as befitting his status. How can one tell whether the father is acting out of love for the son, or out of duty? The answer is, by examining the order in which the father deals with the preparations. If the father first buys the son the jewelry and other luxury items, he is acting out of love for his son, anticipating the joy his son will derive from them. Only then does he attend to the necessities. On the other hand, if the father deals with the necessities first, his love is somewhat less. He feels the need to deal with what is most pressing first; only later will he see to any luxuries he feels like bestowing.

There is a similar distinction regarding mitzvos. Some are absolutely essential to being Jewish. The Shabbos is one such example. There are others, like the construction of the Beis Hamikdash. While it serves to elevate one's holiness, nevertheless, the Jewish people have survived millennia without it.

Before the sin of the golden calf, the Jewish people were beloved by Hashem, having just accepted the Torah with the famous words "we will do and we will listen" (*Shemos* 24:7). Therefore, the luxury (the Mishkan) could precede the necessity (the Shabbos). After the sin of the golden calf, however, the Jewish people were looked upon in a different light. They had to go back to basics; the Shabbos had to precede the Mishkan, to deal with that which was most essential first.

Two Types

This idea of the Beis Halevi, how central Shabbos is to our faith, is a theme that echoes throughout the verses in *parashos Ki Sisa* and *Vayakhel*. Of course, there are different levels of observing it. In the *zemiros* for Friday night, we sing, "All who sanctify the Shabbos as is fitting, all who observe the Shabbos according to the law so as not to desecrate it, his reward is very great according to his actions." The Chofetz Chaim[52] comments on the repetition of the word "all." He says that there are two types of Shabbos observers. There are those who sanctify the day by learning and davening. They are described in the *zemer* as those who sanctify Shabbos "as is fitting." Then there are those who do not sanctify it by any particular action, but still refrain from transgressing its laws. They are described as "who observe the Shabbos according to the law so as not to desecrate it." While both types of Shabbos observers receive great reward, they are not equal. Instead, one is rewarded "according to his actions."

I heard a great slogan regarding an outreach program: Turn Friday Night into Shabbos. While it was aimed at the nonobservant, even those who already keep the Shabbos can benefit from this idea using the principle of the Chofetz Chaim.

Eternal

The verse in *Ki Sisa* says, "the children of Israel shall observe the Shabbos, to make the Shabbos for their generations an eternal covenant" (*Shemos* 31:16). Rav Raphael Hakohen of Hamburg[53] comments on the fact that the word "Shabbos" is used twice. This alludes to the fact that if *bnei Yisrael* will keep two consecutive Shabbasos, they will be redeemed immediately; it will be "for their generations an eternal covenant." The above idea is based on the *gemara* (*Yoma* 38b) that says that if one is presented with the opportunity to do a sin and he refrains from performing it, and then he refrains from committing that sin a second time, subsequently, any time that same sin presents itself, he will not sin. From then on, Hashem will protect that person whenever the chance to sin rears its head again.

Similarly, Hashem promises that if *bnei Yisrael* will keep two Shabbasos, they will be redeemed immediately, and Shabbos will then become "an eternal covenant," as the verse says, "who observe My Shabbos...and grasp My covenant tightly" (*Yeshayah* 56:4). This is also alluded to in the *gemara* (*Shabbos* 119a) that says that if one comes home and finds candles lit and the table set, an angel says, "So should it be that another Shabbos will be like this one." Why doesn't the angel say that all the following Shabbasos should be like this one? Because if he will keep the next Shabbos as well, then all the future ones will certainly be kept, as the Jewish people will be redeemed.

Complete with the Children

Rav Yitzchak Elchanan Spector[54] gives an alternative explanation on the double expression mentioned above. It comes to teach us that one's own observance of the Shabbos is complete only if he teaches his children to follow in his ways after him. This is seen in the verse from *Ki Sisa* cited above. "The children of Israel shall observe the Shabbos" refers to the adults themselves observing the Shabbos. "To make the Shabbos for their generations"; one makes the Shabbos by having his children follow his example. Then it is described as "an eternal covenant," that will be observed for subsequent generations as well. This is achieved only by making it into a positive experience — Turn Friday Night into Shabbos.

He Must Have Made a Mistake

Let us examine a different approach to our question, why Shabbos is mentioned again following the work of the Mishkan. The Chida cites a *gemara* (*Shabbos* 118b) that says whoever observes the Shabbos according to its laws, even if he worshiped idols like in the generation of Enosh, is forgiven. He cites the Beis Yosef, who explains that Shabbos is equal in importance to all the other mitzvos because it teaches us about the way that Hashem guides the world, and that He is Master of creation, renewing His acts of creation every day. It also alludes to the Divinity of Torah. If so, were such an idol worshiper to keep a Shabbos, it would show that he could not possibly have worshiped idols out of conviction, but he must have been misled; the way he observed Shabbos stands in great contrast to his sin and he is to be forgiven. This also explains why Shabbos is repeated again after the incident of the golden calf. Through *bnei Yisrael*'s observance of the Shabbos, that sin could be forgiven.

Flint Stones and Switches

Let us examine a problem that will shed some light on one of the philosophical aspects of observing Shabbos. Following the general warning to observe the Shabbos, the prohibition of *havarah* (making fire) is singled out. We know that there are in fact thirty-nine general categories of prohibited labor; why is making fire the only one that is specified?

Rav Ovadiah Yosef[55] answers that there is a fundamental difference between this and the other categories. With the other thirty-eight categories, the methods of performing them have remained unchanged throughout the generations. Just like it was forbidden to select the waste from food then in the prohibited way, exactly the same method of selection is forbidden now. However, the way of making fire has changed. Originally people would rub two rocks together and from that fire would emerge. This involved great exertion. Nowadays we just flick a switch and the light comes on, with virtually no effort.

One may have thought that this act should therefore be permitted, as it involves little exertion, so the Torah has to specifically warn us against this. The reason is that the categories of labor are forbidden to us not because of the level of physical exertion involved. Technically, one is allowed to move heavy furniture around his house all day (although it may be forbidden rabbinically because the effort involved in doing this is not within the spirit of Shabbos). On the other hand, if one carries a book in one's pocket a few paces in the public domain, he has transgressed a Torah prohibition. The difference is that effort is not the reason for the prohibitions; the acts are all forbidden to demonstrate Hashem's mastery over creation.

A History Lesson

Rav Shimshon Raphael Hirsch[56] elaborates on this idea. The thirty-nine forbidden categories are all derived from the labors performed in the making of the Mishkan. All of them represent man's mastery over the physical world, so by refraining from these acts he is demonstrating that there is Someone more in control than we are. Keeping the Shabbos testifies that we believe in Hashem's creation of the world.

This theory makes sense for thirty-eight of the categories. One type does not seem to fit in with this idea: the prohibition against carrying. This is because carrying does not really alter anything in the physical world.

In *Yirmeyahu* (chapter 17) one sees the prophet bemoaning the lack of Shabbos observance in Jerusalem. He constantly makes a distinction between performing labor and carrying burdens out of one's house. What is it about carrying that is different? He explains that carrying is symbolic of social interaction, taking something from the private domain and placing it in the public, communal domain, and vice versa. The total sum of all social interactions is called "history." By refraining from carrying, one demonstrates that Hashem is the Master not only over the physical aspect of the world, but also over social interactions, namely, world history. Yirmeyahu was telling the Jews of Jerusalem that if they refrained from carrying, demonstrating that they recognized Hashem's mastery over history, then Jerusalem would be saved. If they refused, then Hashem would respond by removing Himself from history, and Jerusalem would be destroyed.

This also explains why in Kiddush we call Shabbos a "remembrance of the Exodus from Egypt," and a "remembrance of the act of creation." By refraining from the other thirty-eight acts, we acknowledge Hashem's acts of creation. By refraining from carrying, we remember the Exodus, and the fact that Hashem is in control of the history of human civilization.

Vayikra

Small Is Beautiful

S efer Vayikra begins, "And He called (*vayikra*) to Moshe." It is very noticeable that the letter aleph at the end of the word *vayikra* is written small. The Baal Haturim comments on this. At the time Moshe was writing down the Torah, he wanted to write the word *vayakar* instead of *vayikra*. That expression was used regarding the prophecy of Bilaam, indicating that Hashem merely chanced upon him. This is in stark contrast to *vayikra*, which, as Rashi explains, is an expression of affection. Moshe, in his humility, wanted to downplay the compliment and use the word *vayakar*. Hashem told him he was not to do so. Instead, Moshe went ahead and wrote it with a small aleph at the end of the word, indicating his humility.

Leftover Ink

The Midrash asks, From where did Moshe's face gain rays of light, as described in the verse (*Shemos* 34:30) "the skin of his face had become radiant"? It answers, the small amount of ink left over on his quill came onto his hand, and he wiped his forehead and it began to shine.

This *midrash* needs an explanation. Firstly, it seems to imply that it was Moshe himself who took the rays; surely they came to him from Heaven. Secondly, he was using special Divine ink. How could it be that he was given even a small amount more than was necessary?

The author of the *Takkanas Ezra*[1] explains that the ink left over was from when Moshe wrote the small letter aleph, which was supposed to have been written larger. The whole reason he was given the rays was because of his great humility. Because he appeared humble, there arose a fear that the people wouldn't treat him with the respect he deserved; therefore, his face shone. This is seen in the verse: "the skin of his face had become radiant, and they feared to approach him." His full humility was revealed at this incident, when he wrote the word *vayikra* with a small aleph, intending to detract from his own importance.

Now we can understand the *midrash*. It asked, From where did Moshe gain the rays? The answer is from the small amount of ink left over on his quill. By his writing the small aleph, the strength of his humility was what made his face shine.

Real Humility

One could ask, Why does the Torah wait for only this instance for Moshe's humility to be revealed? It could have been mentioned at a previous point, before the giving of the Torah, when the verse says, "and Hashem called (*vayikra*) to Moshe" (*Shemos* 19:20). Rav Shmuel Volkin[2] cites an explanation of Reb Chaim Volozhin about the following statement of *Chazal*: Hashem rests His Presence only upon one who is a scholar, mighty, wealthy and humble. We can understand why one needs to be a *talmid chacham*. It is also obvious as to why one must be humble, as Hashem despises the haughty. But why must one be mighty and wealthy? Surely Hashem's Presence could also rest upon someone poor and weak. The Rambam[3] actually explains that "mighty" means one conquers his natural inclinations and tendencies, while "wealthy" means one is happy with his lot. Rav Volkin explains that the main requirement to attain levels of prophecy is humility. However, as long as a person is not wealthy or mighty, there is no proof that he is intrinsically humble; perhaps it is only because of his poverty, but if he were rich he would be haughty. If one is rich and mighty, and yet he is still humble, then he has true humility. This is because humility is relevant only to one who has many fine qualities, but doesn't exalt himself because of them.

Now we can answer our question. In the verse before the giving of the Torah, quoted above, Moshe was still poor. While the rest of the Jewish people were taking of the spoils of Egypt, helping themselves to their hearts' content, Moshe was involved with taking care of the bones of Yosef, making the necessary arrangements for them to travel with them. He became wealthy only at a later stage, when he was dealing in the sapphire shavings from the carving of the second tablets. Therefore, had Moshe's humility been pointed out before the giving of the Torah, since he was still poor, one might have thought that it wasn't true humility. Now that Moshe had carved the second tablets, and subsequently was rich himself, it was evident that he had true humility.

Special Delivery

Let us illustrate these ideas with a parable. There are two different ways of sending a present to a friend. One can send it only with the intention to benefit the recipient. He doesn't care who delivers it, whether the local postman or any other person, as long as it gets to his friend. The second method is when the sender wishes to benefit the deliverer as well. For example, if the sender is a king, the deliverer will feel privileged to send a gift at his command. Alternatively, the sender may wish to grant some payment for the delivery. In these cases the sender will look for or choose someone specific whom he wishes to benefit.

Rav Tzvi Friedman of Liska[4] explains the parable. As mentioned, Moshe, in his humility, wrote the letter aleph small, to try to downgrade the honor bestowed upon him. He didn't feel worthy to give the Torah to *bnei Yisrael*. He wanted the Torah to say *vayakar*, that Hashem just chanced upon him, rather than the word *vayikra*, an expression of endearment. Hashem told him to write the word *vayikra*, indicating that not only did Hashem want to give the Torah to the generation of the wilderness, but that it should be given specifically through the hands of Moshe. Also, Hashem wanted to reward Moshe for this. In Moshe's humility, he wrote the letter aleph small. This ties in with an idea of the Kli Yakar, who quotes the *chazal* that says that Torah is best established only in one of low, humble spirit. Moshe didn't feel worthy of leading *bnei Yisrael*; we find that he even asked Hashem that Aharon should lead. This is seen in the *gemara* (*Eruvin* 13b) which says that when one runs after leadership, leadership runs away from him. Moshe, who ran away from leadership, had leadership chase after him.

Meet Halfway

The *middah* of *anavah* (humility) is one of the many *middos* we are to be wary of. The Rambam[5] writes about *middos* in general that one should not take himself to the extreme in any trait. The healthy path to follow is the middle, balanced way. If, on the other hand, one is at a bad extreme, he must bend himself all the way to the other extreme until he will revert to the middle. The explanation is that the word *middah* means "measure." Each characteristic is neither intrinsically good nor intrinsically bad. Rather, we have to learn how to use it and be in control of it. An example is the trait of anger. It is not good to always have a short fuse, and yet there are times when even anger has a purpose and has to be used. If, however, one has a serious problem with anger, one has to take measures to the opposite extreme to counter his natural tendency.

Rav Yosef Shaul Nathanson[6] says that this idea is alluded to in the verse "any meal offering...you shall not cause it to go up in smoke from any leavening or any honey as a fire offering to Hashem" (*Vayikra* 2:11). The two foodstuffs mentioned, leaven and honey, are opposite types. Leaven is very sharp, while honey is very sweet. Bringing these two foodstuffs, which have such extreme tastes, as part of an offering is not the will of Hashem. However, the verse following this (ibid., 12) continues, "you shall offer them as a first-fruit offering to Hashem." These two verses are symbolic of the idea of the Rambam, about how undesirable it is to go to extremes in one's character traits. However, as we see in verse 12, the two foodstuffs are allowed to be part of a first-fruit offering. This alludes to the fact that before one reaches the middle path he may "first" go to one of the extremes in order to eventually come to the correct point.

While the middle path is the correct one for most traits, the *baalei mussar* say that with one trait, *anavah*, one should go to the extreme. Perhaps one explanation is the *chazal* by the Kli Yakar cited above, that Torah will rest only in one of a humble spirit. The word *Chazal* use is "to remain with," or "rest." This is not to say that one who is arrogant will not be able to learn Torah; rather, it just means that Torah will not have a lasting effect on him. Nothing productive will come of it in the long run. This is possibly because in his arrogance, he won't see that anyone knows more than he does, and he will refuse to learn from others. This is in contrast to the *gemara* (*Taanis* 7b) where Rebbi Chanina says, "Much I learned from my teachers, but more from my colleagues, and I learned more from my students than all of them."

After You...

The following story illustrates these points. Once[7] a *yeshivah bachur* became engaged and he went to his *rosh yeshivah*, Rav Yaakov Ruderman, to ask if he would be *mesader kiddushin* (to officiate at the wedding ceremony). The Rav looked at his diary and much to his regret saw that he would be unable to make it that day. The boy called his father in New York and told him what Rav Ruderman had said. The father, who was close to Rav Moshe Feinstein, asked him if he would officiate at the wedding, and he gladly accepted.

A week before the wedding, the *bachur* went to Rav Ruderman to say good-bye. The Rav told him that things had changed and he was now able to come and officiate at his wedding. The boy was thrilled and told his father, who then informed him that he had already asked Rav Moshe to do it. They argued over who would go to tell Rav Moshe, and they eventually decided to go together.

Nervously they approached Rav Moshe's house. The Rav answered the door, took one look at their faces and said, "I'm not coming to get any honors; I'm only coming as a friend." He then changed the topic. No one will ever know how he knew.

At the wedding Rav Ruderman saw Rav Moshe and said to him, "You're the Rav of New York. You should be *mesader kiddushin*." Rav Moshe replied, "But you're his *rosh yeshivah*. You should do it." Rav Ruderman then responded, "Rav Moshe, you're older, so you should be *mesader kiddushin*," to which Rav Moshe said, "You're right. I'm older so you should listen to me." Finally they brought the *kesubah* to Rav Ruderman, who gave it to Rav Moshe, who asked what he was doing, since he thought they'd agreed who would do it. Rav Ruderman replied, "I'm being *mesader* (arranging) the *kiddushin*, and I'm arranging that you should do it."

Eventually, Rav Moshe read the *kesubah* and said the last *berachos*, while Rav Ruderman was *mesader* with the rest. We see how each of them sought to run from honor and only give honor to each other, each taking the example of Moshe Rabbeinu and the small letter aleph in the word *vayikra*.

PARASHAS TZAV

It's the Thought That Counts

The enumeration of *korbanos* continues into this week's *parashah*. Let us examine some of the underlying philosophical issues of *korbanos*, and some of the reasons behind them. The word *korban* is usually translated as "sacrifice." This translation, however, reflects only part of its real meaning. The root of the word is *karev*, which means "to draw near." The idea is that one who brings an offering to Hashem is actually bringing himself closer to Him.

This is seen in an idea of Rav Dessler.[8] Any interaction between human beings involves either giving or taking. Some people are more giving types, while others are of the more taking persuasion. Rav Dessler asks, When a person gives a gift to another, which would have greater feelings of love for the other, the giver or the receiver? Most people would think the receiver has greater feelings of love, since he benefits from and appreciates the present. Rav Dessler tells us that in fact the giver has the greater feelings of love. The effort he exerts and the thoughts involved will lead to a greater feeling of love for the recipient. The same is true of a parent-child relationship. There is no end to what parents do for their children, while what children do for their parents is more limited. Under such circumstances, the parent will have greater feelings for the child, the recipient of the love, than the child has for the parent. Similarly, when one gives a sacrifice, the effort involved in selecting an appropriate animal and offering the sacrifice will arouse in him great feelings of attachment, love and closeness to Hashem. By giving one becomes closer.

Business or Pleasure?

While the giver will become closer to Hashem because of his offering, we have to examine the clues we are given concerning how Hashem reacts to our offerings. Regarding many of the sacrifices, the Torah says about them, "a pleasing fragrance to Hashem." Rashi comments that it is a source of contentment to Hashem, because He commanded, and His will was carried out. On the other hand, the verse says, "Why do I need your numerous sacrifices?" (*Yeshayah* 1:11). This would seem to contradict the previous scriptural description of the sacrifices.

The following parable[9] will answer this apparent contradiction. There was once a storekeeper who had taken over his father's shop. There was one man in the town who was a big customer of his father but had never done any business with the son. The son was greatly bothered by this and sent friends of his to subtly suggest he come, but to no avail. Eventually he confronted the man and asked him, "Why is it you never even set foot into my shop, when once you were a frequent customer of my father?" The man replied that he would try to come in frequently. So it was, every week he would come in, inquire after the shopkeeper's health and the well-being of his family, but do no business with him. Eventually the shopkeeper snapped at him, "Do you think when I complained to you, I just wanted you to come and say hello and make nice conversation? It was your business that I wanted." Similarly, Hashem isn't interested that when we visit the Beis Hamikdash to make sacrifices, we just "say hello" to Him, and go through the motions. Rather, we must make the sacrifice a more meaningful experience.

Cheap Ingredients

Rav Yaakov Kamenetsky[10] illustrates this point differently. The *minchah* offering that was taken from the first produce was to be brought from barley. Why is such a low-quality ingredient used as a sacrifice in the Beis Hamikdash? Surely the prime purpose of barley is for animal fodder. Secondly, barley is used in the offering of the *sotah* (the suspected adulteress). This was to show that just as her actions were animal-like, so should be her offering. How could it be that the Torah mandates such a low-quality offering? The answer is that the Torah wishes to show that Hashem has no need for our sacrifices, as it says in *Yeshayah*, "Why do I need your numerous sacrifices?" If all the sacrifices were to be of expensive ingredients, one may have mistakenly thought that Hashem has a need for our sacrifices and their ingredients. The Torah actually sets out a sliding scale of sacrifices so that the rich can offer an animal, while the poor can offer mere birds or even flour. We see that it's the act of giving, our becoming closer to Him that really counts, regardless of the actual ingredients. It is really the giver who has the most to gain from the experience.

What Do You Think?

The Midrash at the beginning of *parashas Vayikra* quotes the verse, "Ephraim is My favorite son" (*Yirmeyahu* 31:19). What is the connection between this verse and the sacrifices mentioned in the *parashah*? The Shaarei Simchah answers with a famous *midrash* that talks about an interesting question posed in

Heaven. They asked the *middas hadin* (the Divine attribute of strict justice): "If a man sins, what should his fate be?" It responded, "He should die." They asked the Torah the same question, to which it answered, "Let him bring a sacrifice and gain atonement" (the order of which is laid out in the Torah). They asked Hashem, Who replied, "Let him do *teshuvah* to atone."

The idea behind the Torah's answer, to atone with a sacrifice, is that one has to view what happens to the animal as what should have happened to him. However, Hashem has mercy and takes an animal in place of the person. This is only because of the relationship between the Jewish people and Hashem. Because *bnei Yisrael* (who are referred to as Ephraim) are dear children to Hashem, in His mercy He accepts a sacrifice from them as atonement.

The Imrei Yosef[11] points out that we see from this *midrash* that the *middas hadin* spares the animal yet has no mercy on the man. The advice of the Torah is to save the man but to slaughter the animal. On the other hand, Hashem has mercy on both man and animal. This is seen as we say during *minchah* on Shabbos, "man and animal Hashem saves." This is because for Hashem, *teshuvah* alone suffices. The verse says, "When a person from among you (*mikkem*) will bring an offering to Hashem" (*Vayikra* 1:2). The word *mikkem* can also mean that the offering is literally from the person. That is all Hashem would really require. This is seen in the words "from among *you*...an offering to Hashem." However, in the Torah Hashem laid out the order of sacrifices that would help bring a person to *teshuvah*. Thus, the verse continues, "from the animals...you shall bring your offering." The *teshuvah* together with the sacrifice is "your offering." (We shall see later that the sacrifices are supposed to trigger certain thoughts in the one who offers them.)

Rav Shach[12] looks at the word *mikkem*, "from you," in a different light. He comments that surely the word is superfluous. He answers that it teaches us about the manner in which the sacrifices are to be offered. *Mikkem* comes to teach us that a person has to offer himself as well, by humbling himself in front of Hashem. Only then will the sacrifice be desirable to Hashem. If it is just the animals that are being offered, without any feelings of humility on the part of the giver, then it will not be pleasing to Him.

Who's the Scapegoat?

Let us examine one of the philosophical aspects of sacrifices. We realize that a man must offer up something for his sins, yet why should an animal be made the scapegoat? Secondly, what is it about dealing with the animal in this way that atones for sin? Thirdly, the Gemara (*Berachos* 55a) says that since the destruction of the Beis Hamikdash, the table of a man offers atonement. How can one compare the mundane act of eating to offering a sacrifice in the Beis Hamikdash?

The Yismach Moshe[13] explains that bringing a sacrifice will cause the giver to reflect with the following thought: "I was the one who sinned, and yet the Torah commands me to bring an animal. Surely this is not fair." We can answer this objection with the idea that we bring animals because it is representative of the natural order of creation. Each less developed entity is subservient to the one above it. The giver will then continue, "I didn't create the animals. It is Hashem Who made them and provides them with food, and yet they are slaughtered for my benefit, to save me, just because they are on a lower level on the rung of creation." He will then conclude, "Surely then, man, who was created by Hashem and provided with only good, must therefore be completely subservient to Him, Who is infinitely above us." The sacrifices enable a person to come to this conclusion, which will lead him to repentance and atonement.

Now that the Beis Hamikdash is destroyed, how is it that one can draw such lofty conclusions merely through his sitting at the table and eating meat, as the Gemara suggests? The answer is that he will also ask himself how it is permissible for man to slaughter animals. It is because of the superior status of man in the ladder of development; therefore, animals are subservient to man's needs. If one follows this reasoning through to its conclusion he will realize that man must be subservient to the One above him, namely Hashem, Who is on an infinitely higher level than man is. Therefore, through having the proper intentions, even the table at which one eats can be similar to the altar.

Dibbuk Story

It is related[14] that once a *dibbuk* (soul of another person) entered the body of a young boy. The townspeople tried to persuade it to leave the child but it insisted on remaining. Eventually they threatened to take it to the Vilna Gaon. Suddenly it became very frightened. They asked it why it was suddenly afraid; if it was afraid of the Gaon's fasting and purity, surely it was only in the Gaon's youth that he would fast greatly, but now he was elderly and wasn't accustomed to it anymore. The spirit replied, "You think I'm worried about his fasting; it's his eating that I'm worried about." Even the eating of the Vilna Goan was holy, done in perfect purity. Perhaps having the above intentions made it an event comparable to offering a sacrifice.

A "Treif" Devar Torah

Chazal[15] say that the food we eat has a direct bearing and influence on us. For this reason the Torah permitted some animals to be eaten while forbidding others. If one examines the animals we are allowed to eat, one will discover that they are all herbivores, nonhunting animals. Cows, goats and chickens are all nonaggressive, as opposed to the predators, which we are forbidden from eating. Lions and tigers maul their prey, while the name "birds of prey" speaks for itself. It is as if the Torah wants us to be influenced by the nature of these harmless animals, and not learn from the more aggressive types.

The Ramban writes that the Torah forbids certain foods because they are unhealthy for the body. The Abarbanel asks, How can it be that the Torah is merely acting as a health advisory service? Surely the purpose of the mitzvos is above this. He answers that the reason for the prohibitions is to perfect the soul and attain spiritual, rather than merely physical, health. Reb Chaim of Brisk explains that the forbidden foods and animals are still damaging to one's physical health, but this is precisely as a result of the Torah's prohibition, and not the other way around. This also explains why when a person must eat a forbidden food because of a medical condition, it will not be damaging to his body and soul. It is only when it is forbidden to him that it is damaging.

I'll Have to Chew on It

The Torah mentions two signs that characterize a kosher animal; if either one of them is lacking the animal is rendered *treif*. The first sign is that it must chew the cud. This means that it takes food into its mouth, swallows it, and then brings it up into its mouth to be chewed again. The Shaar Yosef explains that Hashem wanted these animals to be kosher in order to influence people spiritually in this characteristic. The idea is that anything a person experiences should be absorbed and thought about to see what he can learn from it and take away. He should also "chew" upon what he has learned, reviewing and delving deeper into it. Similarly, teachings of *mussar* should be internalized and absorbed while one is reviewing the lessons one has learned. By doing this one will straighten his heart and his character traits to perfection.

The second sign of a kosher animal is that it has split hooves. This is symbolic of the exterior actions of a person, which should be straight and correct. The Torah wanted us to eat and be influenced by animals with both these traits, in order to learn how to perfect the inner self, and how important it is that a person's outer self is straight. On the other hand, the camel, hyrax and hare only chew the cud. This symbolizes that while they only are in control of their inner side, their outer self is neglected.

Look at Me...

The most famous prohibited animal is the *chazir* (pig). *Chazal* actually compare the wicked Esav to a *chazir*. Why did they see fit to compare him to a pig in particular? Rav Moshe Mordechai Epstein[16] explains that Esav was called a "man of hunting" (*Bereishis* 25:27), to which *Chazal* say he would trap people with his mouth. He would speak with them about the importance of mitzvos between man and his fellow, for example, that of honoring one's parents. He would then claim that he was following the legacy of his grandfather, Avraham Avinu, the epitome of *chessed*. Because he involved himself in these mitzvos, which manifest themselves externally for all to see, he was successful in trapping people and convincing them of his righteousness.

Another way of interpreting the symbolism of the two signs a kosher animal should possess is as follows. The split hooves represent purity of hands — in other words, a man should have good relations with his fellow — while chewing the cud represents inner purity. The mitzvos between man and Hashem are not always visible to the outside world, but as we know, Hashem discerns the inner thoughts of a man.

Esav is comparable to a *chazir*, which has only one of these signs, the outer, external one, the split hooves. Although he had a good external appearance, he was lacking any inner feeling. Therefore, he was impure. This also manifests itself in the hooves of a *chazir*, which stretch outwards. It is as if it's trying to say, "Look at my feet. The whole of me is kosher." However, even the feet are detestable and *treif*. Similarly, the mitzvos Esav claims to have done are also *treif*. This is seen when it says, "for hunting was in his mouth" (*Bereishis* 25:28), to which *Chazal* say he would "hunt" married women and take them away from their husbands. The outer façade was there, but really he was nothing but a deceiver.

You Must Be Joking!

Chazal ask, why is the pig called a *chazir*? They answer that the word *chazir* means to return, indicating that in the future, it will become permitted to Yisrael. The question is asked, Surely not one detail of the Torah will be retracted. How then could the *chazir* become permissible? The Ohr Hachaim answers that in the future, the nature of the *chazir* will change. It will actually begin to chew the cud, which will render it kosher. The Chofetz Chaim[17] comments that we see from here that it is not by definition that the animal is *treif*; rather, it is the lack of one of these requirements that causes it to be prohibited. Therefore, if the *chazir* begins to chew the cud, it can be considered kosher.

Generous Discrimination

One of the prohibited birds is called a *chassidah*. Rashi says that it is called this because it does *chessed* with others of its kind by giving them food. That being the case, surely it should have been a kosher species, since it contains a desirable characteristic. The Imrei Emes[18] answers that it is excluded because it does *chessed* only with its own kind.

When Reb Naftali Tropp was in Russia he reported on the harsh actions of the Communists. They wanted to make everyone equal, and in so doing would steal and plunder from the rich and give to the poor. They would claim that they were doing this in the name of equality, altruism and social justice. Rav Naftali explained that the same applies to the *chassidah*, and that is why it is considered an impure bird. The food it distributes so generously is not its own but has been stolen and plundered from its fellow birds. While it is involved in *chessed* in one respect, it is looked at unfavorably because of the source of its generosity.

Seeing What You Want to See

Another impure bird is the *daah*. The Gemara (*Chullin* 63b) says that it is also known as the *re'ah* (literally to see). It is so called because it can stand in Bavel and see a carcass as far away as Eretz Yisrael. Rav Meir Shapiro[19] explains that the *re'ah* is placed amongst the impure birds because of its outlook on life. It stands in Bavel, where *Chazal* decreed that automatically one is impure upon entry, and sees Eretz Yisrael, the holiest and purest of lands, and chooses to focus on a carcass. Instead of seeing its own impurity, it looks around and finds something impure in none less than Eretz Yisrael. This is alluded to by the prophet: "May Hashem denounce you, O Satan. May Hashem Who chooses Jerusalem denounce you" (*Zechariah* 3:2).

We notice that there are two denunciations in the above verse, which allude to two types of Satans (accusers). One accuses against anything that does not find favor in its eyes, not differentiating between that which is holy and that which is not. This type of Satan needs only one denunciation. The second type of Satan chooses to make accusations even against Jerusalem, the holy city. To this Satan, the rest of the world is perfect; it is only with Jerusalem that it finds fault. This accuser needs two denunciations.

In *Tehillim* (128:5) we say, "and may you see the goodness of Jerusalem all the days of your life." This means one should look for only the good of Jerusalem. One application of this is that we know of the sin of the spies and are warned about slandering the land. Secondly, the *re'ah* is criticized for its ability to look only at the bad and never at the good. Because of this undesirable trait, it is impure and we should not learn from it.

Empty Vessels

The Torah goes on to speak about a situation where the carcass of an impure animal falls into an earthenware vessel. If it has entered the space inside the vessel, the vessel becomes impure. If the carcass only touches the outside of the vessel, however, the vessel remains pure. The reason is because an earthenware vessel has no intrinsic value attached to it; it is useful only because it can hold objects. That is why it doesn't become impure if a carcass touches its outside, since only its inside is what counts. On the other hand, a silver vessel also becomes impure through contact on its outside; its outside is what is valuable in this case.

The Kotzker Rebbe[20] uses this distinction to explain why in *mussaf* on the *Yamim Nora'im*, we compare man to an earthenware vessel. As mentioned, its value is based only on what is inside and what it can contain. Similarly, man's heart and inner thoughts, rather than what is merely going on outside, is what is really important. This is also seen in the *mishnah* in *Avos* (5:27), "Do not look at the vessel, but rather that which is inside it."

Solitary Confinement

Solitary confinement is widely regarded as one of the worst forms of punishment. Keeping someone isolated, as an outcast with no place in society, is one of the harshest punitive measures one can take. In prisons, only the worst criminals are placed there, since for various reasons they are unfit to be amongst even the other prisoners. The Torah actually prescribes a similar punishment. A person afflicted with *tzaraas* has to tear his clothing and leave his hair uncut. In addition, he has to live alone outside the camp of *bnei Yisrael* for a limited period, warning those approaching him that he is impure.

The Gemara (*Nedarim* 64b) says that a *metzora* is considered as a dead person. Reb Chaim Shmuelevitz[21] explains that this is not because of the pains and suffering caused by the afflictions. This is seen in Hallel, as the verse says, "Hashem has chastened me exceedingly, but He did not let me die" (*Tehillim* 118:18) — all the suffering is not equivalent to death. The reason a *metzora* is like a dead person is because of the isolation he is placed in. He is cut off from everyone else, having no contact with the outside world, a reject from civilized society.

The Gemara (*Arachin* 16b) says that since the *metzora* caused discord and separation between man and wife, and between

man and his fellow, the Torah decreed that he too must be separated from his fellow Jews. The commentators compare him to a
mazik, one who does damage wherever he goes. Therefore, the
Torah ordained he sit outside the camp so that his impurity does
not spread; he is thus prevented from causing any more damage.
Why is he dealt with in such a way and what can we learn from
the various practices he has to undertake?

You Can't Pick and Choose

Rav Yisrael Salanter[22] asks why the laws of the *metzora* follow
the Torah's enumeration of the laws dealing with kosher and
nonkosher animals? It is well known that the plague of *tzaraas* is
caused by the sin of *lashon hara*. While many people are meticulous about what they eat, in order not to make themselves impure through forbidden foods, they are negligent about what
comes out of their mouths. The *yetzer hara* makes a person
think, "How can these words be damaging?" or one convinces
oneself that what he is about to say is permitted. Alternatively,
one uses ignorance of the laws as his excuse.

The Torah is teaching us that even if a man guards his tongue
from forbidden foods, eating only *glatt* kosher to the highest
standards, he still has to guard his mouth from the impure
words that come out. The Chofetz Chaim[23] writes that with
lashon hara, one can transgress up to seventeen negative commandments and fourteen positive ones; in addition, three
curses could apply to him. With kashrus, the number of prohibitions is far less. From the rest of the *parashah* we see the extent of
the severe impurity that is caused by a slip of the tongue.

A Visit to the Local Kohen

The first thing a *metzora* would do was to visit the *kohen*, who
would examine him to determine whether he was contaminated

or not. One of the reasons for going to the *kohen* was for him to guide a person to the correct way of atonement. The *kohanim* served as the spiritual leaders of *bnei Yisrael*, and their guidance and teachings were essential to enable a person to forsake the sin that brought all this upon him in the first place.

Reb Chaim Volozhin[24] gives a second reason why the *metzora* was brought to the *kohen*. He explains that the word *vehuva*, "and he be brought" (*Vayikra* 14:2) means that he can be brought even against his will. He says that often the *lashon hara* is directed against a nation's leaders, in this case the *kohanim*. Because of this, a person may be reluctant and embarrassed to go to the *kohen*. Therefore, the Torah had to teach us that he be brought even against his will. Let him seek atonement through the one he ridiculed and should have had more respect towards.

The Vayakhel Moshe cites another reason why the *metzora* is brought specifically to the *kohen*. One of the reasons why the sin of *lashon hara* is such a great stumbling block is because people often justify their sinful speech by thinking that it is in fact a mitzvah to say it, to warn other people of the shortcomings of a particular person. (See the *Sefer Chofetz Chaim*, where he explains the fallacy of this argument, as well as the circumstances and strict conditions that must be met for speaking negatively of others to be permissible.) For this reason, the Torah commands that the *metzora* must be brought to Aharon HaKohen. The outstanding quality of Aharon was that he was the lover and pursuer of peace. Often, in order to make peace between a husband and wife he would have to hide the truth or say something not exactly true. The Torah is telling us that the "lies" of Aharon, which make peace between man and his fellow, are more dear to Hashem than the "truths" of the *metzora*, which sow nothing but strife and discontent. Because of this, he must go specifically to Aharon to learn from his example.

Finally, on this point, there is a rule that a *kohen* who is afflicted may not examine his own *tzaraas* but must go to another to determine its status. This is because his own self-interest may prevent him from making an objective decision. Similarly, one can always see the faults of others, but it is infinitely harder to see one's own faults. Therefore, one must approach the *kohen*, who is an objective source, to help determine his status. We shall return to this idea later.

Outside Influence

One of the wonders of the affliction of *tzaraas* is that if one has a small discoloration on him he will be impure, yet if he is covered from head to toe he is rendered pure. How can we account for this paradox? The Shaarei Simchah explains that it is harder for people who are well known and established as wicked to influence others, as everyone knows about their wickedness and will keep away. One should, however, be more afraid of a person whose evil is hidden in his heart. These people do come into regular contact with others and their influence, although subtle, can be very damaging.

Along similar lines, the Kli Yakar explains that a *chazir* has an extra degree of impurity because it stretches out its split hooves in order to deceive people into thinking it is a kosher animal. Esav is compared to a *chazir*, as he too would deceive people with his mouth. A *metzora*, whose sin is *lashon hara*, would have to sit outside the camp. He would warn others from approaching, as the verse says, "he is to call out, 'Impure, impure' " (*Vayikra* 13:45), revealing his sin and wickedness. If, on the other hand, he is covered from head to toe with *tzaraas*, his wickedness is obvious to everyone and people will know not to get too close. There is no further purpose in placing him outside the camp, as everyone will see and be warned.

The Chofetz Chaim[25] takes a different approach to answering this question. The purpose of the *metzora's* isolation is to give him time to reflect on his situation. He will reach thoughts of repentance, realizing how odious his ways are, and will resolve not to speak more *lashon hara*. The laws of the *metzora* deal only with a case where the *tzaraas* does not cover one's entire body. In such a case, the *metzora* may view his affliction as a freak occurrence or medical condition. Therefore, by his leaving the camp he will get the wake-up call that will cause him to repent, since he will have the time to reflect properly on his situation. If his entire body is covered, he will immediately realize the root cause of it; he doesn't need anything else to cause him to repent.

What's the Definition of a Bad Driver? That Which Everyone Else Is

Let us examine the significance of the *metzora's* having to call out the words "Impure, impure." The Vayedaber Moshe gives an esoteric explanation of the verse. *Chazal* say that there is a tendency amongst people to talk about the failings of others, and yet the gossiper himself will possess some of these failings. We can see this idea if we read the verse the following way. "Impure," refers to the one doing the calling out, the impure one. It then continues, "impure he shall call out"; he calls out to other people that they are impure. The ludicrousness of such a person's actions is evident. With this we can understand the statement of *Chazal*, "A person sees all deficiencies except his own." The very faults that bother a person about another are the exact same ones that he himself has.

Rav Sorotzkin[26] explains that the *metzora's* calling out, "Impure, impure" is in fact a part of the *teshuvah* process. Prior to this he was used to speaking *lashon hara*; now it is only appropriate that he should use his speech in a positive way. It is a mitzvah for him to warn others about his impurity, so that they should not become infected. This mitzvah is the beginning of his repentance, wherein he is taught that speech can be used in a positive way as well.

The Way Home

At the end of the *metzora's* intensive recovery program the Torah says, "the *tzaraas* affliction has healed from the *metzora*" (*Vayikra* 14:3). Rav Raphael Hakohen of Hamburg[27] asks why he is still called a *metzora* even after the affliction has healed completely. The Rambam (*Hilchos Teshuvah* 2:1) asks, What is complete *teshuvah*? He answers that it is when the same situation arises, and the person has the same opportunity to sin as before, but instead he conquers his evil inclination, because of his *teshuvah*. Similarly, with the *metzora*, even when he repents for the *lashon hara* he has spoken, he has not done complete *teshuvah*. While he was dwelling outside the camp in isolation, it was impossible for the opportunity to speak *lashon hara* to arise and for him to consequently be able to show that he would not stumble anew. Therefore, the Torah still calls him a *tzarua* until he returns to the camp, surrounded by the rest of *bnei Yisrael*. Under such circumstances, if he refrains from further *lashon hara* he is welcomed back.

Forget Nepal

eople are always looking for spirituality, some out of despair at what the material world has to offer, others as if attracted by a magnet for no rational reason. People will go to all sorts of faraway places and try out all kinds of interesting things in the search for a meaningful existence. Without moving an inch, before heading to the travel agent or the local institute for kabbalistic studies, let us examine what the Torah and our Sages have to say on the matter. *Parashas Kedoshim* begins, "You shall be holy (*kedoshim tehiyu*), for I Hashem your God am holy" (*Vayikra* 19:22). Rashi explains, "Be removed (*perushim*) from forbidden relations and from sin, for wherever you find restrictions in these areas, you find holiness juxtaposed to it." The idea is that just like some things are forbidden to you, there are equivalent and similar things which are permitted and which one can make use of. There are forbidden meats, but others that are permitted. There are forbidden relationships, but then there are those that are permitted through marriage.

The Ramban questions Rashi's interpretation of holiness; surely the Torah has warned us regarding separating from these prohibited things elsewhere, he says. Why is it necessary to inform us of them again here? Rather, the Ramban explains, the separation mentioned here is to separate from even that which is permitted to us. By voluntarily refraining from even that which is permitted we avoid being a *naval birshus haTorah* (a boor with the Torah's license).

What does this mean? There are many activities permitted by the Torah. The commandment to be holy is coming to warn us not about the actions themselves but rather about the way in which they are being performed. By exercising restraint, one can reach a higher level in his Divine service. One can, for example, buy the meat of an animal that was slaughtered in the finest way, wash for his meal, make *hamotzi*, *bentch* with the greatest *kavanah* and yet still be called a *boor*. Why? Because the extreme quantities one ate were not in keeping with the Torah's guidelines of restraint, and therefore he didn't fulfill the mitzvah to be holy.

A Good Cup

Rav Yerucham Levovitz[28] illustrates this idea with a parable. There was once a doctor who suggested that weak people not drink coffee. If they found it difficult to refrain completely they should drink only decaffeinated coffee. To an outsider the person seems to be drinking the same coffee as before; the grains look the same, the resulting brew looks the same. Similarly, permissible unions or foods are essentially the same as those forbidden. The difference is that the permitted has had the caffeine removed, while the forbidden is dangerous.

In like manner, the Torah gave us guidelines regarding which actions are full of spiritual caffeine and therefore like poison. This commandment suggests that we further guard our spiritual health by imposing restrictions even on that which is permitted in order to restrict overindulgence in that which is even remotely dangerous. This is what the Ramban means when he says to avoid becoming a boor even with the license of the Torah. By leading a life of self-restraint and not overindulging in one's desires even in permitted activities, one fulfills *kedoshim tehiyu*.

The Midrash on the verse says, "If you sanctify yourselves, I will consider it as if you have sanctified Me." Rav Shmuel Rozovsky[29] says that all that was created was for the purpose of sanctifying Hashem's Name, as in the verse "all that is, I have created in My Name and in My honor" (*Yeshayah* 43:7). The idea behind this is that when one elevates himself over his natural instincts, either by restraint or by performing a mitzvah, he is testifying that he was created to manifest the glory of Hashem in this world. As long as one simply exists within a mundane life, doing everything normal people do, following his urges, he will not become anything holy. Doing something which will cause him to be elevated above the mundane will cause a link with that which is holy.

Now we can understand the Midrash. If one sanctifies himself, doing something because it is the will of Hashem, he is publicly testifying that he recognizes that he was created to sanctify Hashem's Name.

In Public View

Rav Yonasan Eibeschutz[30] places a slight limitation on this idea. He cites Rashi, who says that this portion of the Torah was stated in front of all of *bnei Yisrael*. The publicity was meant to teach us that even the limitations one accepts upon himself must have defined parameters.

During the time of the Second Temple there were people called the Essenes, who would go off and live in the desert, cutting themselves off from worldly pleasures. The Sages, known as the Perushim (separators), placed great value on limiting one's indulgences; at the same time, however, they taught that one's actions must be pleasing not only to Hashem but to one's fellowman as well. One is not allowed to change the natural order and not be part of society. The commentators write that with regard to limiting one's indulgences, one is not allowed to take himself to an extreme by not marrying or not eating meat. The commandment to be holy was given in the presence of all of Yisrael to illustrate that one should practice controlling his desires, but only within the boundaries that allow him to remain a part of society.

Live and Let Die

Let us examine a different explanation of holiness. Regarding our commandment the Midrash cites the verse "And you who cling to Hashem your God, you are all alive today" (*Devarim* 4:4). What has this verse got to do with our commandment? The Ksav Sofer cites a cryptic statement of *Chazal*: One who wants to live should cause himself to die, while one who wants to die should cause himself to live" (*Tamid* 32a). The explanation is that "causing oneself to die" means reducing his worldly pleasures. While Hashem created everything to benefit man, one has to act with caution, since an abundance of pleasure could cause him to rebel against Hashem. He should "kill himself" a little and refrain from indulging in too much worldly pleasure to remain safe.

On the other hand, there is a person whose actions are all for the sake of Heaven; through his eating, drinking and sleeping he intends to serve his Creator better. All his worldly pleasures are therefore turned into mitzvos. Even when he is asleep he is getting closer to Hashem. Such a person doesn't need to "kill himself" in this world in order to merit the World to Come; he doesn't stumble through eating and drinking. This is seen in the above verse: "And you who cling to Hashem your God," by doing your actions for the sake of Heaven, then "you are all alive today," even in this world. According to the Ksav Sofer, holiness is merely a change in one's attitude. One has to think to himself that every action he does, even if it is merely a normal activity, is for the sake of Heaven so that it will cause him to serve Hashem better.

The commandment to be holy is followed first by the commandment of Shabbos and then by the commandment to honor one's parents. When these are mentioned in the second set of tablets, they are both followed by the words "as you were commanded by Hashem your God" (*Devarim* 5:12,16). The Aruch Hashulchan[31] explains the reason for this. These two commandments have something in common, that even without following the Torah one could still have come to the same decision to observe these practices. Everyone needs a day off from work, while honoring parents is necessary for a civilized society. The Torah therefore tells us not to observe these because of natural instincts, or what local trading laws allow, but because they are the commandments of Hashem.

In the first set of tablets, this instruction was not necessary; the people were on the level of angels. Following the sin of the golden calf, this instruction became necessary. When the Torah says, "You shall be holy," it is to be done through the mitzvos of Shabbos and honoring parents, precisely for the sake of Heaven and not just because of what logic dictates.

From this we learn that all our physical needs should also be fulfilled in order to serve Hashem. That is what is meant by holiness. With this we can understand the statement of *Chazal*, "Sanctify yourself with that which is permitted to you" (*Yevamos* 20a). Holiness is attained not only through spiritual matters, but also through that which is permitted to a person, by his recognizing that he is human and not an angel.

Holiness in Everyday Mitzvos

Let us conclude with one final explanation of holiness. Rav Yisrael Salanter[32] writes that many people mistakenly think that holiness and purity are associated only with spiritual things like mysticism and other esoteric pursuits. He explains that in fact we find the rest of the *parashah* filled with commandments relating to man's everyday life and his dealings with other people: "do not steal," "do not be a talebearer amongst your people," as well as commandments about correct weights and measures. Rav Salanter is telling us that one fulfills the commandment to be holy through following these laws of basic human interaction as mentioned in the rest of the *parashah*, rather than involving oneself only in purely spiritual matters.

The Beis Av[33] also comments on the juxtaposition of the commandment to be holy and that of honoring one's parents and observing Shabbos. By carefully observing these everyday mitzvos, a person sanctifies his life. When we recite a *berachah* on a mitzvah we say *asher kiddeshanu bemitzvosav*, "Who has sanctified us through His mitzvos." This shows that it is these well-known mitzvos which cause a person to sanctify his life.

"Making" Yom Tov

This is the time of year for festivals. Beginning with Rosh Chodesh Shevat until Shavuos, there is a major or minor festival every two weeks. (In between Rashei Chodashim we have Tu BiShevat, Purim, Pesach and Pesach Sheini.) The section of the festivals begins, "Hashem's appointed festivals, which you shall designate (*asher tikra'u osam*) as callings of holiness. These are My appointed festivals. Six days labor shall be done, and the seventh day is a day of complete rest..." (*Vayikra* 23:2-3).

Why does the Torah first state, "Hashem's appointed festivals," and then talk about Shabbos? Surely it should continue speaking about the festivals. Let us examine three answers. Rashi, as explained by the Me'am Loez, comments that one may have thought that the Shabbos is far superior to the festivals, since it was established at the time of creation, to be on the seventh day eternally. One may think that the festivals, whose dates are determined by the *beis din* (as we shall examine later), are therefore of lesser importance, since their dates are determined by man's sighting of the new moon. Rashi therefore tells us that the reason for the juxtaposition of Shabbos and the festivals is to show that "whoever desecrates the festivals is considered to have violated the Shabbos, and whoever upholds the festivals is considered as if he upheld the Shabbos."

"Making" Shabbos

Rav Tzvi Friedman of Liska[34] provides a second answer. He cites the *chazal* that says that one who observes the Shabbos is considered Hashem's partner in creation. Each Shabbos we observe is in itself a new creation. We thus find the verse *laasos es haShabbos*, "making the Shabbos" (*Shemos* 31:16). It is as if we are creating the Shabbos by observing it. As we have mentioned above, the word *osam* refers to our authority in determining the festivals. It therefore seems that our ability to consecrate the months is the result of being considered a partner to G-d in creation, through observance of the Shabbos. The Torah alluded to this idea by first proceeding to talk about the Shabbos, and only then going on to talk about the festivals.

Rav Yonasan Eibeschutz[35] gives a different answer. He explains that the determination of the festivals has a direct bearing on the Shabbos, as it may happen that a festival will cause a temporary suspension of the laws of Shabbos. This could happen if Rosh Hashanah or Yom Kippur were to fall on a Shabbos. One example is that the festival sacrifices override the Shabbos. The mention of Shabbos before the festivals teaches us that Yisrael's determination of the time of the festivals is valid even though it may cause the laws of Shabbos to be suspended.

Being Sociable

The Meshech Chochmah[36] examines a philosophical aspect of the difference between Shabbos and Yom Tov. There are two types of mitzvos. There are those such as tefillin, tzitzis and mezuzah, whose purpose is to strengthen the bond between man and Hashem. Other mitzvos serve to strengthen the bond between man and his fellow. Examples are the laws of charity, *terumah* and *maaser*. A similar difference exists between Shabbos and *yom tov*. Regarding Shabbos we are commanded, "Let every man remain in his place" (*Shemos* 16:29); one has to remain within certain boundaries. Both carrying and preparing food are also forbidden. This shows us that Shabbos is more of an individualistic day; the extra time should be spent learning and davening, strengthening the bond between man and Hashem. On the other hand, *yom tov* is supposed to strengthen the bond between people. If a hundred guests turn up at one's home, one is allowed to cook for them. The whole of *klal Yisrael* would go up to the Beis Hamikdash to rejoice in front of Hashem. Therefore, there are no restrictions on traveling or carrying, thereby promoting social interaction.

A Royal Invitation

On the festivals there is a specific mitzvah in the Torah to ensure that the poor are able to rejoice as well. One could be punished for failure to perform this mitzvah. On the other hand, there is no such punishment for neglecting the poor on Shabbos. How can we account for the difference?

In the introduction to the *Shev Shemaisa* we find the following parable. Once a king decided to visit a certain villager. Much to his disgust, he wasn't treated in the way deserving of a king, which angered him greatly. Later, a messenger invited the king to a different villager's home. Should this villager not treat the king well, he would be even angrier than he was with the first host. At least with the first, the king came of his own accord, while with the second, he was actually invited by the villager. He would be angry not only with the villager, but also with the messenger who delivered the invitation.

Shabbos was fixed and given as a sign between Hashem and *bnei Yisrael* that He created the world in six days and rested on the seventh. *Bnei Yisrael* are not punished if the poor do not join in with them; it is Hashem's determined time. *Yamim tovim* are different. As we shall see, *bnei Yisrael* would determine the exact days on which they would fall. Therefore, if they do not honor the festivals as fitting by inviting the poor and destitute, to enhance the latter's enjoyment of these times, then they are worthy of punishment. This is seen in the verse "My soul detests your new moons and your appointed times" (*Yeshayah* 1:14). Hashem will detest not only the festivals, but even the Rashei Chodashim, because they are the "messengers" which announce the festivals.

Sanctify the Festivals on Earth

Let us examine a fascinating insight into calculating the dates of the festivals. The Gemara (*Rosh Hashanah* 25b) explains from our verse that since the Torah wrote the word *osam*, alef-taf-mem, instead of the full version that would have included a vav as well, it is alluding to the word *atem*, which literally means "you." This refers to the fact that the power to determine the days of the festivals are given over by G-d to man. We would rely on a system whereby a pair of witnesses who would witness the new moon would come to the Sanhedrin. After a thorough investigation of the witnesses the *beis din* would declare the new month. The *beis din* determined whether the festivals would be earlier or later, affecting the observation of a festival on a particular date.

Another very important task for the *beis din* was to determine a leap year. The consequences of this were that if an extra month were added, Pesach, and subsequently all festivals, would be observed a month later. (Leap years are needed because of the discrepancy of eleven days between the solar and lunar years; adding an extra month ensures that Pesach will always fall in the spring.) The Rambam (*Hilchos Kiddush Hachodesh* 2:10) explains that when the *beis din* declares a leap year, the extra month is still observed even if they declared it mistakenly. Even though it is known to be wrong one must still rely on their decision, as the verse says: *asher tikra'u osam*, "which you shall designate." One may think the results would be catastrophic, but in fact the Gemara says that Hashem does not sanctify the months in the Heavenly courts until the earthly court has done so.

Using this idea, the Tosefes Berachah explains why only in a leap year do we add the words: *ulechaparas pesha*, "and for willful transgression" in the Rosh Chodesh *mussaf Amidah*. This is because through our calculations we could have been mistaken in our determination of the extra month. If this were the case we could be mistakenly eating on the real Yom Kippur or eating *chametz* on Pesach. For this reason it is appropriate to ask for forgiveness for this particular type of sin specifically during leap years.

We have seen that with Shabbos, the sanctity is determined by Hashem, while with Yom Tov it is determined by men. This idea also manifests itself in the verse "you shall be for Me a kingdom of priests" (*Shemos* 19:6). Rav Meir Shapiro[37] explains that two distinct entities are referred to in the verse: kingship and the priesthood. While the priests' status is conferred upon them from above, the kingship is only at the request and acceptance of the people. At Mount Sinai, *bnei Yisrael* were told of two facets of holiness. The first is that which comes from Heaven, and the second is that which comes from themselves through their own actions. Therefore, it was not coincidental that the day of the giving of the Torah was on a Shabbos, as well as Yom Tov.

Why Shavuos Is Different

In relation to the current period, the verse says regarding Shavuos, "And you shall declare on that very day." Why does the Torah refer to Shavuos as "on that very day," an expression we do not find in relation to any other festival? Rav Yitzchak Ze'ev Soloveitchik[38] explains that there is a difference between Shavuos and the other festivals. He cites the Rambam (*Hilchos Kiddush Hachodesh* 3:16), who explains that the Sanhedrin had the authority to sanctify the months retroactively. For example, if witnesses for a particular month turned up only at the end of that month rather than at the beginning the court could re-count the days from which the witnesses claimed the moon appeared. The Torah could not have written "on that very day," as the date could have been changed. While all the other festivals could thus be retroactively rescheduled, Shavuos is different. The day of its celebration is not dependent on any day of the month; rather, it is always forty-nine days after the Omer offering was brought. The timing of the giving of that offering was based on the month of Nissan, which could not be changed once that month was over. This is why Shavuos is described as taking place "on that very day."

Shabbos and Yom Tov "Equals" Shemittah and Yovel

Let us conclude with an idea from next week's *parashah* that is related to our subject. The Meshech Chochmah comments on the fact that the expression *Shabbos laShem* is used in the context of both Shabbos and the *shemittah*. He explains that the sanctity of Shabbos is fixed eternally to be on the seventh day. *Yamim tovim*, however, are sanctified on earth, in that the *beis din* has the power to determine their dates as a result of witnesses sighting the new moon. The *Meshech Chochmah* explains that the same difference exists between the *shemittah* year and the *yovel* (the jubilee year). Whatever we are accustomed to observing during the *shemittah* we observe during *yovel*. However, the *yovel* is sanctified only if it is treated as a *yovel*, in that the shofar is sounded, slaves are released and lands are returned, while *shemittah* is sanctified regardless of earthly acceptance or proclamation. This explains why, in reference to *shemittah*, it says, *Shabbos laShem*, "a Shabbos for Hashem," while regarding *yovel* it says: "and you shall sanctify" and "holy it shall be to you," which is similar to what is said about Yom Tov: "a holy convocation it shall be to you." The comparison of *yovel* with Yom Tov is even more apparent when we realize that *yovel* is the time for releasing slaves, which alludes to the going out of Egypt, and *yamim tovim* are, as we say in their Kiddush, a remembrance of the going out of Egypt, and our release from slavery.

A Year Off

This week's *parashah* begins "And Hashem spoke to Moshe on Mount Sinai, saying... When you come into the land which I give you...on the seventh year there shall be a complete rest for the land, a Sabbath for Hashem" (*Vayikra* 25:1–3). Rashi asks why the laws of *shemittah* are specifically mentioned as being given at Mount Sinai; surely all the other commandments were also given there. He answers that it teaches us that just as with *shemittah*, where all its general rules, details and finer points were stated at Sinai, so too, all the other mitzvos, their general rules, details and finer points were given over at Sinai.

The Best Proof

According to Rashi's interpretation, why does the Torah inform us of this idea specifically at this instance, as opposed to at our introduction to any other mitzvah in the Torah? Let us examine four approaches to this question. The Chasam Sofer[39] explains that the mitzvah of *shemittah* is proof that the Torah is *min haShamayim* (given from Heaven). The way of farmers, he explains, is to sow their fields several years and then leave them to replenish their strength for a while. The Torah in fact tells one to sow continuously for as long as six years. Then it states that during the sixth year, when one would think the land is at its weakest, it will produce enough for the coming three years, until the crop of the ninth year is ready. If the Torah were not Divine, people would simply starve. No man could have ever made such a promise, as he could not guarantee this happening. That Moshe Rabbeinu gave over this mitzvah containing such promises is proof that the Torah must be from Hashem. This explains the intent of Rashi, when he says, "just as *shemittah* was mentioned at Sinai." The mitzvah of *shemittah* proves that the Torah was given and taught at Sinai, by Hashem and not on Moshe's own accord. It therefore follows that the rest of the Torah was also Divinely given.

Seven Up

The Bris Shalom[40] suggests an alternative answer to the above question. He explains the juxtaposition of *shemittah* and Mount Sinai based on a rather mystical idea brought down in *Pirkei D'Rabi Eliezer*. There are seven main lands out of which Hashem chose Eretz Yisrael. There are seven mountains from which Hashem chose Mount Sinai. There are seven days of the week; Hashem chose the Shabbos. The Midrash explains that all sevens are dear to Hashem. Regarding the seven ancestors — Avraham, Yitzchak, Yaakov, Levi, Kehas, Amram and Moshe — it was Moshe who received the Torah. With regard to years, it is the seventh year that is special. Similarly, at the end of every seventh *shemittah* cycle is another special year, namely, the *yovel* year. All this is alluded to in the above verse: "And Hashem spoke to Moshe," the seventh of the forefathers, "on Mount Sinai," the seventh of the mountains, "saying...When you come into the land which I give you," the seventh of the lands. The

verse continues: "the land shall observe a Sabbath for Hashem."
Rashi there explains: "For the sake of Hashem, just as it is said regarding the Shabbos of creation [i.e., the weekly Shabbos]." This
refers to the fact that the same term, *Shabbos laShem*, "a Sabbath
for Hashem," is used in reference to the *shemittah* as well as the
weekly Shabbos. Just as Hashem chose the seventh day of creation to be holy, He chose the seventh year to be holy, and similarly, after seven complete *shemittah* cycles, the fiftieth year is
also holy. We see this from the fact that all sevens are dear to
Hashem.

Shabbos and Shemittah

The Ponovezher Rav[41] once explained regarding our weekly
Shabbos that not only are there numerous laws and prohibitions
that characterize it, but also there is an extra element of
kedushah present. Similarly, a human being is invested with holiness. However, in the course of the other six days of the week,
he is involved in the darkness of nonsacred matters. Comes
along Shabbos, which is all holy, as it says, "And Hashem
blessed the seventh day and sanctified it" (*Bereishis* 2:3), and re-
juvenates this *kedushah* in man. These two holy elements, the
laws of Shabbos and the extra *kedushah*, combine to make a holy
Shabbos for the Jewish people.

The same is true regarding the land of Israel. Its essence is
kedushah; however, in the course of six years of working the land
it is involved only in the profane. Comes along the seventh year
and reunites it with the holiness of Eretz Yisrael. The mitzvah of
shemittah is only as a result of a holy people and a holy land together, a spiritual dimension which no other nation or land can
claim. Just as we are under the *hashgachah pratis* and direct control of Hashem, it is also written about the land, "the eyes of
Hashem your G-d are always upon it, from the beginning of the

year until the year's end" (*Devarim* 11:12). Hashem is constantly overseeing it and performing miracles there.

In the *shemittah* year, the people live a life of holiness, keeping its mitzvos, having to observe its laws and treat the fruits of that year with a special sanctity. This is similar to what takes place on Shabbos, when more sanctity is bestowed on us. We say in the Shabbos *mussaf Amidah*, "they shall rejoice in Your Kingship"; similarly, we must rejoice under the Kingship of Hashem, and then the continuation of the prayer will be fulfilled: "the people that sanctify the seventh, they will all be satisfied and delighted from Your goodness." Shabbos is described as the source of all blessing. If we rejoice in the Shabbos and the *shemittah*, observing their laws, we will receive all the blessings that will take effect during the rest of the week, and similarly, the remaining six years.

Giving Strength

Rav Shmuel Bloch[42] quotes his Rebbe, the Chofetz Chaim, who suggests a third approach. He compares Hashem's descending to Mount Sinai to a king who decides to visit a certain village. The presence of the king will certainly require the villagers to clean up the place and act with a certain reverence, carrying out his will, and have gratitude for his presence. So too, Hashem came down to this world to give the Torah. We have to pay attention to His every word and fulfill His will. For this reason, the Torah mentions Mount Sinai in conjunction with *shemittah*. The laws of *shemittah* are a great test and demand great sacrifice. They are a test of faith and trust in Hashem, where one has to rely on the Torah's promise that he will have sufficient produce despite the year of rest. By mentioning Mount Sinai along with these laws, the Torah sought to give us strength and reinforce our commitment to keeping Hashem's commandments.

In fact, the Midrash calls those who observe the *shemittah* "mighty warriors who fulfill His word" (*Tehillim* 103:20). This is because it is unusual for one to observe a mitzvah for an entire day, week or month, and yet here the Torah ordains that a farmer leave his field abandoned, and still he remains silent for an entire year. Every day he will walk past the field thinking of what he could be earning, and yet he restrains himself. Because he overcomes such strong natural tendencies, he is called a warrior.

Rav Aharon Kotler[43] asks why these *shemittah* observers should be called heroes, since anyway Hashem promised that He would increase His blessing in the sixth year to provide enough food to last until after *shemittah*. He answers that we see from this the power of the *yetzer hara* in battling a man and perverting his thoughts. A man's natural desire is for material success. Even though he has three years' worth of crops, and he knows of the great miracle that brought it there, he still will look at his field lying fallow and think about how much he is "losing." Only a hero can overcome this natural reaction and follow the Torah's will.

Making It Up

The Chida gives a different answer to our question. We find in the Gemara (*Berachos* 35b) that Rava would tell his students not to be seen by him during the months of Tishrei and Nissan; since these were the times of harvesting and gathering, they should occupy themselves with their *parnasah* to enable them to learn the rest of the year. We find that two months of the year they were not involved in as much Torah learning as during the rest of the year. In the course of six years they would not be learning for a total of twelve months. Therefore, the *shemittah* year came to make up for the lack of learning in those months.

Mount Sinai is mentioned next to *shemittah* to allude to the *mishnah* (*Avos* 6:2), that says that every day a Heavenly voice comes from Sinai and says, "woe to people for the neglect of Torah." The mitzvah of *shemittah* would come precisely to make up for the neglect of Torah.

Don't Only Look Down; Look Up As Well

I would like to conclude with one final idea. The Alshich writes that people are mistaken when they think that Hashem's commandment to make the land rest is just like that which people are accustomed to doing anyway, sowing one year and leaving fallow the next so as not to diminish the land's strength. The Alshich tells us that when the Torah says, *Shabbos laShem*, "a Sabbath for Hashem," it is telling us that it is to be observed purely because it is a commandment from Hashem, not because the land needs a rest. The commandment was given only in regard to Eretz Yisrael, a land directly under Hashem's influence, "a land that Hashem your G-d seeks out; the eyes of Hashem your G-d are always upon it" (*Devarim* 11:12).

We see that the land's produce is a direct result of Hashem's blessing. As mentioned, one would think that the earth would be weakest in the sixth year, while in fact it is at its strongest, producing enough for the next three years. This miracle demonstrates the results of Hashem's blessing, as well as our reliance on Him. The farmer is being reminded that instead of always looking down to the ground for the source of his nourishment, he must look up as well. This is the message of the *shemittah*, that we should trust in Hashem and realize that He is the ultimate Source of all good.

Bemidbar

Division of the Camp

This week's *parashah* contains the instructions regarding the formation of the camp in the desert. The Mishkan was placed in the center of the camp, which was called the Camp of the Shechinah, and an inner circle surrounded this. To the east were Moshe, Aharon and his sons. Then there were *bnei Gershon* to the west, *bnei Kehas* to the south and *bnei Merari* to the north. This was called the Camp of the *Levi'im*. Outside of this was the Camp of the Israelites. On the eastern side were Yehudah, Yissachar and Zevulun. To the south were Reuven, Shimon and Gad. To the west were Ephraim, Menasheh and Binyamin. Finally, to the north were Dan, Naftali and Asher.

Various reasons are given to explain why each tribe was placed accordingly. For example, one particular side, to the east, is the direction in which the sun rises, from where light spreads to the world. Here we find Yehudah, who is the sole source of kingship in Yisrael, as it says, "the scepter shall not depart from Yehudah" (*Bereishis* 49:10). Next to him, we have Yissachar, whose role was learning Torah, and next to him, Zevulun, who would engage in commerce and support Yissachar in his learning. It is as if the light of Torah spreads to the world from these three tribes. Rashi (on ibid., 3:38) points out that from here we see how much good one merits by having good neighbors, as these three tribes were next to Moshe and Aharon, and they all merited greatness in Torah. The Kli Yakar and Ramban both give explanations for the placements of the other tribes; see there for more details.

How to Make Arguments

The Midrash relates that when Hashem commanded Moshe to arrange the camps by their tribes and in their particular places, Moshe became worried and said, "Perhaps now there will be arguments and strife amongst *bnei Yisrael*. If I tell one tribe to be on one side, they will complain that they want to be on another side. Similarly, another tribe will also want to be elsewhere." Hashem replied to Moshe that the tribes already knew their placements from the funeral of their forefather Yaakov. During his lifetime, Yaakov had given specific instructions as to the location of the brothers when carrying his coffin.

This *midrash* needs some explanation. We are dealing with the generation of the *midbar*, which had witnessed the splitting of the sea and the revelation at Sinai, amongst other miracles. Why would Moshe have thought that people on such a high spiritual level would have such petty claims, bickering about their positions? Also, what is the connection between their positions in the desert and those surrounding Yaakov's coffin?

The Division of Labor

One answer[1] is that in fact the concern was not about the physical locations of the tribes, but rather what the locations around the Mishkan actually represented. This can be compared to an army. For it to be successful there will be many different types of roles. The success of each unit is dependent on all the others working in coordination with each other. No one will dream of switching his role for something he is not suitable for, as it will put in danger not only himself but everyone else as well. The positions of the tribes were symbolic of their contribution to the nation as a whole.

For *klal Yisrael* to function there must be a division of labor. Different people must be priests, some judges, others scholars and others supporters of Torah. For the nation to be successful, everyone must have specific roles, with everyone using their particular strengths, working for the common good and towards a higher purpose.

Moshe was worried that when he would assign each tribe its roles, one would say, "We don't want to be the priests; we want to be judges instead," and so on. However, Yaakov had already assigned each tribe its unique role before his death. At the end of *parashas Vayechi*, we find the blessings given by Yaakov to his sons. Upon closer examination some of them seem more like criticisms. The commentators explain that this is in fact a great blessing. Yaakov was not interested in merely chastising them; rather, he was pointing out their particular strengths and weaknesses, based on their natures. This revealed to them what their roles in life should be. Hashem told Moshe not to worry about assigning their roles. They would not resent it or rebel, as Yaakov had already assigned their roles to them.

The Mishkan as a Unifying Force

Rav Yaakov Kamenetsky[2] observes that the positioning of the tribes took place only in the second month of the second year of *bnei Yisrael*'s journey through the desert. Why was there such a delay? Why couldn't this have taken place in the first year? He answers that there was a difference between the first and second years. In the first year, the Mishkan was not yet built. By the second year the Mishkan was in existence. What difference should this make? Without the Mishkan in the center, there was no unifying purpose, no common goals to work for, and argument and dissension could prevail. With the advent of the Mishkan, *bnei Yisrael* had a mission in life, to spread the *Shem Shamayim* and sanctify the Name of Hashem.

There are two types of unity. When you take people at opposite ends of the spectrum, each with his own agendas, goals and aspirations which run contrary to the others, and try and make them work together, the results are not likely to be successful. If you take people without much in common, but with similar desires and aspirations, the result will be peace, since each will be working for the common good.

In the first year, the Mishkan didn't exist, and Moshe was worried that there would be discontent regarding each tribe's allotted location. Once infused with a higher purpose, as symbolized by the building of the Mishkan, they all looked towards the common goal. This is how real peace and unity is achieved.

Tosafos (*Megillah* 31b, *klalos*) explains that we read *Bemidbar* before Shavuos, in order not to place the curses of the previous *parashah*, *Bechukosai* next to Shavuos. Rav Moshe Feinstein[3] gives an alternative reason for this. There are people who downgrade their own status when they think to themselves, "Who am I? My level is so low. Even if I were to learn I wouldn't reach a level of any substance." He says that because of this they become slack and lazy in their Torah studies. Therefore, we read *parashas Bemidbar*, which includes the counting of the people, before Shavuos. This teaches us that every Jew, great or small, is counted and has significance and importance in his or her own right, and is an integral part of the community. The reading of this *parashah* with the understanding of this idea should give encouragement before *Matan Torah*.

With this understanding we can give another reason why we

read *Bemidbar* before Shavuos. It says, "and Yisrael camped (*vayichan*) there opposite the mountain (*Shemos* 19:2). The word *vayichan* is in the singular to indicate that when *bnei Yisrael* encamped in preparation to receive the Torah, it was "as one man with one heart." This can be achieved by reading the above portion in *Bemidbar*, where everyone had his own role and appreciated that of others. That is how a nation can function successfully, with each person recognizing his role, and realizing his unique contribution to the nation.

Is It Another Flood?

We find a similar idea also relating to Shavuos. There is a fascinating *gemara* (*Zevachim* 116a) that says at the time the Torah was being given to *bnei Yisrael*, the nations of the world were otherwise occupied. They gathered together to Bilaam Harasha, and asked him: "Is there a flood coming to the world?" He replied, "Hashem will give might to His people." The nations replied, "Hashem will bless His people with peace" (*Tehillim* 29:11).

We need to understand why the nations thought a flood was being brought on the world, and why Bilaam and the nations responded as they did. Rav Meir Shapiro[4] explains that unity is usually the result of a danger or threat to both parties. Different groups, which would otherwise be enemies, suddenly become friends to save themselves. Obviously, this is not true unity; as soon as the danger disappears they become enemies once again. Since the flood, until Sinai, there was no time when such diverse groups had banded together. In the time of Noach, all sorts of animals lived in peace together in the ark, where they were saved from the floods ravaging the earth outside. This type of peace is not what we hope for. Instead, we desire peace even when quiet and tranquility are the order.

When Yisrael camped in preparation to receive the Torah, it was "as one man with one heart." The nations saw this and thought that maybe this was because of a flood coming to the world. Bilaam subsequently replied, "Hashem will give might to His people," meaning that this is true unity, that the Torah is a true unifying force. That is why the nations replied, "Hashem will bless His people with peace"; in other words, this peace is not a result of curse in the world, but instead a result of blessing.

We now see the connection between *parashas Bemidbar* and *Matan Torah*. The Torah is the true unifying force of the Jewish people: "Its ways are ways of pleasantness and all its paths are peace" (*Mishlei* 3:17). Following the instructions laid out in the Torah and observing all its mitzvos lead to a society functioning perfectly, each of its members performing his unique role and living in complete harmony with everyone else.

At All Costs

O nce[5] a man came to Rav Mordechai Gifter with his wife to explain his *shalom bayis* problems. During their discussion, it emerged that there was nothing wrong with the woman other than that the husband felt she didn't have enough *derech eretz*. He was learning in *kollel* and therefore felt it was beneath his dignity to take out the garbage on his way out of the house. Rav Gifter told them he needed two days to think about it, upon which they should return. The next day there was a knock at the door. It was the Rav. "I've thought about it and decided it is beneath your dignity," he said. "Therefore I've come to take out the garbage myself."

Erasing the Divine Name Brings the Divine Name

In this week's *parashah*, we find the procedure for the investigation of the suspected adulteress: "The *kohen* shall inscribe these curses on a scroll and erase it into the bitter waters. He shall cause the woman to drink the waters that curse" (*Bemidbar* 5:23-24). This dissolved scroll contained the holy Name of Hashem. *Chazal* say that although it is usually forbidden to erase the Name, and one who does so is liable for lashes, never-theless, Hashem commanded that it be done in order to bring peace between man and wife, upon her being proven innocent. The Maharal[6] explains that when there is marital harmony, the Divine Presence dwells between the couple. Although on one hand we are erasing the Divine Name, the peace that will ensue following her being proven innocent will in fact once again cause the Shechinah to dwell between them.

The laws of the *sotah* seem somewhat out of place at the be-ginning of *Sefer Bemidbar*, where we mainly find the designation of the tribes' positions, the counting of *bnei Yisrael* and the allo-cation of roles. The Mikdash Mordechai explains that in fact there is a very important connection between the laws of the *sotah* and these other topics. During the opening chapters of *Bemidbar* we find the phrase *lemishpechosam leveis avosam*, "ac-cording to their families, according to their fathers' houses." This phrase is repeated over and over again, stressing both the fact that the Jewish people and its tribes are made up of family units and the importance of that unit to the nation's survival. We can now understand why the *parashah* of *sotah* is inserted here: to tell us that when the family unit breaks down, *klal Yisrael* as a nation breaks down as well. Without a secure family unit, the result is a suspected *sotah*, and eventually the whole structure collapses, precisely because there is no *lemishpechosam leveis avosam*.

A Machlokes about Peace

The Mikdash Mordechai then resolves a dispute in the Sifri. After the portions of *sotah* and the *Nazir*, we find the portion of *birkas kohanim*, which ends: *veyasem lecha shalom*, "and He shall grant you peace" (*Bemidbar* 6:26). According to R. Chanina Segan Hakohanim, this phrase refers to peace in the home, while according to R. Natan this refers to peace on a national level.

It seems rather strange to have an argument on the meaning of the word peace! The Mikdash Mordechai says that there is no contradiction and reconciles the two opinions. Everyone agrees that the concern is for national peace within *klal Yisrael*. This consists of both peace on her borders, as well as internal peace. However, in order to achieve peace on a national level, there must be peace in the home first, precisely because *klal Yisrael* is made up of a collection of family units.

Birkas Kohanim

If we look at the text of the *birkas kohanim*, we see another manifestation of this idea. The Toldos Yitzchak[7] explains that the first verse contains three words. This alludes to the three forefathers, in whose merit Hashem blesses us. The middle verse contains five words, alluding to the merit of studying the five books of the Torah. The final verse contains seven words, which alludes to the seven firmaments. Alternatively, the first verse alludes to the three people who are called up to the Torah on Mondays and Thursdays. The middle verse alludes to the five people called up on *yamim tovim*, while the final verse alludes to the seven called up on Shabbos. Since it says, *veyasem lecha shalom*, "and He shall grant you peace," in order that there shall be no arguments between *kohanim* and *levi'im* on one hand, and *yisraelim* on the other, the Rabbis determined that each set receive eight *aliyos* in a week. The *yisraelim* receive five on Shabbos morning, one at Shabbos *minchah*, and one on Monday and Thursday. *Kohanim* and *levi'im* together receive two on Shabbos morning and *minchah*, and two on both Monday and Thursday. This shows how the Rabbis, in fixing the law, made no room for quarrels to arise.

The Me'am Loez comments on the fact that the *birkas kohanim* is written in the singular. He says that, strictly speaking, it should have been in the plural, addressing the multitude. This is to allude to the fact that all these blessings apply only when all of Yisrael are dwelling in harmony and considered like "one man with one heart." This is why they were said in the singular, as if to say that these blessings will take effect only when there is *achdus* and not when *machlokes* is rife. Similarly, when the final blessing concludes with "He shall grant you peace," it alludes to the idea that the previous blessings are all dependent on peace.

Respect

The Gemara (*Berachos* 20b) says that the ministering angels said to Hashem, "Surely it says in the Torah, 'Who does not show favor and Who does not accept a bribe' (*Devarim* 10:17), and yet You show favoritism to Yisrael, as it says, 'May Hashem lift His countenance to you' (*Bemidbar* 6:26)." Hashem then replied, "How can I not show favoritism, since it says, 'You will eat and you will be satisfied and you will bless' (*Devarim* 8:10), and they are particular until an olive's worth or until an egg's worth."

The measures mentioned are referring to the minimum amounts one eats for which he will be obligated to make an after blessing. While Hashem instructed after blessings only for when one is satisfied, *Chazal* established them for even lesser amounts.

Why does the Gemara say that they are particular about "until an olive's worth or until an egg's worth"? It would have been more correct to say, "an olive's and an egg's worth." Rebbi Yehoshua Mikutna[8] explains that this reflects the amount of food required by Rebbi Meir, who would require a minimum of an olive's worth in order to make an after blessing, while Rebbi Yehudah would require an egg's worth.

This *gemara* in fact teaches us about the conduct of their students, were they to be at a meal together. If the students of Rebbi Meir would eat an olive's worth and *bentch*, the students of Rebbi Yehudah would get upset, thinking they were wrong and making a blessing in vain. On the other hand, if the students of Rebbi Yehudah would eat an olive's worth and not *bentch*, the students of Rebbi Meir would claim they were eating without *bentching* afterwards. Therefore, in order that there should be unity, they were both meticulous so as to eat either less than an olive's worth, so that according to both opinions they would not be obligated to say *birkas hamazon*, or to eat more than an egg's worth, to be obligated according to both opinions. What they would be careful not to eat was the amount "until an olive's worth and until an egg's worth"; in other words, from an olive's worth until an egg's worth. What resulted was that despite the fact that they both thought the ruling was with them, they both respected each other and lived in peace and harmony, not doing something to deliberately contradict the other. Therefore, because of this, Hashem also acted towards them within the letter of the law, and treated them favorably. This is seen in the verse that the angels used for their claim: "May Hashem lift His countenance to you." This was in the merit of their keeping the remainder of the verse, "and establish peace for you." The peace that was between them made Hashem look favorably on *klal Yisrael*.

Let us examine a verse in *parashas Terumah* that illustrates this point: "from every man whose heart motivates him you shall take My portion" (*Shemos* 25:2). The Midrash says that Moshe said to Hashem, "Are *bnei Yisrael* able to fulfill this?" to which Hashem replied, "Even one of them is able to do it," as the verse says, "from every man whose heart motivates him."

What is this *midrash* coming to teach us? The Imrei Shefer[9] explains that Moshe was saying that surely this matter would lead to disputes, as each one would want to donate the table or the ark himself. Hashem replied that even if one of *bnei Yisrael* were to donate the entire lot, everyone would look at him with an *ayin tovah* and would not be jealous. Instead, everyone would be happy that the will of Hashem was done, so what difference would it make whether he or someone else fulfilled it?

Twelve Are Considered as One

At the end of the *parashah*, after the long description of what each prince brought on his particular day, it says, "This was the dedication of the altar, on the day it was anointed, from the leaders of Israel" (*Bemidbar* 7:84). Between the words "this was" and "dedication of the altar" a vertical line is placed in the text. Rav Yisrael Isser Shapiro[10] explains the reason for this with the following *midrash*. The Torah refers to the inauguration ceremony as "the day it was anointed," which makes it sound like the whole process took place on one day rather than twelve. The verse comes to teach us that all the tribes are equally dear to Hashem, and therefore Scripture considers them to have all offered their tributes on the first day. That is why there is an interruption between the words, to tell us that although the dedication was interrupted and each prince brought a tribute on a separate day, it was considered as "on the day it was anointed," as if they all brought offerings on the same day.

In fact, the commentators say that they all desired to bring their offerings on one day together. However, Hashem commanded that only one prince per day bring a tribute, and they accepted this with joy and satisfaction. They didn't try and outdo the other by pushing to be first. Rather, there was peace and unity in doing the will of Hashem, and that is why they are all considered to have offered a tribute on the same day.

Aharon's Disappointment

The *parashah* begins with the instruction for Aharon to kindle the lights of the menorah. Rashi asks why the passage dealing with the lighting of the menorah was placed next to the offerings of the princes during the inauguration of the Mishkan, at the end of last week's *parashah*. He cites a *midrash* that says that when Aharon saw the inauguration ceremony involving the princes, he felt bad that neither he nor his tribe were involved in the offerings. Hashem replied to him, "By your life, your role is greater than theirs is. You will kindle and prepare the lights of the menorah."

This *midrash* is very puzzling. Firstly, why was this particular mitzvah a consolation prize for Aharon? Secondly, what was Aharon's complaint? Surely being *kohen gadol* meant he would offer up all of the offerings in the Temple, so how could his complaint be justified?

The Future Chanukas Habayis

The Ramban answers that in fact, Hashem was telling Aharon not to worry, because in the future there would be another inauguration, following the Chanukah miracle, where his descendants would play a great part. The Chanukah victory was brought about through the Chashmona'im, who were all *kohanim*, and involved in the reestablishment of the kindling of the menorah. This miracle is commemorated through the Chanukah lights. The mitzvah of kindling the Chanukah candles was to be even greater than performing the sacrifices in the Temple. While the latter was performed only when the Beis Hamikdash was in existence, the lights of Chanukah were to be kindled even after its destruction. Similarly, the mitzvah of *birkas kohanim* is performed throughout all generations. This explains why the three passages — the priestly blessings, the inauguration offerings of the princes, and finally our portion of the kindling of the menorah — all follow one another. With those two eternal mitzvos, Hashem appeased Aharon.

The Real Significance of the Chanukah Miracle

Rav Shneur Kotler[11] brings down a famous *chazal*, which says that the menorah and its lights are an allusion to Torah. The verse says, "For a candle is a mitzvah, and the Torah is light" (*Mishlei* 6:23). In order to light a candle one needs a flame. That flame is the Torah, and through its study one is able to perform the mitzvos properly.

When Hashem said to Aharon, "your role is greater than theirs is," He was saying that while all the sacrifices are offered by Aharon, nevertheless, his role is to be even greater than that. The verse says, "For the lips of the *kohen* should safeguard knowledge, and people should seek teaching from his mouth" (*Malachi* 2:7). The lights that the *kohen* was to kindle allude to the light of Torah. They were to spread Torah to *klal Yisrael*, a job which would remain even after the Temple was destroyed, while the sacrifices were brought only as long as the Temple existed.

This idea ties in with that of the Ramban. The Chanukah

story involved the Greeks' attempt to obliterate Torah study and observance. During that period, all Torah study was moved underground, as it was strictly forbidden. Victory over the Greeks led to the reestablishment of the lighting of the menorah in the Temple, which had been defiled, and a reinstitution of Torah study. We commemorate the miracle with the Chanukah lights, which symbolize Torah, and it was the *kohanim* who had a special role in rejuvenating its study.

Desire Also Counts

The Gemara (*Berachos* 40a) says that regarding the ways of Hashem, a full vessel can hold more, while an empty one cannot contain any more. What is behind this puzzling statement? Rav Chatzkel Levenstein[12] says that when a person strives after more and more mitzvos, he can absorb and contain more, as if he is still lacking. This is seen in the *gemara* (ibid., 64a) that says that *talmidei chachamim* have no rest, neither in this world, nor in the World to Come, as in the verse "They advance from strength to strength" (*Tehillim* 84:8). They will not hear of rest in their quest to carry out more mitzvos. On the other hand, an empty person, devoid of mitzvos, feels that he is satisfied and has no desire to fill himself with more mitzvos. Even when an easy mitzvah comes to his hand he will push it off, claiming how busy he is.

The Shemen Hatov explains that when Aharon was told "your role is greater than theirs is," it was not referring to any particular service to be performed; instead, it was meritorious that he was depressed at being unable to perform a mitzvah. What gave Hashem satisfaction was Aharon's desire to be close to Him through performing another commandment. Rather than being satisfied with those he could already do, he desired more opportunities to fulfill the will of Hashem.

The concept of the menorah symbolizes this very idea. The Midrash says that it is absurd to say that Hashem actually needs the light emanating from the menorah. Rather, it is the act of devotion and intentions of the *kohen* in performing the will of Hashem that is significant. Since Aharon had such a great desire to fulfill more mitzvos, he was rewarded with the lighting of the menorah, which embodies this concept.

What's Really behind Tzitzis

This concept is seen in a story about the Vilna Gaon. Shortly before his death, he held a pair of tzitzis in his hands and cried about his future inability to perform this mitzvah. He remarked that in this world, one can buy a pair of tzitzis for a few coins, but in the World to Come it is impossible to fulfill this mitzvah. Rav Yaakov Ruderman[13] remarked on this incident that we are compared to children dressed in splendor, in a palace of gold, but who do not understand the significance of the place. In the same way, we don't understand how to measure the significance and reward for observing a mitzvah from the Torah.

The Vilna Gaon was different. In all his greatness he experienced real pleasure and delight in fulfilling the will of Hashem. He knew the extreme importance of each mitzvah, and of carrying out each commandment to perfection. That is why he found it so difficult to separate from this world, because it would prevent his performing this one mitzvah that the rest of us take for granted. Similarly, we can understand why Aharon was upset. On his high level, he felt great pleasure and closeness to Hashem with every mitzvah he performed, fulfilling it with all his strength. That is why he expressed such disappointment at being unable to perform more.

The verse writes about Aharon's lighting of the menorah, "Aharon did so...as Hashem had commanded Moshe" (*Bemidbar*

8:3). Rav Simcha Zissel of Kelm[14] asks, Why do we need a whole verse to tell us that Aharon did as he was instructed, and would it really enter our minds that he would do otherwise? He answers that the preparation of the lights for the menorah was considered one of the easier tasks in the Mishkan. It merely involved preparing the wick for use. Aharon, to whom Hashem had allocated the tasks of the service of the incense and the many sacrifices, may have viewed this job as one of the lighter tasks. The Torah comes to tell us that even this easy job was considered by Aharon to be just as important and vital as the others were. Because it was still a commandment of Hashem, it required preparation to do it, "as Hashem had commanded Moshe."

The People's Complaint

Later on in the *parashah* we see another example of the value of desiring to do more mitzvos. Some of *bnei Yisrael* were impure and prevented from offering the *korban Pesach*. They asked, "Why should we be left out by not offering Hashem's offering in its appointed time?" (*Bemidbar* 9:7). How could it enter their minds to make such a request? They were impure, and surely, the rule's the rule. Also, when this request was made the time had already passed to offer the sacrifice, so what was the point of their asking? Rav Chatzkel Levenstein[15] says that even though they were impure, they still had a desire for and did not give up hope of offering the *korban Pesach*. They did their part and made the request to Moshe. In the end, they merited to offer the *Pesach Sheini* a month later than the regular Pesach, for people who were impure on the first one. The *Pesach Sheini* reminds us that if one has the will to perform a mitzvah, he will be granted *siyatta di'Shmaya* to fulfill more mitzvos.

The Letters on Their Heads

Later on in the *parashah* we find the famous verses *vayehi bineso'a haaron...*, "and it was when the ark would journey..." (*Bemidbar* 10:35-36). An inverted letter nun surrounds these two verses on either side. Exactly why this is placed here is subject to much debate. The Ramban explains that it is placed here in order to separate between two sets of punishments. It is obvious what the second set of punishments is for; following the second nun is the incident of the complainers, followed by those who desired more earthly food, rather than manna from Heaven. What the punishment before the first nun was for is not as clear.

The Gemara (*Shabbos* 116a) relates that the previous verse, "and they journeyed from the mountain of Hashem" (*Bemidbar* 10:33), alludes to the fact that *bnei Yisrael* left Mount Sinai like a "child let out from school, a captive released from prison." While they were there, they were murmuring amongst themselves that they wished they could leave. They were learning so much there. Every day they were receiving more mitzvos to observe and life was becoming burdensome. Now that they were free, they felt life would be easier for them, away from the confines of Sinai.

The Me'am Loez also comments on the two inverted nuns. Before Sinai, when they declared the famous words *naaseh venishma*, "we will do and we will listen" (*Shemos* 24:7), each person received two crowns, one for *naaseh* and one for *nishma*. In those days *bnei Yisrael* were dearer to Hashem than the angels and were on an exalted spiritual level. Now they wanted to separate themselves from the burden of Torah and mitzvos, and fled from Sinai in great haste.

The two nuns allude to the words *naaseh venishma*. Just as *bnei Yisrael* overturned their desire to do and to listen, so too, the letters alluding to that declaration are inverted. This is in great contrast to the example of Aharon, and many years later, the Vilna Gaon.

We have seen in one *parashah* two very differing examples of adherence to and desire to perform mitzvos. By following in Aharon Hakohen's footsteps, desiring another mitzvah, another opportunity to learn Hashem's Torah, one can be a true *eved Hashem*.

What You See Is Not What You Get

This week's *parashah* contains one of the most tragic events for *bnei Yisrael*. The incident of the spies would delay their entry into the Promised Land for forty years and have repercussions throughout all generations. "Send forth for yourself men, and let them spy out the land of Canaan that I give the children of Israel" (*Bemidbar* 13:2). The particular word used here for spying (*veyasuru*) differs from that used in *Devarim*, when Moshe recounts the history of *bnei Yisrael* in the desert: "Let us send men ahead of us and let them spy out (*veyachperu*) the land" (*Devarim* 1:22). A third Hebrew term for spying is used several verses later in *Devarim*, when it says, *vayeraglu osah*, from which we get the name of this incident, the event of the *meraglim*. There are vast differences between these three expressions, even though they all have the same English translation.

The Kli Yakar explains the difference between them. The first expression, with the root *lasur*, is used in our *parashah*. It was the word Hashem used and therefore has only positive connotations, as we find elsewhere in *Bemidbar*, when it mentions that the ark would travel before the camp of *bnei Yisrael* "to search (*lasur*) for them a resting place" (*Bemidbar* 10:33). There was no need for spies in the usual sense of the word, as Hashem had already promised them that it was a land flowing with milk and honey. Whether the people there were strong or weak would make no difference; Hashem had promised *bnei Yisrael* that they would be victorious. Hashem only wanted to show them the goodness of the land, as well as its spiritual potential, so that they would return and tell *bnei Yisrael* of its greatness, thereby strengthening their resolve and desire to follow Hashem.

The second expression, *veyachperu*, is used in connection with *bnei Yisrael*'s intentions in sending the spies. The root of the word is *cherpah*, which means "disgrace." This refers to the fact that they were always looking for a pretext to return to Egypt, remembering the "good life" they had there. They hoped that by sending the spies, they would bring back a negative report, giving them an excuse to demand a return to Egypt. What they didn't intend was for outright falsehoods and slander to be spread as a result.

The third expression, *vayeraglu osah*, has the root *leragel*. This word always has negative connotations, as when Yosef accused his brothers, "You are spies (*meraglim atem*); you have come to see the land's nakedness" (*Bereishis* 42:9). This expression is used specifically to describe how the spies corrupted their mission, bringing back lies and falsehoods, demonstrating a denial of Hashem. Rashi comments that the term *ragel* is the same expression as in the verse "do not be a talebearer (*rachil*) amongst your people."

Moshe Prays Only for Yehoshua

The Torah goes on to list the names of the men to be sent from each of the twelve tribes, at the end of which Moshe changes the name of Hoshea to Yehoshua, by adding an extra letter yud to his name. Rashi tells us that it was added because Moshe had to pray for him, "May God (Yud-Heh) save you from the plot of the spies."

Why did Moshe specifically pray for Yehoshua and not for the other spies, and in particular, why not for Kalev? The Kehillas Yitzchak explains that a person can commit two types of sins. The first are those which a person knows are wrong, but finds it hard to separate from. The second type are those where the *yetzer hara* deceives a person into thinking that what he is doing is actually a mitzvah. Obviously, the sins in the second category are far harder to repent for, as a person doesn't realize he has done anything wrong, and even if he were to question his act for a moment, he would convince himself of the correctness of the "mitzvah" he has performed.

The *Zohar* relates that the spies brought back an evil report because they thought that if *bnei Yisrael* would enter the land of Israel, Moshe would appoint new princes in their place. Therefore, they sought to prevent this, reporting back as they did.

The Midrash explains that in fact at the time of sending, the spies were people of great spiritual stature, leaders of the people and righteous in their deeds. Therefore, Moshe did not suspect that they would pervert their mission by bringing back false reports about the land. This was despite the fact that they were biased in the matter, as they thought that they stood to lose their leadership. Moshe never imagined that they would stumble into such an obvious sin as this.

However, regarding Yehoshua, Moshe was afraid. Yehoshua had been witness to the incident of Eldad and Meidad, who had prophesied that Moshe would die and Yehoshua would lead the people into the land, and at whom Yehoshua became very angry and demanded, "My lord Moshe, make an end of them" (*Bemidbar* 11:28). Moshe was worried that Yehoshua would deliberately distort the truth about the land, in order that *bnei*

Yisrael would not go up to fight and would remain in the wilderness. Moshe would therefore remain alive, in contradiction to the prophecy foretelling his death as a precondition to their entering the land.

With this in mind, we can understand why Moshe prayed only for Yehoshua, "May God save you from the plot of the spies." Moshe was telling Yehoshua that perhaps it would enter the other spies' minds to tell lies about the land, but Yehoshua should know it is only because they wish to remain the princes. They would therefore realize immediately that this is a sin and would refrain from all falsehood. However, with regard to Yehoshua, Moshe was worried that he would tell falsehoods, thinking it was a mitzvah in order to keep his teacher alive, and would not refrain from speaking badly about the land.

This explains why Moshe prayed for Yehoshua, but why didn't he pray for Kalev? As we have explained, the reason the spies brought false reports about the land is because they stood to lose their princely status on entry. How did they know that by entering the land they would lose that title? The Knesses Yechezkel[16] answers that in fact, they knew that on entering the land, a king would be appointed. Kingship was to always come from the tribe of Yehudah, as it says, "the scepter shall not depart from Yehudah" (*Bereishis* 49:10). Since Kalev was the prince of Yehudah, he was to become king. All the others would lose their status to princes emanating from Yehudah. Therefore, Moshe did not have to pray for him; he would anyway have no desire to prevent their entry into the land, as he would be king.

Seeing Isn't Believing

The spies described the land as "a land that devours its inhabitants" (*Bemidbar* 13:32). Rashi explains that wherever they went they saw people burying their dead. Hashem had actually made this happen for their benefit, so that the inhabitants would be otherwise occupied and not notice the spies. This being the case, what was the sin of the spies? Surely what they were saying was in fact the truth; they did indeed see many funerals going on. The Kotzker Rebbe[17] explains that not everything that is merely not a lie is the truth. A man who says an apple is green is no more than "not a liar," but he would not necessarily be called a man of truth. A man of truth looks at not only what his eyes behold; he looks at what is beyond the surface, searching for the depth of the matter. The camera may lie and something other than what his eyes perceive may be going on.

This was the essence of the sin of the spies. What they spoke could not be called lies, but it also wasn't the truth of the matter. They failed to get a deeper understanding of what was going on. When they saw people burying their dead, they thought it was characteristic of the land, but they didn't see that Hashem orchestrated these events for their benefit, in order that they should not be discovered. On the other hand, only Yehoshua and Kalev were able to perceive what was really going on.

The Camera Lies

There is a fascinating similarity between certain expressions used within our *parashah*. Regarding the spies, the Torah says, *u're'isem es haaretz*, "and you shall look at the land" (*Bemidbar* 13:18). At the end of the *parashah* it says regarding tzitzis, *u're'isem oso*, "and you shall look at them" (ibid., 15:39). Rabbi Yissachar Frand explains that since the same word is used, we can see that the Torah is telling us an important message, namely, that the spies failed to learn the lesson of tzitzis. *Chazal* say that the message of tzitzis is that one should look at them and be reminded of all the mitzvos of Hashem. This happens because the tzitzis contain in them a thread of *techeiles* (blue). The *techeiles* resembles the sea, which in turn reminds one of the sky, which reminds one of the *kiseh hakavod* (the Divine throne), which causes one to remember all the commandments of Hashem. We learn from the mitzvah of tzitzis that one is capable of seeing much more than meets the eye.

On the other hand, the spies were also told to "see" something, namely the land. All they saw was that which was right in front of their eyes: giants, oversized fruits, a land that was intimidating and frightening, and they felt "like grasshoppers." What they didn't see was the holiness of the land, its spiritual potential, as well as a future resting place for the Shechinah.

Why is it that the spies refused to see beyond that which is tangible, completely overlooking the land's spirituality? The answer is because of self-interest; as mentioned, they stood to lose their positions of honor and leadership. That is why they refused to see beyond the physical. This is in contrast to the lesson of tzitzis, which tells one to open up his eyes to what is really going on. This lesson likewise applies to other mitzvos, and in particular to Torah study. The results are often intangible in the physical sense, but one knows that their performance strikes a spiritual chord in *Shamayim*. The mitzvah on tzitzis tells us to look beyond that which is only quantifiable and physical, to that which is spiritual.

Trouble and Strife

This week's *parashah* begins by telling us that Korach "took" (*Bemidbar* 16:1), but does not specify what it was that he was taking. Rashi tells us that he took himself, meaning that he separated himself from the rest of *bnei Yisrael* by raising objections regarding his exclusion from the priesthood. He then caused others to join him in his dispute.

Well, What Did He Take?

The Gemara (*Sanhedrin* 109b) gives another explanation. When the verse says, "And Korach took," it means that he took a bad purchase for himself. What does the Gemara mean by this statement? Rav Noach Mainds[18] explains that this purchase was in sharp contrast to the Torah, which is called a "good purchase" as it says, "For a good purchase I have given you" (*Mishlei* 4:2). *Chazal* explain that an example of a good acquisition is when two people teach each other a chapter that the other didn't know before. The result is that each has knowledge of two chapters, while previously each knew only one. That is what *Chazal* call a good deal. Another type of transaction is when a seller sells an object to a friend at a mutually agreeable price. The seller has lost the object, but has gained money, while the buyer has gained an object but lost his money. This is described as a medium type of purchase. Korach, however, undertook a bad purchase. He persuaded people with his money to join him (*Chazal* say he was one of the wealthiest people ever). The result of this purchase was that the ground swallowed up all of them, as well as their property. The decision to get involved in such a dispute was considered a bad purchase.

The Vilna Maggid[19] gives a slightly different explanation. He explains that the nature of a sale is that it is usually mutually beneficial to both parties. Another type is where either the buyer or seller is better off, while the other is worse off, depending on the circumstances. In this "transaction," one would think that only Korach and his group lost and they were the only party involved. However, in fact another party benefited. *Bnei Yisrael* were subsequently given the commandment "do not be like Korach and his congregation" (*Bemidbar* 17:5). This was a warning to guard themselves from all forms of *machlokes*. Seeing the severity of the sin and its punishment would serve as a warning causing people to think twice before being involved in such disputes.

Saved by His Wife

At the beginning of the *parashah*, we find one of Korach's accomplices mentioned: Onn Ben Peles. Later on, when the main perpetrators are listed as the earth swallowed them up, his name is noticeably absent. The Gemara (*Sanhedrin* 110a) relates that his wife caused him to withdraw from the dispute. She told him that either way he wouldn't have anything to gain by getting involved. If Aharon won, Aharon would remain in his position; if Korach won, Korach would be *kohen gadol*. The Gemara then applies the following verse to her (*Mishlei* 14:1): "The wise among women builds her house," as she saved her husband from *machlokes*. On the other hand, the rest of the verse, "but the foolish one tears it down with her hands," is applied to the wife of Korach, who spurred her husband on to dispute the priesthood, causing his downfall (literally).

Surely logic dictates that if one has nothing to gain, one shouldn't get involved in the first place. Why then is the wife of Onn Ben Peles considered so "wise among women," having told him such a basic fact? The question is stronger when we consider the odds of winning such a dispute. On one hand there was Aharon, the established prophet, appointed by Hashem. On the other hand was Korach, who felt his claim was stronger; as the Midrash tells us, he saw Shmuel HaNavi, whom Scripture describes as equal to Moshe and Aharon, descended from him. What he didn't realize was that it was his sons who would repent in the future and that Shmuel would be descended from them. Then we find two hundred and fifty men each bearing fire pans to burn incense. They all knew that the punishment for offering incense by an unauthorized person was death. Only one person involved in the entire episode could come out alive. What sort of bookmaker would offer anyone odds on those people actually winning?

Rav Chaim Shmuelevitz[20] explains that at the time of *machlokes*, when tempers are running high, it takes a wise man (or woman in this case) to see the truth under such circumstances. To not get involved in the dispute in the first place is elementary and obvious to everyone. However, once one is involved in the dispute and the fires of rage and hatred are burning with accusations, and falsehoods are prevalent, it takes a wise man to see the truth of the matter and break out of the dispute, however illogical the claims may be. That is why his wife was described as the wisest of women, since she was able to see beyond the dispute and realize what its consequences would be.

Along the same lines, it is interesting to note that in *Pirkei Avos* (5:17) it asks: "What is a *machlokes* that is not for the sake of Heaven? That of Korach and his congregation." Why does it not say, "the dispute between Korach and Moshe?" Surely they were the real disputants. Rav Yonasan Eibeschutz[21] explains that in fact the dispute was precisely between Korach and his followers. Each was seeking the honor for himself, despite his minimal chances of attaining his goal. Moshe's intentions were only for the sake of Heaven, to establish who was the chosen one. It was only the followers of Korach that were all divided on which one of them should lead.

This is the insanity of that *machlokes*, that all those people followed Korach, believing that he was fighting their cause. They all knew the consequences, and yet despite this, they were so caught up in the dispute that they did not realize that they stood to lose their lives.

The same *mishnah* describes what is a *machlokes* for the sake of Heaven: that between Beis Hillel and Beis Shammai. The difference was that despite the halachic dispute, the two schools loved and respected each other's opinions. Under such circumstances, there can be a *machlokes* for the sake of Heaven. With Korach and his followers, their *machlokes* was out of hate for Moshe, with each seeking the honor for himself. This is the fundamental rule: Whether the differences arise as a consequence of love or hate will determine the fate and results.

Where Does It All Come From?

Everyone knows the power of *machlokes*, what it leads to and the harm it does. No one comes out unscathed from a dispute, even the one who is right. Why do we then find it so prevalent amongst us? Rav Hirsh Michel Shapira[22] explains with a very interesting idea. All Jews were created with an extra *koach* (strength) for *machlokes*. This can be channeled in one of two ways. Ideally, one should use it to make *machlokes* between the *yetzer tov* and *yetzer hara*, the good and evil inclinations. One should resolve to overcome and battle the temptations with which the *yetzer hara* presents us and follow that which one knows is right and just. Another expression of this strength is in Torah study, where one is constantly trying to question various opinions and delve deeper into his learning in order to gain a fuller understanding of our Sages. If this energy is not used up in these pursuits, it manifests itself in other ways, as we see with Korach. If channeled into the right areas, great growth can be achieved.

Following the downfall of Korach and his followers, the verse says, "The entire assembly of *bnei Yisrael* complained on the next day against Moshe and Aharon" (*Bemidbar* 17:6). Rav Leib Chasman[23] says that we see from here the power of *machlokes*. The congregation had seen all that was done to Korach and his followers, the fires from Heaven and the opening up of the ground. What clearer evidence can you have to testify to the truth of Moshe and Aharon being Hashem's chosen ones? Despite all this, the fires of *machlokes* continued to burn amongst them. We then find that twenty-four thousand of them died in a plague, and yet there was still the need to take a staff from each tribal leader in order to prove once and for all who was right. The staffs were left in the ark overnight and Aharon's staff sprouted almonds and flowers, proving forevermore who the chosen one was. Even after the plague, there was still a need for this. Such is the power of *machlokes*; its fires still rage long after they should.

It's Effort That Counts

Let us conclude with an important lesson from the challenge

of the staffs. As mentioned, Aharon's staff sprouted both flowers and almonds. Normally, when a fruit is produced, its blossoms fall away. What is the significance of this incident, where the blossoms remained with the fruit? Rav Moshe Feinstein[24] explains that the flower is the preparation for the forthcoming fruit. Having both the blossom and flower remain teaches us that in matters of spirituality, the preparation and effort are important. In contrast, in the secular world it is only results that count. The hours one spent studying for that exam are irrelevant; it is what happens on the day that counts. All the comments usually heard afterwards — that subject wasn't on the syllabus, we weren't taught that, I was ill, the room was too hot, it was too noisy outside, and so on — all count for nothing. Two years of study all boil down to what happens on the day. We find the opposite with Torah and mitzvos. What is important to Hashem is one's efforts and application. How one really devotes himself to His will, the determination one learns with, and one's preparation for mitzvos are all considered important. This staff was hidden for eternity with its flowers and its fruit to teach us this lesson.

Just Don't Ask Questions

There is an interesting difference between the descriptions following the death of Aharon and that of Moshe. In *parashas Chukas*, it says that the entire house of Israel wept for Aharon, while concerning Moshe, the commentators explain that only some of *bnei Yisrael* mourned. Why was it that when Aharon died the entire people wept, while not everyone wept following Moshe's death?

There was a fundamental difference between the two. Aharon was loved by the entire population. He was called the "pursuer of peace," as *Chazal* tell us that when he knew of a couple at odds with each other he would try and resolve their differences. Similarly, if two men were quarreling, he would go privately to one and tell him how he had heard that the other was regretful of their quarrel, how wrong he was, and how he wished they were at peace again. Then he would go to the other and tell him the same, and the next time the two would meet, they would be reconciled.

All of Aharon's words were gently spoken, and he was always doing *chessed*. The Yalkut Shimoni relates that when he would see an evil person, he would not ignore him or turn his nose up at him. Instead, he would greet him with a smile and inquire after his welfare. The next day, when that person sought to commit a sin, he would think to himself, "How can I possibly do such a thing, when Aharon the *kohen gadol* takes the time to speak to me in such a way? I'll be so ashamed next time I see him," and the person would then refrain from sinning. That is why he is described as one who "saved the multitudes from sinning," and it is because of these qualities that the whole congregation mourned for him. Such characteristics were irreplaceable.

Moshe, on the other hand, could not enjoy such a role. In his position as leader, he often had to give rebuke in order to set people straight and prevent rebellions. In his role as judge, he had to issue uncompromising rulings, in order to adhere to the truth rather than just teach that which was popular. This is why we find such a difference in reactions following each of their deaths.

Just Get the Hint

There is a fascinating *midrash*[25] concerning the events leading up to Aharon's death. It says that it was as if Hashem didn't have the desire or willingness to personally tell the ultimate man of peace of his death, but instead instructed Moshe to inform him of it. It is interesting to note that we do not find that Hashem had a similar problem telling Moshe. Perhaps it was this character trait of being the pursuer of peace that gave Aharon this special status.

Moshe also felt that he could not tell Aharon straight out. Instead he came to him early in the morning and told him that the previous night he had been taught something by Hashem which he wanted to relate to him, but he had forgotten it. He knew that it was from *Sefer Bereishis*, so they took out a scroll and began to learn. They read the story of creation, and after each day

Moshe said, "It is good that which Hashem made." When they reached the creation of Adam HaRishon, Moshe said about him, "Look what great evil he caused; through him death came to the world." Aharon replied, "Surely it is forbidden to talk like that. Hashem has decreed death upon us and that is the end of all man. Look at Adam and Chavah, whom He created and personally tended to in the Garden of Eden, and yet their end was to return to the ground." Moshe then counterargued, "But surely we reached a higher level. I ascended to Heaven to receive the Torah amongst angels. You stopped the plague of death with incense after the incident of Korach, prevailing over the angel of death himself. After all this our end is just going to be the same!"

Despite this, Aharon failed to take the hints. Moshe then read the verse where Hashem tells Avraham of his forthcoming death, and said, "Who knows if our day to die hasn't come? If Hashem came to you and said you will die in twenty years, would you accept it with love?" To which Aharon responded, "Righteous is He and righteous is His judgment." Moshe asked him the same question several more times, each time decreasing the number of years, with Aharon giving the same answer as before. Finally he asked him what if it were to be decreed for today, to which Aharon replied, "Righteous is He and righteous is His judgment, blessed is the One Who decrees." Moshe then informed him of his forthcoming death. What is remarkable to see is how Aharon was unquestioning of the ways of Hashem, accepting His decree with love.

Even Science Can't Explain

We also learn this lesson from the unique and special mitzvah of *parah adumah* at the beginning of our *parashah*.

The *parah adumah*, or red heifer as it is known, is the biggest mystery to mankind. If a person became impure through contact with a dead body, he was sprinkled with water mixed with the ashes of the *parah adumah* on the third and seventh days. The difficulty lies in the fact that one who was impure would be purified through its ashes, while anyone involved in the preparation, carrying or sprinkling the ashes, would become impure. The *parashah* begins, "This is the statute of the Torah" (*Bemidbar* 19:2). A statute is a mitzvah for which we have absolutely no comprehension of the reason; it must be fulfilled purely as a decree of Hashem. The commentators ask why this mitzvah is described as "the statute of the Torah" as opposed to "the statute of the heifer," or "the statute of impurity." Why is it given such a title, as if encompassing all of the Torah?

Rav Aharon Kotler[26] explains with a very powerful and fundamental idea. With all other mitzvos, one can try to come to some kind of understanding of the reasons behind them. The mitzvah of the *parah adumah* though, is impossible to even begin speculating about. Even Shlomo Hamelech, who was the wisest of men, was forced to admit that this was beyond him. When one is faced with the *parah adumah*, one is forced to realize that his own knowledge is limited, and he cannot fathom the ways of Hashem. He concludes that in fact the reasoning behind all the mitzvos is beyond his comprehension.

All of Torah is described here as a *chok* (statute), entirely beyond human understanding. In fact, the Beis Halevi writes that the *Sefer HaChinnuch*, which explains reasons for the mitzvos, was written only to give one *chizuk* (encouragement to perform mitzvos), while in fact the absolute reason for the mitzvos is beyond us. Proof of this is that the Midrash tells us that the forefathers kept all the mitzvos and that they ate matzah despite the fact that the Exodus was yet to take place. The mitzvos are kept purely for the sole reason of fulfilling the will of Hashem.

Moshe was given the title of "a faithful servant," which indicates how praiseworthy he was, that all he did for *bnei Yisrael* in the desert was only as a servant of Hashem. Similarly, before the giving of the Torah, *bnei Yisrael* declared, "we will do and we will listen" (*Shemos* 24:7). This indicated their commitment to performing the mitzvos, even before they knew what they were.

The Midrash relates that Hashem first offered the Torah to *bnei Yishmael*. When they saw the commandments prohibiting immorality they rejected it. Similarly, *bnei Esav* were offered it, but when shown the prohibition against murder, they also turned it down. What kind of offer was Hashem making the nations? If He wanted them to accept it, surely He should have shown them more positive aspects: *cholent*, cheesecake, Purim, Simchas Torah. The explanation is that the nations needed to know what was written in the Torah in order to accept it. As soon as one asks this before he's accepted it, he'll never be able to fully keep it. Only if one declares, "we will do," regardless of what's in it and what its reasons are, will he be able to fully accept and observe it.

This Obviously Doesn't Apply to Me

The Mishnah in *Shabbos* (1:3) states that on Friday night one should not read by candlelight. The Gemara (*Shabbos* 12b) explains the reason for this prohibition: maybe one will come to tilt the lamp in order to adjust it, causing it to be extinguished. The Gemara continues that when Rebbi Yishmael heard this reason he said, "I'll read by candlelight and will just be careful not to touch it." The story continues that one Friday night he was reading by such a light and he began touching the wick, causing it to be extinguished. He then exclaimed, "How great are the words of the Sages, who taught that one should not read by candlelight."

The simple understanding of this statement is that Rebbi Yishmael was praising the Rabbis, who knew someone would come to sin and therefore made the prohibition. He thought that he wouldn't stumble and yet he still came to sin. The Vilna Gaon[27] teaches that when Rebbi Yishmael said, "How great are the words of the Sages, who taught that one should not read by candlelight," he was specifically praising the Rabbis of the Mishnah, who gave a blanket prohibition rather than giving a reason. Once you start giving reasons, an opening is created to say, "Surely that doesn't apply here," or "That was for then but this is now." The message of the *parah adumah* is that "This is the statute of the Torah," that one must accept its laws whether one understands them or not.

No Idea

There is another extremely important lesson to be learned from the paradox of *parah adumah*. As stated above, Hashem deliberately hid the reasoning behind this mitzvah from all men, even from Shlomo Hamelech, who understood everything else. Why did this lesson have to be taught in relation to this mitzvah as opposed to any other statute? The Be'er Yosef explains that sometimes in life events happen that are unexplainable, events with terrible paradoxes which appear to make no sense. In particular, the most difficult area of comprehension is that of *tzaddik vera lo* (a righteous person and bad befalls him), and on the other hand, *rasha vetov lo* (the wicked prospering). Logic would dictate just the reverse: one who follows Hashem's commandments should live a good life, while a wicked person should suffer misfortune and pain. Yet we often find exactly the opposite.

Hashem is educating us through this paradox. The Shemen Hatov adds that death came to the world only as a result of Adam and Chavah eating from the tree of knowledge. The motive behind their act was the desire to know why. Rather than following Hashem's commandment without reservations, they needed to know why it was forbidden and what the consequences of transgressing the commandment would be. This desire to know brought death to the world.

It is precisely following a death that the laws of the red heifer are applicable. This is why death was an appropriate punishment for the sin. The question of why led man to be confronted by *parah adumah*, whose very essence is to teach us that we cannot understand everything. Precisely then, at the moment following a death, one has many questions beginning with "why," but one is taught that at least during this lifetime, it is impossible to know the answers.

Results You Never Imagined

The story of Bilaam the prophet contains many important messages for us. Balak, king of Moab, seeing the annihilation of the surrounding nations at the hands of *bnei Yisrael*, felt threatened and disturbed. In his despair he hired Bilaam to curse the Jewish people in order to cause their downfall. The Chofetz Chaim[28] observes that when a Jew is in trouble he goes to a tzaddik to seek his blessing, and to ask him to pray to Hashem to save him. This is in stark contrast to the nations of the world. Balak, in his fear of the Jewish people, didn't ask to be blessed, but rather sought to curse Yisrael. This, says the Chofetz Chaim, is the nature of the wicked. They seek not their own blessing, but only the downfall of others.

In this vein, Rav Yisrael Salanter[29] explains that there are two ways one can raise oneself over one's fellowman. One is by elevating himself through his actions and good deeds until others recognize his greatness. Alternatively, he can lower the other person's reputation in the eyes of others, thereby causing his degradation. Both ways exalt one person over the other. Obviously the former is the way of the righteous and of *bnei aliyah* (people seeking spiritual growth). The second is of negative, empty people who don't seek their own elevation, but nevertheless can't stand the very sight of others achieving what they themselves have no desire for.

You Call That a Blessing?

The most famous verse in this week's *parashah* is said when Bilaam tries to curse *bnei Yisrael* and finds that he is only allowed to bless them: "How goodly are your tents, O Jacob, your dwelling places (*mishkenosecha*), Yisrael" (*Bemidbar* 24:5). Rashi remarks that Bilaam was praising the fact that the openings of Yisrael's tents were not aligned opposite each other, so that they couldn't see into each other's tents.

The Midrash quotes a verse appropriate to this time of year: "Hashem vented His fury, He poured out His burning anger, He kindled a fire in Zion which consumed its foundations" (*Eichah* 4:11). This teaches us that Hashem had to punish the Jewish people for an accumulation of sins, but instead of annihilating them, He released His anger on the wood and stone of the Beis Hamikdash in order to preserve Yisrael.

Chazal say that the First Temple was built in the merit of Avraham. Since he fathered Yishmael, it was not everlasting. The Second Temple was built in the merit of Yitzchak, and since he fathered Esav it too was not everlasting. The Third Temple will be in the merit of Yaakov. Since no blemish issued from him, it will therefore be eternal.

The Shaar Bas Rabbim comments that although Bilaam uttered a blessing, in his heart he wished to say a curse. When he said, "How goodly are your tents, O Jacob," he was alluding to how he desired the First Temple to be in the merit of Jacob. This was because then it would be a *mishkenosecha Yisrael*. The word *mishkenosecha* has a second meaning, namely, a pledge. Bilaam, in his wickedness, was saying how good it would be if the First

Temple were built in the merit of Jacob; since it could not be destroyed, Yisrael themselves would have to be taken as a pledge for their sins and be destroyed. Hashem in His mercy released His anger on the Temples, but saved *bnei Yisrael*.

The Navi Sums It All Up

Why is it that the First Temple, which was destroyed for the three cardinal sins of murder, immorality and idol worship, was rebuilt after seventy years, while the Second Temple, which was destroyed because of baseless hatred, remains unrestored after two thousand years? The commentators explain that it is because of the importance of mitzvos between man and his fellow, and the consequences if they are neglected, that the Temple's reconstruction is being delayed.

Let us have a look at this week's haftarah. The Kochav MiYaakov explains that we find that Michah the prophet is doing a self-analysis: "With what shall I approach Hashem…shall I approach Him with burnt offerings…Will Hashem find favor in thousands of rams?" (*Michah* 6:6-7). He is really asking, "What is it I can really do to appease Hashem?" If it is with offerings, which there is a basis to, as they are enumerated in the Torah, this is only a kindness of Hashem that He accepts these, since anyway they are His. If it is with something that is considered more one's own, namely, his children, *Chazal* say that there are three partners in the creation of a person: Hashem, his father and his mother. Therefore, children also belong to Hashem. Rather, the concluding advice is "He has told you, O man, what is good, and what Hashem seeks from you, only the performance of justice, the love of kindness, and walking humbly with your God" (ibid., 8).

What is the meaning of this verse? The Malbim explains that "the performance of justice" refers to the mitzvos between man and his fellow. How one treats others in business, his honesty and integrity, are typical examples of mitzvos in this category. "The love of kindness" is the other aspect of this category of mitzvos. This includes interpersonal relationships and the kindness he bestows on others. "Walking humbly with your God" refers to mitzvos between man and God, and in particular, according to the Radak, those which are hidden in the heart, as we say in Shema, "you shall love Hashem your God with all your heart." We see that this verse encompasses all of a person's Divine service. One thing that stands out is the emphasis placed on mitzvos between man and his fellow, and the importance of *chessed*. The following incidents illustrate this point.

A Night in the Home of the Chofetz Chaim

When Rav Elya Lopian[30] was the *rosh yeshivah* of Kfar Chassidim, he traveled to Gateshead to raise funds for the yeshivah. He was told that there was a wealthy man in the community who supported all types of Torah causes — yeshivos, shuls, mikvaos, and so forth. The man was not *shomer Shabbos* and Rav Elya didn't want to take that money to build Torah. The community told him, however, that it would be a *chillul Hashem* if he didn't go to visit the man, and that he would be offended and wouldn't support the other Orthodox institutions, so Rav Elya decided to meet him anyway but resolved not to take any money from him. At the end of their meeting, when the rich man announced he would like to make a donation, Rav Elya replied that he had come only to visit, not to take money. The man persisted and eventually the rabbi asked him, "Why is it you are so generous to Orthodox institutions and yet you yourself are not keeping Torah and mitzvos?" The man replied that he was the first rabbi to ask him that, and then told him the following story.

When the man was young, his parents wanted him to study in yeshivah. He didn't want to; he just wanted to run wild and wasn't ready for it. Despite this his parents packed a case for him and sent him to Radin to the yeshivah of the Chofetz Chaim. He spent a whole day traveling, and then had an interview with the *mashgiach*. It didn't take long for the rabbi to work out that he was not the type of student they were looking for, and that he had no desire to become that type. He told the boy it was not the place for him. Not too disappointed, he asked the *mashgiach* if he could just spend the night in the dormitories, as his train was not leaving until the next day. The rule was that unless one was a student of the yeshivah one could not spend the night in the dormitories, but the *mashgiach* told him that if he got permission from the Chofetz Chaim he could stay.

The Chofetz Chaim lived on the other side of town. The boy traveled there and knocked on the door and explained the situation. The Chofetz Chaim confirmed to him that it was the rule, but told him that instead he could stay at his house for the night. He gave him some of his meal, and personally made his bed, as he was accustomed to do for his guests.

That night the boy couldn't sleep. The events of the day were racing through his mind, and he thought about what he would tell his parents, and the irony that he wasn't allowed to sleep in the yeshivah dormitory but could sleep in the Chofetz Chaim's home. Suddenly, the Chofetz Chaim entered his room. The boy pretended to be asleep. He looked at the boy, and exclaimed, "Oy, my guest is cold." He took off his long coat and placed it over the boy. The Chofetz Chaim learned in his shirtsleeves on a bitter Polish winter night so that his guest remained warm.

The man concluded his story by saying, "I may not keep Torah and mitzvos yet, but that cloak warmed my body as well as my soul to what Torah and mitzvos mean." The Chofetz Chaim never once imagined that his actions would result years later in the support of such causes. All that he had in mind was the well-being of his guest.

On the other hand, we are never aware of what failing to perform a mitzvah might cause. There was once a young *avreich* from Lakewood who went to an out-of-town community to interview for the position of rabbi. He inspired the congregation with his *drashos*, and when the people took a vote, they unanimously decided to accept him as rabbi. The *avreich* informed the congregation that he would accept the position on one condition: that they put up a *mechitzah* in the shul, as it did not yet have one.

The committee had a meeting and all present voted for the motion, except one, who happened to be the president and had veto power. Apologetically, they informed him of the decision.

In his disbelief, the *avreich* requested to meet the president to try and convince him to change his mind. They told him it would be no use, but he went to meet him anyway. At the meeting, the young *avreich* told the president how the shul could grow and be inspired if they would just accept his condition. The president told him, "I like you and believe it would be good for the shul. However, my shul will not become Orthodox." He then took him over to the window and continued, "You see that house over there? For twenty-five years I have been the neighbor of the owner of that house, and each year he puts up a Sukkah. I don't, as I'm Conservative. Not once did he ever invite me in. If that's Orthodox Judaism, I don't want any part of it, and my shul will not become Orthodox."

They'd Come for Me?

Some actions can inspire people to completely change their perspectives. There is a boy in Jerusalem who recently passed a test on a whole Gemara by heart (not word for word, but the content of each and every page). This is the story of that boy. One day a rabbi received a call from a new father, who was not religious and had found his number in the phone book. He told him that his baby had been born with a serious heart problem, and he wanted to know why God had done this to him. The rabbi answered that before answering the question, they would have to answer the question of who is God and why He is good, and so on. They arranged to meet and spent six weekly sessions discussing the issues. At that stage the baby was to go through the first of what was to be about twelve open-heart operations. At the time, the father mentioned in passing to the rabbi that he would take blood only from the children's blood bank, as in those days the screening process was not as good, and adult blood was more likely to be problematic. The rabbi told him that he would send some of his students who had that particular blood group to the hospital, and that he should schedule time for ten people to give blood. The man replied, "Why would they come for me? I'm not religious, and they don't know me," but the rabbi assured him that they would come.

The day that the students were scheduled to give blood arrived, and the father was waiting for them in the hospital. A minute passed, then two, then five. When after ten minutes the boys still hadn't shown up, the man told himself, "I knew they wouldn't come for me." Suddenly, all the way down the corridor, he saw one yeshivah student, then another, until a group of about fifteen boys started walking through the corridor. They stopped the man and asked, "Excuse me, sir. Where do we give blood?" At that point the father started crying, and said to himself, "If this is Torah Judaism, then I need to find out more about it." Currently all this man's children are learning in various yeshivos, and his whole family are observant and practicing Jews.

These stories show the importance of our deeds, and that

simple actions can have ramifications that we never dreamt of. In these troubled times, when we remember the destruction of the Beis Hamikdash and its causes, we should take note of the words of the prophet and particularly seek the "performance of justice" and "the love of kindness."

The First Peace Prize

S*efer Bemidbar* is full of tragic events that occurred in the desert. We find complaints about the food, the incident of the spies, the rebellion of Korach, the sin of the striking of the rock, the deaths of Miriam and Aharon, plagues amongst the people — one tragedy after another. The latest incident was when Bilaam, taking a parting shot at *bnei Yisrael*, advised Balak that if he wanted to bring about the downfall of the Jews, he should get them involved in immorality, as Hashem particularly despises that and will punish them greatly for it. The Midianite women enticed *bnei Yisrael* to practice the basest form of idolatry as well as immorality. A great plague came upon them, causing twenty-four thousand deaths, until Pinchas, seeing a prince of the tribe of Shimon involved publicly and brazenly with one of these women, stepped up and killed them both with one spear. The plague then stopped and Pinchas was promised great reward: a covenant of peace and eternal priesthood.

Surrounded by Big Brothers

If one looks at the second half of *Sefer Bemidbar*, one sees that there are five *parashos*. In certain years *Chukas* and *Balak* are read as a double *parashah*, as are *Mattos* and *Massei*. In the middle, sandwiched between these two pairs, we find *parashas Pinchas*. This teaches us a very important lesson. One reason why Pinchas's act was so praiseworthy was that he went against everything that was going on around him. He decided that now was a time to act for the honor of Hashem. This is alluded to in the sequence of the *parashos*. He is stuck in the middle, surrounded on both sides by two lengthy double *parashos*, and yet "small" Pinchas arose above them all and made his mark on history. So too, if one wants to achieve anything in matters of observance, one has to rise above the various distractions of our times.

Real Peace

Why was Pinchas rewarded with a covenant of peace? One would have thought that for someone who had killed, this would be the last thing he should receive. Perhaps he could have instead received the award for zealotry, or stopping a plague, but a peace prize?

Rav Chaim Soloveitchik[31] says that people have a misconception of what peace is. They think that it means there must be peace at all costs; as long as there are no fights or disputes between anyone, then all is fine. He explains that the root of the word *shalom*, is, in fact, *shaleim*, which means perfection. The ultimate state of perfection is where there is peace between man and Hashem. If a husband and wife are united, following the Torah's laws, then there is *shalom* between them and also with Hashem. If there is complete peace amongst Yisrael, but there is friction between them and Hashem, if the law they are following is different from that of Hashem's, then that is not called a state of *shalom*.

During the plague, there was no other way to achieve this

shalom. Pinchas had to act as he did in order to restore that peace. This shows us that by overriding peace, momentarily creating *machlokes*, he restored a more important and effective peace for *bnei Yisrael*, that between them and Hashem.

The Netziv[32] answers the above question differently. He explains that it could have been that a spirit of brazenness and zealotry would have resided in Pinchas for a long time after the act, which subsequently would have been counterproductive, causing him to stumble. Therefore, Hashem blessed him that he should have peace, and that he would revert to enjoying serenity and a peaceful existence. This was only granted to him because his actions were for the sake of Heaven, to avenge the desecration of Hashem's Name.

We find a similar promise given regarding an *ir hanidachas*, a city where the majority of its residents are practicing idolatry. Following the commandment to enter and destroy the city and its population, the Torah says, "and He will give you mercy...when you listen to the voice of Hashem" (*Devarim* 13:18). The promise is that even though the people performed a destructive act, a spirit of mercy would subsequently enter their hearts. It is precisely because they followed the Divine commandment and listened to the voice of Hashem that they would merit this. So too, Pinchas did not follow any warlike instincts, but rather sought to do the will of Hashem, which is why on the act's completion he was rewarded with a covenant of peace, despite the fact that it seems contrary to the very deed he did. As soon as the act was completed, he could return to his previous status.

Against His Nature

Exactly why was Pinchas's act so heroic? The verse at the beginning of our *parashah* records Pinchas's lineage as the "son of Elazar the son of Aharon." Why does the Torah need to go so far back? Surely we know Aharon was the father of Elazar. The *Me'am Loez* explains that this was in order to tell us of the greatness of his act. If he were a man of war, trained in weapons, then it would not have been such an outstanding deed. However, he was a *talmid chacham*, son of the high priest Elazar, who was the son of the great pursuer of peace, Aharon. The verse is telling us to see who this man was, who his father and grandfather were and how this act of killing was so foreign to him. *Chazal* say that he needed twelve miracles to enable him to perform the act. However, since he initiated the act, he was given help from Heaven to complete it. He was willing to give up his life for the mitzvah, risking being killed by a supporter of the guilty party. Despite his lack of skill in weaponry, he nevertheless did what was necessary, making certain to "avenge My jealousy" (*Bemidbar* 25:11) and make Hashem's anger subside.

Hashem gave Pinchas the ultimate approval for his actions "when he zealously avenged My vengeance amongst them" (*Bemidbar* 25:11). The Ohr Hachaim comments that there are three separate praises contained in this verse. "He zealously avenged" praises him for the fact that he risked his life for the sake of Hashem. Secondly, what he did was only for the sake of Hashem and for no ulterior motive. This is described as the verse continues, "My vengeance." The third praise is that he performed the act in front of the whole of *bnei Yisrael*. In particular, the entire tribe of Shimon was standing nearby when their leader was killed. Therefore, the verse says "amongst them," that he was not afraid to do what was right in public.

Why These?

Why was it that Pinchas was promised these particular rewards of eternal priesthood and a covenant of peace? The commentators explain that he was rewarded *middah keneged middah* (measure for measure). As stated above, he risked his own life in order to per-form the act. For that he was rewarded with a "covenant of peace"; he would never die but would instead live forever. The Midrash explains that he in fact became Eliyahu Hanavi, who never died, but instead ascended to Heaven alive. Secondly, his act atoned for *bnei Yisrael*, making *shalom* between them and Hashem. As the job of the priests is to atone for the Jewish peo-ple through their sacrifices, it was only appropriate that he was granted eternal priesthood for himself and his descendants.

The Midrash on our verse says, "by right he took his reward." Exactly what does this mean? The Chasam Sofer[33] questions the reward for Pinchas with a *gemara* (*Kiddushin* 39b) which says that there is no reward for a mitzvah in this world. This is because a man could become ruined with an abundance of good, as the verse says, "and Yeshurun waxed fat and kicked" (*Devarim* 32:15). Another reason is to ensure that his reward for the next world will not become diminished. How then could Pinchas receive such great promises, especially in this world? The Chasam Sofer ex-plains that the statement is applicable only to ordinary people who do mitzvos. People who bring merit to the multitudes are different, as it says, "whoever merits the multitude, sin will not come about through his hands" (*Avos* 5:18). Pinchas sanctified the Divine Name, and caused great benefit to the masses as he turned away Hashem's anger. Therefore, he could receive his re-ward immediately, since it was certain that he would not corrupt his ways. That is why the Midrash says "by right he took his re-ward"; it was appropriate he receive it even in this world.

Above the Call of Duty

The Dubno Maggid[34] asks why Pinchas was offered such great reward, the likes of which were never offered to anyone else. He explains with a parable. Once there was a young man who worked for a wealthy merchant, receiving a room and meals in return. One day the merchant, his family, and the worker were enjoying a Purim meal. In the middle of it, a stranger who wished to make a large business deal came to the door. The worker rose and asked the merchant for the keys to the warehouse and went to help the customer. The transaction took several hours, after which the worker came back and told the merchant of the great profit.

The next day, the merchant asked him what he would like as compensation for his services, which were well above the call of duty. The worker refused, saying that the agreement he made with him was only that he receive his basic needs. The merchant, however, insisted that since he saw how zealous he was in his work, he should increase his reward. The worker, on the other hand, felt he had no right to claim a reward, as he was deeply indebted to his employer, who had treated him so well for many years.

It is the same between Hashem and man. He gives us life, health and food. We are forever indebted to him. Any good we do is nowhere near sufficient to repay Him for His kindness. How then could Pinchas lay claim to this reward for what he did in the service of Hashem?

In *Pirkei Avos* (2:21) it says that the granting of reward for the righteous is reserved for the next world. We are granted reward for our mitzvos only because Hashem desires it, not because we have a right to reward. Pinchas, however, went above and beyond the call of duty. He put his life in danger in order to fight for the cause of Hashem. For this, he was deemed worthy of a special reward. Pinchas could never have asked for such gifts of his own accord, but Hashem wished to give them to him for his extraordinary deed. I would compare his actions to a fireman, who when putting out normal fires is just doing his job. When he jumps in to save others, putting his own life at risk, that is when he is deserving of special praise.

First Things First

There is an interesting request in this week's *parashah*. The tribes of Reuven and Gad asked Moshe for permission to separate from the rest of the tribes and settle on the other side of the Jordan River. Due to their abundance of cattle and livestock, they would require that region's vast lands to contain them. Moshe became angry, and compared their request to that of the mission of the spies, as they were discouraging the rest of *bnei Yisrael* from entering the land of Israel. After some clarification, Moshe acceded to their request. Were the tribes of Reuven and Gad justified in asking to settle where they did, and if not, where did they err? In addition, why did it all end in disaster years later when they became the first tribes to go into exile?

Dwelling in Sukkos

Rav Aharon Kotler[35] explains that the reasoning behind their request was correct. Yaakov Avinu had also settled in those lands across the Jordan in a place called Sukkos. This is seen in the verse which says that after his parting from Esav, "But Yaakov journeyed to Sukkos and built himself a house, and for his livestock he made shelters (sukkos); he therefore called the name of the place Sukkos" (*Bereishis* 33:17). Why does the Torah tell us that he made shelters for his animals, and furthermore, why was the place named after the booths that his flock dwelt in, rather than his own house?

Chazal say regarding Avraham that every plot of land he walked on was given to him and his descendants afterwards. Yaakov also inherited this promise, and therefore journeyed to Sukkos to prepare that place for his descendants. This was achieved by building not only a house for himself, but also shelters for his livestock. By calling the place after the booths, he simultaneously prepared that place for the animals of his descendants. The tribes of Reuven and Gad were therefore claiming the inheritance from Yaakov; now they were coming with their abundance of animals and felt it was their right to dwell there.

When the verse says, "The children of Reuven and the children of Gad had abundant livestock, very great" (*Bemidbar* 32:1), it places the tribe of Gad next to the words "abundant" and "very great." This is because they were the main initiators of the request, since they had the most livestock. This is alluded to in the rest of the narrative, where Gad is mentioned first, as they had the most interest in the request. In addition, in *Sefer Yehoshua*, it says that the place Sukkos was given specifically to the tribe of Gad. Because of their abundance of livestock as compared to Reuven, they merited that particular place. This was all because their ancestor Yaakov had paved the way.

Where Did They Come From?

Further on in the narrative we find that half of the tribe of Menasheh joined the group that settled on the other side of the Jordan River. How did they become involved, when we never find that they actually requested to become cosettlers? Furthermore, why wasn't their settling there contingent upon the same conditions that were set for the other two tribes, who had to promise that they would help conquer the rest of Eretz Yisrael first before being allowed to settle in their own land? The Yerushalmi (*Bikkurim* 81) relates that Moshe had actually instructed this part of the tribe of Menasheh to go. He saw that the strength of Torah there would be weak, so he sent them to live there, since he foresaw that many Torah scholars and heads of yeshivos would emanate from them.

An alternative answer is derived from a *gemara* (*Bava Basra* 123b), which tells us that Yaakov Avinu saw that the children of Esav would only be defeated by the hands of the children of Yosef: "And it shall be that the house of Yaakov shall be a fire, the house of Yosef a flame and the house of Esav straw" (*Ovadiah* 1:18). Scripture also relates that when David Hamelech waged war with Amalek, they merited victory because of the leaders of the tribe of Menasheh. Also, later on in the *parashah* we read that Menasheh conquered the area of Gilada. We see, according to this answer, that they were sent to reside over the Jordan because of their physical prowess, acting not only to protect those tribes, but also as the first line of defense against attackers from the east.

There was once a professor of time management who came to give his lecture carrying a large jar and some stones. He placed the stones in the jar until it was full and asked the class, "Is the jar full?" They all replied "yes." He then brought out some smaller pebbles from under the table. He poured them into the jar, and again asked the class if the jar was full. Again they replied that it was. He repeated the motions, this time with sand, to which the class sounded sure that it was finally full. He then poured in some water, finally admitting that it was now full. He asked the class what the lesson from this experiment was. One person replied, "No matter how full one's day is you can always squeeze in something else." The professor replied that it was good but he had something else in mind. "If you don't get the large stones in at the beginning," he said, "you won't get them in later. One has to have priorities."

A Change of Perspective

Reb Chaim of Volozhin[36] asks the following question. Following Moshe's response, in which he admonished them to put their trust in Hashem, the tribes of Reuven and Gad replied, "Your servants shall do as our master instructs" (*Bemidbar* 32:25). What was it Moshe had instructed? Surely he had only agreed to their request and set out the conditions. What was the specific thing they had to do?

If we look at Moshe's response to their request, we find several major differences between what he said and the tribes' request. The tribes said, "We will arm ourselves swiftly for *bnei Yisrael*" (*Bemidbar* 32:17), without mentioning Hashem's Name. They continued confidently, "our children will dwell in fortified cities," implying that they could rely on the strength of their own hands without any Heavenly assistance. Moshe corrected them and said, "If you will arm yourselves before Hashem for the battle...and every armed man among you shall cross the Jordan before Hashem...and the land shall be conquered before Hashem" (*Bemidbar* 32:20-22).

Moshe was teaching them that they would succeed only if they placed their trust in Hashem. They had to recognize that only if Hashem decides that an enterprise will be successful will success be achieved; otherwise, the use of all the effort and armies in the world will be futile. This explains why Moshe told them that they would "Build...cities for your small children" (*Bemidbar* 32:24), not mentioning that they would be "fortified," as the two tribes had suggested. With Hashem's help they could leave them as open, unwalled cities.

Now we can understand their response, "Your servants shall do as my master instructs," i.e., we shall put our trust in Hashem only. "And your servants shall cross over, every armed person of the legion, before Hashem to do battle, as my Lord speaks" (*Bemidbar* 32:27). The tribes of Reuven and Gad had noted the rebuke of Moshe and had taken it to heart. Now that they realized the source of their strength and their reliance upon Hashem, they were ready to proceed.

What's Really Important

There is another criticism of these two tribes found in the *parashah*. It says, "Pens for our flocks shall we build here for our livestock, and cities for our small children" (*Bemidbar* 32:16). The Midrash says that they were at fault in their request, in that they made the *ikar* (that which is primary) into *tafel* (that which is secondary), and they made that which is *tafel* into the *ikar*. This was because they placed their possessions before their bodies, worrying about their flocks before their people. The Midrash then applies the following verse to them: "If an inheritance is seized hastily in the beginning, its end will not be blessed" (*Mishlei* 20:21).

Rav Shmuel Rozovsky[37] makes an inference from the words of the above *midrash*. He says that they were at fault on two separate accounts. Not only did they make the *ikar* into *tafel*, they also made that which is of lesser importance into the main item. Rav Rozovsky continues that it actually follows that when a person has this distorted value system he will then proceed to relegate that which is of vital importance to that of negligible value. He is highlighting the importance of placing one's priorities in the correct order based on the Torah's outlook, and not following what the rest of the world dictates.

Rabbeinu Bachaye explains the verse in *Mishlei* cited by the Midrash above, that if there is an inheritance that is not due to come to a person from Heaven, but rather he runs and grabs it, the outcome will be that it will not bring blessing. On the other hand, if an inheritance does come from Heaven, its outcome will result in blessing. He then cites the fact that there were two exceedingly wealthy men in the world, Korach and Haman. Both of them were destroyed together with their property. This was because their wealth was not decreed from on high; instead, they stole and extorted from others.

The tribes of Reuven and Gad were exceedingly wealthy with their abundance of cattle, which, as mentioned, they held dearer to them than their own children. For this, Hashem said, "By your lives, you will not see a sign of blessing from this property." So it was that the venture of the tribes over the Jordan ended in tragedy when they were exiled prematurely, before the other tribes. Rabbeinu Bachaye then applies to them the verse "For neither from sunrise nor from sunset, nor from the wilderness comes greatness. For Hashem is the Judge; He lowers this one and raises that one" (*Tehillim* 75:7-8). This teaches us that it is not one's travels and ventures which raise a person and make him wealthy; rather, all is dependant on Hashem. He raises and He lowers, as those tribes tragically discovered years later.

Let us conclude with an idea related to the period we are currently in, which ties in with the previous idea. The Kitzur Shulchan Aruch (121:1) discusses the purpose of a fast day: to awaken the heart to repentance. He then goes on to say that the *ikar* of the day is not the fasting, but the repentance. Proof of this is found in *Sefer Yonah*, where it says (3:10), "And Hashem saw their ways." The Sages comment that it doesn't say that He saw their sackcloth and fasting, but that He saw their deeds, that they had repented for their evil ways. Thus, fasting should be viewed only as a preparation for repentance.

What is interesting is that the Kitzur Shulchan Aruch then goes on to say that people who fast but spend the day involved in other matters "grab onto the *tafel* and leave the *ikar*." This is exactly the same criticism leveled by the Midrash at the two tribes. Surely there is an important lesson in this. Firstly, when we read this *parashah* we are between two major fasts. Perhaps the message from the Kitzur is that we should not be content with going through the motions of fasting, but instead should try to focus on what the day is really about. Secondly, in life there are always distractions. However, one of the lessons from the *parashah* is that one must never lose sight of his true goals and priorities.

Devarim

The End Is in Sight

There is a very dramatic contrast that we see on Tishah B'Av. Before midday, the atmosphere in shul is very depressing — the lights are dimmed, the *paroches* is removed, and people are sitting on the floor. Comes the afternoon, we get up off the floor and restore the shul to its previous splendor. Why is there such a vast difference between the morning and afternoon of this day? A simple parable[1] will provide an insight.

Once there was a great artist who decided he was going to paint his greatest masterpiece. He journeyed with his companion up a mountain and found the perfect view to paint. After several days the painting was complete. He began to view his work from different angles to see what improvements could be made. He started walking backwards, admiring his work. He then continued to pace further backwards, focusing only on his work, until eventually, he came to within a few meters of the edge of the mountain cliff. His companion realized the danger he was in and called to him to stop, but he paid no notice. When he was only seconds away from certain death, his friend shouted at him to stop, but the artist was too engrossed in his work to pay attention. Finally, the friend picked up a knife and ran to the picture and slashed it, destroying the masterpiece. "What are you doing?" the artist cried out, having come to his senses. "Look behind you and you'll see why I did it," replied his friend.

Similarly, the Jewish people had sinned greatly and seemed destined for destruction. All morning of the Ninth of Av, all those years ago, the Jews were terrified that perhaps their fate was destruction at the hands of the enemy. At midday the fires began to burn. Hashem had vented his wrath on the Beis Hamikdash rather than on the Jewish people themselves. This explains the change in the level of mourning during the day. All morning there was the threat of the impeding annihilation, which is why the mood is so depressing, encompassing the fear and uncertainty of the Jewish people. In the afternoon, they realized that although the Beis Hamikdash was aflame, nevertheless their bodies were spared. That is why certain aspects of mourning cease by the afternoon, despite the fact that the major part of the destruction began only then.

Related to Pesach

It is interesting to note that the only other day where we find such a split within the day is on *erev Pesach*. One may eat *chametz* during the first few hours of the day, after which it becomes forbidden. It is also interesting to note that the first day of Pesach always falls on the same day of the week that Tishah B'Av occurs. This would suggest that there is a link between the two.

On Pesach, the first part of the Seder, until the meal, is dedicated to the previous Exodus, from Egypt, while the text after the meal alludes to the future redemption. One reason for the egg on the Seder plate is to symbolize our mourning for the destruction of the Beis Hamikdash (eggs are the traditional first meal given to mourners). So too, the last meal before Tishah B'Av consists of an egg dipped in ashes. There is also another aspect to Tishah B'Av. It is brought down that it is the day upon which Mashiach is born, symbolizing the beginning of the redemption process. It is also related that in the messianic era, Shivah Asar BeTammuz and Tishah B'Av will become *yamim tovim*, with the rest of the three weeks becoming Chol Hamoed for these new festivals. This is alluded to in the fact that we don't say *Tachanun* on Tishah B'Av.

Many of the *kinos* that we recite not only talk about the past destruction, but also mention our longing for the Jerusalem of the future. One of the most famous chapters describes the dramatic differences between the going forth from Egypt in all its glory, to the misery our people suffered when going forth from Jerusalem. It ends, though, with "gladness and joy, while anguish and sighing will flee, when I return to Jerusalem" (*Kinah* 31). Similarly, in *minchah* we insert a paragraph into the *Amidah* which ends: "You consumed her with fire; You will rebuild her with fire." All this shows that although we mourn for the great tragedies that befell us, we must also hope and long for the end of this bitter exile.

A Very Long Drashah

Now, however, we are in exile. What is our status and what does this week's *parashah* teach us about our predicament? At the beginning of our *parashah* Scripture relates, "On the other side of the Jordan, Moshe began clarifying this Torah" (*Devarim* 1:5). Rashi cites a *midrash* that says that Moshe explained the Torah to *bnei Yisrael* in seventy different languages. What does this mean? Here you have a whole nation, after forty years of wandering, about to enter their final destination, and the rabbi begins a *drashah* explaining not just a few nice points on the

Torah, but the whole Torah, and in seventy languages? What was the purpose of this?

The Ksav Sofer explains that the intention was to remove an idea from the hearts of those who wish to deny the truth. They could say that the Torah was given to be kept either in the desert, while *bnei Yisrael* dwelled in solitude, or in the land of Israel, as it says, "they shall not be reckoned with the nations" (*Bemidbar* 23:9). However, in exile, amongst the nations, there is no need to practice the mitzvos. In order to dispel this belief, Moshe explained the Torah in seventy languages, to show that in any place, amongst any nation who speaks any language, we need to keep the Torah and its mitzvos and not change them in any detail or depart from them in any way.

The Ksav Vehakabbalah questions this interpretation of the Midrash. What purpose would there be in explaining the Torah in seventy foreign languages? The question is strengthened in light of the *chazal* that says that one of the merits of *bnei Yisrael* in Egypt was that they didn't change their mother tongue. Rather, the Midrash is referring to a concept we have called *shivim panim laTorah*, that there are seventy facets to Torah. Besides the simplest explanation of each detail of Torah, there are seventy other explanations, and deeper understandings of what is in the Torah, which all adhere to Hashem's will. That is what Moshe was revealing here by explaining the Torah in such a way.

Not for the Desert Only

The next verse continues with Moshe relating that after the revelation at Sinai, Hashem instructed, "You have had much dwelling by this mountain. Turn yourselves and journey, and come to the mountain of the Emorite and all its neighbors..." (*Devarim* 1:6–7). Rashi cites a *midrash* that explains that Hashem was telling *bnei Yisrael* that there was much reward for their dwelling at that mountain: they had made the Mishkan, the menorah and its implements, received the Torah and appointed the Sanhedrin. It seems that after all that was achieved at Sinai, they were ready to begin being told other laws and ideas which would maintain them in their lofty status. Surely now it would be beneath their dignity to merely journey to the lowly "mountain of the Emorite and its neighbors."

The Lomzer Rebbe[2] explains that one may think like this, because, after all, they had received the Torah directly from Hashem, with all its many laws and details, and therefore they should dwell in solitude in the desert away from inferior beings. Moshe therefore explained to them that, on the contrary, the Torah is a living Torah, and that it is meant to be observed amongst members of a society, surrounded by other people and nations. This is because the Torah contains the answers to all questions in life, including those relating to human interaction. In fact, if the Jewish people keep their part — "and you shall guard them and do them" — then, the verse continues, the nations shall say, "Surely a wise and understanding people is this great nation" (*Devarim* 4:6). This is what the *midrash* is relating to us. After all the spiritual heights *bnei Yisrael* achieved at Sinai, it shouldn't enter their minds to remain there in solitude, but rather they should journey on and become a nation surrounded by the other nations. The Torah is designed for this, "for it is your wisdom and understanding in the eyes of the peoples" (ibid.).

Later on in the *parashah*, Hashem says, "Enough of your circling this mountain; turn yourselves northward (*tsafonah*)...you are passing through the boundaries of your brothers, the children of Esav who dwell in Seir" (ibid., 2:3–4). Using a play on the word *tsafonah*, *Chazal* derive from this verse the instruction *hatsfinu atzmechem*, hide yourselves from the persecuting nations while in exile. The Gemara asks where one should flee, to which it answers, flee to Torah.

We see that the root of the word *tsafon* means Torah, from the verse "He has secured (*yatspon*) the eternal Torah for the upright; it is a shield for those who walk in innocence" (*Mishlei* 2:7). The Kehillas Yitzchak explains that the verse is giving us advice as to how to survive in exile. By "hiding" oneself by learning Torah, which is "our life and the length of our days," he will save himself from harm in *galus*, until the redemption comes. Proof for this idea is that the verse speaks about passing through the territory of Esav, whose very name is associated with exile and persecution of the Jewish people. Under such conditions, we are advised by the verse in *Mishlei*, Torah is a shield, assured to protect one from harm.

These lessons are all crucial for us to absorb on Tishah B'Av. Moshe imprinted this idea on *bnei Yisrael*, that Torah and its study applies equally wherever they may be. The advice to flee to Torah is not only for physical protection, but also the key to the future redemption. May Tishah B'Av turn into a day of joy for all of *klal Yisrael*, speedily in our days.

PARASHAS VA'ESCHANAN

Pray Silence

Moshe continues recounting *bnei Yisrael*'s journey in this week's *parashah*. He recalls how, after the conquest of the lands on the other side of the Jordan, he prayed for a revocation of the decree barring his entry, and asked that he be allowed to enter the Promised Land before he died. The commentators explain that since they had conquered the lands which would belong to the two and a half tribes who would settle over the Jordan, Moshe thought that perhaps since he was allowed into those lands, the decree had been rescinded and he would be allowed into Eretz Yisrael as well. Hashem, however, responded, "It is much for you; do not speak to Me further about this matter" (*Devarim* 3:26).

Stop Praying

Why did Moshe's request warrant this particular response, not to approach Hashem again about this matter? Moshe's actual request was "Please (*nah*), let me cross and see the good land..." (*Devarim* 3:25). The Midrash says that Moshe pointed out to Hashem that it says in His Torah that there may be a situation whereby a slave completes his servitude and wishes to stay with his master and declares, "I love my master, my wife and my children; I shall not go free" (*Shemos* 21:5). In reply to this statement of Moshe, Hashem gave the above-mentioned response.

What was the meaning of Moshe's claim and why was Hashem's response appropriate? The Chanukas HaTorah explains this using a *gemara* in *Kiddushin* (22a). It derives from the above verse that a slave requesting to stay has to repeat his request, "I will not go," for it to be effective. Now we can understand the conversation. Moshe was telling Hashem that it says in His very own Torah, "But if the slave shall surely say" (the slave referring to Moshe) "I love my Master" (referring to Hashem) "my wife" (referring to Torah) "and my children" (referring to *bnei Yisrael*). He was saying that surely if he were to repeat his request, Hashem would have to keep him alive, and let him cross the Jordan, in order to fulfill that which is in Hashem's own Torah about such a "slave." That is why Hashem told Moshe not to repeat the request a second time, as He would then have to keep Moshe alive, which He could not do, and we shall suggest why later.

The Vilna Gaon[3] explains the verse differently. Moshe knew that if the word *nah* were said twice during prayer, his prayer would be accepted. We see this regarding his prayer for Miriam after she was stricken with *tzaraas*: "Please (*nah*), Hashem, heal her (*nah*) now" (*Bemidbar* 12:13). In this instance, when Moshe said, "Please (*nah*), let me cross," he wanted to use the word *nah* again, upon which his prayer would have to be answered. That is why Hashem told him not to speak anymore regarding that matter, using the word *nah*, since the decree forbidding him to cross the Jordan was a decree that could not be revoked.

We still have to understand why Hashem had to prevent Moshe from finishing the prayer. If Hashem would have desired to fulfill his request, even without the word *nah* the prayer would have sufficed, and if He didn't wish to fulfill it, then how should saying *nah* twice have helped? The Vilna Gaon answers that prayer is a statute, set into the nature of the way Hashem guides the world. Our prayers are heard and can have the power to tear up decrees. Therefore, since He didn't desire to change the rules according to which prayer works, He instead requested that Moshe not complete that prayer.

Well, Why Not?

Both of the above answers suggest why Hashem told Moshe to stop praying. Why did Hashem not wish to accept the prayer and accede to Moshe's request? Rav Y. Z. Soloveitchik[4] cites the Rambam (*Hilchot Yesodei HaTorah* 10:7–8) who says that if a prophet prophecies punishment, but the punishment didn't come about, this is not a contradiction to his prophecy, because Hashem in His mercy revoked the decree. Perhaps the people repented and they were forgiven. If, however, the prophet prophesied about good events and they failed to come about, then he is certainly a false prophet. This is because any good that Hashem decrees is never rescinded, while Hashem does rescind bad decrees.

The claim of Moshe was that since Hashem can annul bad decrees, so too, perhaps He would annul the decree forbidding Moshe to enter the land. Hashem responded that Moshe should not continue to speak about the matter, and then continues to say, "command Yehoshua...for he shall cross before the people and cause them to inherit the land" (*Devarim* 3:28). He was informing Moshe that the time had come for Yehoshua to lead, as it had been decreed that he, and not Moshe, would lead the people into the land. Since that part of the decree was good in nature, Hashem could not change the decree and had to let it be.

The Yalkut Chamishai comments that the verse where Moshe tells Yehoshua, "so will Hashem do to all the kings where you cross over" (*Devarim* 3:21) is immediately followed by the first verse of our *parashah*, where Moshe relates how he prayed for the decree against entering the land to be rescinded. The closeness of these two verses is an example of what the Gemara (*Berachos* 10a) says, that even if a sword is resting on one's neck, he should still ask for mercy (from Hashem). Here, Moshe already knew of the decree of his not entering the land, and yet he still prayed for it to be rescinded. He was teaching a lesson to all generations, that in times of trouble, even when a decree has been passed, one should still seek mercy.

On Four Conditions

Moshe's prayer begins, "And I implored (to) Hashem at that time, saying..." (*Devarim* 3:23). The Ohr Hachaim says that one's prayers should meet four conditions in order that they be accepted. His supplication should be with a broken heart, like a poor person collecting at the door, as the verse says, "A poor person utters supplications" (*Mishlei* 18:23). Secondly, he should pray that his request be accepted with the Divine attribute of mercy. Thirdly, the time should be fitting for acceptance of his prayers, as we say during *minchah* on Shabbos, "As for me, may my prayers to you, Hashem, be at an opportune time" (*Tehillim* 69:14). Fourthly, the supplicant should express his prayer as specifically and clearly as possible.

All four attributes are found in the above verse. The words "And I implored" suggest that he used a language of supplication. "To Hashem" refers to the particular Name of Hashem associated with the characteristic of mercy. "At that time" refers to the fact that it was a particularly favorable time. Finally, it continues with the word "saying," informing us that the prayer was clear and specific.

Later on, the *parashah* speaks about the Jews in exile. It says,

"From there you (in the plural) will seek Hashem your God, and you (in the singular) will find Him, if you search for Him with all your heart and with all your soul" (*Devarim* 4:29). Why is there a change within this verse from the plural to the singular tense? The Vilna Gaon[5] explains with a *gemara* (*Rosh Hashanah* 18a) that talks about two people who went on trial for a crime punishable by death, with exactly the same circumstances surrounding their crimes, yet one was saved and the other condemned. Why were the prayers of one answered, while the other were not? The Gemara answers that it was because one had a *tefillah sheleimah* and the other didn't. Rashi explains this to mean that one prayed with *kavanah* (intent and feeling), while the other did not.

Our verse alludes to this concept. The words "you will seek," in the plural, refer to two (or more) people who sought Him out. The words "and you will find Him" refer to an individual supplicant. This refers to the fact that although many pray, only a small amount are answered because they pray with intent. The verse then ends, "if you search for Him with all your heart and with all your soul." It is only because the individual prays with complete devotion, concentration and intent that he is answered.

It's Written in Black and White

Once there was a man who needed help from Heaven for a particular problem. As part of his efforts, he wrote his Hebrew name in the siddur of a great rabbi, at the appropriate point for this type of prayer, in the hope that the rabbi would pray on his behalf. A few weeks later he felt bad that he had brazenly written in the rabbi's siddur without asking for permission, so he decided to ask the rabbi for forgiveness for this.

Awkwardly, he explained what he had done and apologized profusely for it, to which the rabbi replied, "You don't need to apologize. I never actually noticed you had written anything there." The rabbi had never taken his eyes out of his prayer book, not even from the words he was saying, to look at the margins. He would concentrate only on each and every letter of every single word. He wasn't thinking about what else he had to do that day, or looking at his watch wondering when the service would be over. He was just praying, asking for Divine mercy from the King of kings. Davening is a hard *avodah* to do, requiring concentration and sincerity. If we are at least aware and remind ourselves to Whom we are praying and what we are praying for, acting appropriately for a *beis haknesses*, then we can sincerely request that our prayers be accepted.

Shabbos Nachamu

Let us finish with a beautiful comment on this week's haftarah from Rav Meir Shapiro.[6] This Shabbos is called Shabbos Nachamu, as we begin seven haftaras of comforting and consolation, having just read the three haftaras about punishment and retribution. The Midrash says that at the time Hashem exiled the Jewish people amongst the nations, He said to the nations, "I am giving over my children to you; I seek from you that every so often, you comfort them from their sorrow and pain." The Jewish nation on hearing this cried, "To whom are you giving us to, and whom are you letting comfort us?" to which Hashem responded "I only wanted to test you, to see if you would be content with comfort from the nations, but now that I see you don't want this, I Myself will comfort you."

Rav Meir Shapiro explains that with this we can understand the order of the first four haftaras of comfort. This week's haftarah begins with the well-known phrase, "Comfort, comfort

My people" (*Yeshayah* 40:1). Hashem is giving instructions to the nations to comfort His people. Next week's haftarah begins, "And Tzion said, "Hashem has forsaken me" (ibid., 49:14), referring to the fact that the Jewish people complained that He had instructed the nations to comfort them rather than comforting them Himself. Following that, Hashem revealed that He had only wanted to test them to see if they would be consoled that way, as the haftarah for *Re'eh* begins, "O afflicted, storm-tossed, unconsoled one" (ibid., 54:11). Finally Hashem says that He will fulfill their request, as it says in the following week's haftarah, "It is I; I am He Who comforts you" (ibid., 51:12).

Why Fear?

This week's *parashah* contains a crucial lesson for us, which is one of the fundamental principles of Judaism: "And now, O Yisrael, what does Hashem your God ask of you? Only to fear Hashem your God, to go in all His ways, and to love Him" (*Devarim* 10:12). What is the meaning of the fear of Heaven that we are being instructed about? Perhaps we can define it as having an awareness that there is One Who is above us, watching over all our actions. This is referred to in the Mishnah: "Look at three things and you will not come to sin. Know from where you came from, to where you are going, and in front of Whom you are going to give account for your actions" (*Avos* 3:1). This awareness, that there is a Presence that oversees all, and that we are held accountable for our actions, is an enlightening thought.

The verse mentions that there is to be both a fear of, and a love of Hashem. The Alshich gives two explanations of the relationship between the two. He explains that there are two types of fear: the fear of punishment, and the reverence of something superior. If one has only the latter, he may be negligent or inadvertently omit aspects of his service. Fear of punishment prevents this. Therefore, both types are necessary. If one had only fear one would not serve Hashem with self-sacrifice, since only a love of Hashem could cause one to risk his life. On the other hand, Hashem is not interested in our love unless we have fear as well. If one were only full of love for Hashem, he would constantly be negligent, relying on Hashem's forgiving nature. Moshe was telling *bnei Yisrael* that they should combine both elements in their Divine service.

The Alshich's second approach to the subject of the relationship between love and fear of God is as follows. There are two sets of commandments, those between man and Hashem, and those between man and his fellow. One would usually understand the former as being built on the amount of fear of Heaven one has. Regarding commandments between man and his fellow, one would think that the most important thing is that one has a loving element within him towards others. Without this fear and love one cannot fulfill the mitzvos. Hashem is telling us that the opposite must be true as well. He wants us to also observe commandments towards our fellow human beings out of a fear of Heaven, and to observe the mitzvos between man and Hashem out of love.

The Gemara in *Berachos* (33b), referring to the above verse, says, "Everything is determined from Heaven, except for *yiras Shamayim* (fear of Heaven). The explanation[7] is that keeping all other mitzvos is dependent on help from Heaven, to the extent that the resources one is given enables one to perform them. Only if one has a roof over his head can he place a mezuzah on his doorposts. The mitzvah of *yiras Shamayim* is different in that no Heavenly assistance is provided, or indeed necessary, to enable one to fulfill it. Since it is dependent on thought and frame of mind only, it can be observed even in a prison where one can't fulfill any other mitzvos. This point can also be derived from the fact that the verse talks about what Hashem asks "of you." This demand is something that is fulfilled "from you" — only from within you and not with Heavenly assistance.

So What Do You Do?

The following incident illustrates this point. The Beis Halevi once asked a former student, "What do you do?" to which he replied, "I work as a merchant." He then repeated the question, to which he received exactly the same answer. He then asked a third time, "But what do you do?" to which he received the same answer. He then said to him, "Do you think I didn't hear your first and second answer? I was asking you what you do, what your input is regarding matters within your power to control, and all you told me was what you did for a livelihood, the outcome of which Hashem anyway determines." He then related the following: "People are faced with all types of situations. Whether they are rich or poor, have *simchah* or sorrows, are all things that depend on Divine Providence. If I wanted to know about monetary matters, I would have asked, "How are Hashem's actions affecting you?" to which you could have replied whether or not Hashem was paving your way with *mazal* and blessing. However, I was asking "What do you do?" In other words, what is your input into matters, particularly those pertaining to spirituality. You should have answered how many hours you set aside for Torah study, or other acts of kindness that you are involved in."

Half Man or Whole Man?

Let us develop this idea a stage further. Shlomo Hamelech's *Megillas Koheles* is full of the most profound advice, counseling people not to go after the materialistic world, but rather to focus on spiritual matters. How does the *sefer* end? What is the parting advice that Shlomo Hamelech wishes to make an impression on us? "The sum of the matter, when all has been considered, fear God and keep His commandments, for that is a whole man."

Firstly, one sees that fear of Heaven is the crucial feature that Shlomo Hamelech advises is to be employed, indicating its importance and centrality. Secondly, as Rav Elchanan Wasserman[8] explains, one shouldn't think that fear of Heaven is merely a higher level, and that even without it one can still be considered a man, just lacking this one aspect. Instead, the verse tells us that one who fears God is considered the "whole man." One who doesn't fear God cannot be considered a man. The reason for this is that since he does not feel accountable to anyone higher than human beings, when it suits him he will just go after his base instincts. Man's refinement and placement above the animal kingdom exist only because he separates himself from his animal instincts.

Rav Elchanan is telling us that the "quality" of a man is dependent on his level of *yiras Shamayim*. If he has much, then he is a great man; if he has little, he is a "small" man; and if he has none, he is simply no different from an animal, aside from his being dressed up in human form.

You Have Everything…Except the Most Important Thing

Rav Elchanan explains that we also see this idea in *Sefer Bereishis*. Avraham and Sarah journeyed to the land of Gerar, where, upon their arrival, Sarah was abducted. Hashem appeared to Avimelech, the king of the land, in a dream and threatened to kill him because of this sin. In the morning, Avimelech returned her to Avraham, upon which he asked him, "Why didn't you tell me that she was your wife? Why did you do such a thing to bring such punishments upon me by not telling me?" To this, Avraham replied with the famous answer, "Because I said, there is but no fear of God in this place and they would slay me because of my wife" (*Bereishis* 20:11).

Avraham was telling Avimelech that indeed his society was a civil one. It had culture, a legal system with high courts of justice — everything one could need. However, despite all this, there was but one element lacking: *yiras Elokim* (fear of God). When people in such a society would face a battle between their emotions and lusts, and their man-made laws, then emotions would prevail, since what the heart desires will overcome the intellect. That is what could lead a person in that society to take a man's wife away. In such a society, where man decides what is correct, anything can be legislated into law, as with the people of Sodom, who had all forms of wickedness inscribed into law. Only when one has fear of God, knowing that He is eternal, watches all of one's actions and holds him accountable for them, will one comply with a higher, unchanging, timeless value system.

A Comforting Thought

Let us conclude with an idea on this week's haftarah. It is recorded that when the Ramban[9] came to Eretz Yisrael and saw the abundance of produce and trees growing there, even during the exile of its people, he became so disturbed that he fainted. After he was revived he said that actually this abundance brings hope and comfort. It can be compared to a nursing mother, who as long as the child is alive will do all she can to prevent the milk from ceasing. If the child dies, *rachmana litzlan*, she will do all she can to make the milk stop. The comparison is that if Eretz Yisrael is dried up completely during its desolation, then it is a sign that the land has been forsaken forever. Now that Hashem provides Eretz Yisrael with fruit in abundance, it is a sign that the Jewish people will return to it. This is alluded to in the haftarah (*Yeshayah* 51:3): "For Hashem shall comfort Tzion; He shall comfort all her ruins." The verse then tells us with what she shall be comforted: "He shall make her wilderness like Eden, and her wasteland like a garden of Hashem." The abundance growing there was a sign that Hashem would surely remember the land and bring His people back to it.

Making a Prophet

This week's *parashah* contains the commandment neither to add to nor to take away from the mitzvos of the Torah. It is obvious why it is forbidden to subtract from them, but what is the problem with adding new commandments? The Dubno Maggid[10] answers with a parable. Once someone borrowed a plate from his friend, and upon returning it he gave a saucer in addition, telling him that the plate had had a baby. The friend gladly accepted this addition. A few weeks later he borrowed a jug, and upon returning it, presented his friend with a small jug, again informing him of the new addition. A month later he borrowed a silver candlestick. When time passed and he had not returned it, his friend inquired after it, to which he informed him that it had died. The friend asked him if he thought he was so gullible to believe this, to which the borrower replied, "If you accepted the births of the saucer and jug unquestioningly, then you should also believe that candlesticks can die." So too, if we were allowed to add mitzvos, we would soon forget the Divinity of the Torah. We would perceive it as partly man-made and discard any mitzvos which were too difficult or inconvenient. Therefore, we are forbidden not only from subtracting from it, but also from adding to it, in order not to weaken the Torah's stature.

Frum Idol Worship

We see that there is a connection between the prohibition against adding mitzvos, idolatry and false prophets. The beginning of the *parashah* talks about the curse "if you stray from the path that I command you today, to follow the gods of others" (*Devarim* 11:28). Rashi explains that this teaches us that one who serves idols has strayed from the entire path that we are commanded about, and therefore is like one who denies the entire Torah.

What extra information is Rashi informing us of here? Surely it is obvious that idol worship removes one from the Torah's way. The Beis Av[11] explains that in fact the Torah here is specifically referring to one who serves idols in tandem with keeping the rest of the mitzvos. Although at first glance he is keeping the Torah, nevertheless, he is also serving a foreign entity besides Hashem. This was the sin of the golden calf; *bnei Yisrael* didn't deny Hashem's existence, they just believed in other powers as well. He quotes the Rambam, who says that this is in fact the main type of *avodah zarah* that the Torah is warning us about.

Now we can understand what Rashi is telling us, that one who worships other gods, even if he does so along with performing the mitzvos, is still considered as one who denies the entire Torah, as he has removed himself from the path which Hashem has instructed us about.

He's Not the Messiah…

The false prophet is one such example of one who could be observing the rest of the Torah, yet errs in particular areas. The verse says, "If there should stand up in your midst (*bekirbecha*) a prophet (*navi*) or dreamer of a dream..." (*Devarim* 13:2). In our version of the Baal Haturim we find no comment on this verse. Rebbi Akiva Eiger[12] explains that in his day, there was a version of the text of the Baal Haturim that comments on the Hebrew word meaning "in your midst" (*bekirbecha*). It says there that it has the same *gematria* as the words *zu ha'ishah* (the woman), which is 324. Rebbi Eiger explains that at the time of the Baal Haturim, the Jews were put under tremendous pressure to convert to Christianity. In order to convince them to convert, they tried to bring proof from the Torah that the future Messiah would be born miraculously from a Jewish mother. The Baal Haturim tried to refute their claims and revealed a hidden secret. The above mentioned verse speaks about a false prophet who encourages people to go after other gods. The real *drashah* that should have appeared in the Baal Haturim is that the words *bekirbecha navi* (a [false] prophet in your midst), have the same *gematria* as the words *zu ha'ishah u'venah* (the woman and her son), which is 387. This is an obvious reference, and refutation, to the most well known false prophet, who they say was born through only a mother. The censors had got hold of the real text, which Rebbi Akiva Eiger had, and erased the words "and her son," in a despicable effort to show the Jews that the Messiah would be miraculously born from a Jewish mother. The above comment, however, remained in the text, and it took Rebbi Akiva Eiger to decipher its true meaning, working backwards to understand the true intentions of the comment.

The next section speaks about a person who secretly tries to entice others to idol worship: "If your brother, the son of your mother...will incite you secretly, saying, 'Let us go and worship the gods of others' " (*Devarim* 13:7). Why does the verse talk about only one who is your brother through your mother and not of one who is your brother through your father? The Yalkut Peninim[13] explains that the Torah is hinting to the well-known enticer, about whom they say has no human father. Therefore, according to that, he is only "your brother, the son of your mother," and so the Torah instructs, "you shall not take kindly to him and you shall not listen to him."

It is related[14] that at the time of Shabbetai Tzvi, many people followed him, including great rabbis. The Taz spoke to Shabbetai Tzvi's son to try and find out what was below the surface. His son told him that all his days he had never seen any blemish or flaw in his father's actions, only that when he slept, he lay on his back. The Taz responded, "If so, there is no doubt that he's not the Messiah, because the Gemara (*Berachos* 13b) says that the real Messiah will not transgress even the smallest of rabbinical decrees. The end of Shabbetai Tzvi proved his true identity: Together with his followers they eventually committed many severe sins, and were imprisoned by the Turks. He converted to Islam to save himself and died in disgrace, all the while still believing that he was the Messiah.

Hide and Seek

Let us return to the section dealing with one who tries to entice others to join in his idolatrous activities. The verse says, "You shall not take kindly to him and you shall not listen to him; your eye shall not take pity on him; you shall not be compassionate and you shall not cover it up for him" (*Devarim* 13:9). Surely, regarding other capital cases, we are obligated to try and find merit for the defendant, so that he should be spared. Yet here, not only are we not instructed to find a merit for him, we are given directions to specifically expedite his condemnation, such as that he doesn't need to be warned first, while usually one does need this in capital cases. Also, judges who would usually be disqualified are allowed to judge him. Furthermore, his punishment is stoning, the harshest form of the death penalty.

In addition, while we always need witnesses to a sin in order to punish the perpetrator, here, after the accused told someone to worship with him, we "framed" him, and had witnesses hide behind a wall while he was asked to repeat his claim, in order that witnesses could testify about his guilt. Surely, we have a prohibition not to place a stumbling block before the blind, and yet here such behavior is endorsed with the Torah's license. Why do we deal so strictly with the "enticer," and why is he treated in such a different way?

Rav Aharon Kotler[15] explains, citing a statement of Rav Chaim of Volozhin. The world was created only in order that a man should do good and benefit others, as it says, *olam chessed tibaneh.* Since the enticer brings only bad to other people, causing them much spiritual harm, he loses his merit to exist. The Sages say that one who causes his friend to sin is worse than one who kills him. This is because one who kills someone only removes him from this world, while one who causes another to sin drives him out of this world and the World to Come. All other types of sins mentioned in the Torah by definition are capable of being performed on an individual level, without involving anyone else. This sin by definition involves bringing others down with the sinner, which is why it is dealt with so severely. Since the transgressor is defeating not only his purpose in the world, but that of others as well, and because the transgression is idolatry, which was described by Rashi above as a denial of the entire Torah, such evil cannot be tolerated.

Opposite Enticement

Scripture goes on to describe the enticer's end: "you shall pelt him with stones...for he sought to make you stray from near Hashem" (*Devarim* 13:11). The Alter of Kelm[16] explains that because "he sought" he is killed, even though he was not successful in his efforts. It is well known that the Divine attribute of reward is many times greater than that of punishment. The Alter points out that if this is what happens to those who flout the Divine will, bringing others to sin, even though they don't succeed, how great will the reward be for those who try to bring people in the opposite direction — to *teshuvah*, Torah and mitzvos. Even for the effort alone — despite the fact that one is not always successful — the reward will surely be great.

A Royal Appointment

Once I did the customary *bein hazmanim* outing of taking an American to see the sights of London. We went to the Tower of London and made our way to the main attraction: the crown jewels. We were impressed by the wide array of crowns, scepters and other royal attire. I could not help but notice the security arrangements for the jewels. They were set behind thick glass walls with a laser system to detect foreign incursion. In my curiosity, I asked a guard, "You see that diamond ball thing over there? How much is that worth?" He gave a knowing chuckle at the absurdity of the question and said, "Oh, there's no price on these." It was shortly before Elul, when we prepare ourselves for Rosh Hashanah, and the following thought occurred to me. *Chazal* say that one of the reasons we have earthly kings is to help us understand in some small measure the greatness of Hashem's Kingship over us. This is seen in the blessing we recite upon seeing a king; "Who has given of His glory to human beings." Presumably, this statement was made for when one sees a real king (or dictator) whom one trembles before, as life or death is in his hands. One is supposed to realize how much infinitely greater is the Kingship of Hashem, Who controls and orchestrates events.

This week's *parashah* contains the landmark commandment of placing a king over *bnei Yisrael*. This was to take place only once they were settled in Eretz Yisrael. We find that many years later, Shmuel Hanavi rebuked the people for requesting a king. If it is a positive mitzvah, how was Shmuel justified in this? The commentators[17] explain that the mitzvah to appoint a king is different from other mitzvos. It is similar in nature to the mitzvah of writing a *get* in order to divorce one's wife. When one is in need of such actions, he has to fulfill the mitzvah, but it is preferable not to need it in the first place. So too, Shmuel was rebuking *bnei Yisrael* for the fact that they had come to the level that they would request a king. It would have been better had they not needed one in the first place.

Rav Yisrael Salanter[18] answers differently. There are two positive purposes in appointing a king. Firstly, a king has the strength and power to watch over his subjects' observance of mitzvos, to strengthen and encourage the fulfillment of them. We find this with Chizkiyah Hamelech, who thrust a sword into the floor of the *beis midrash* and said, "Whoever doesn't occupy himself with learning Torah, this sword should pierce him." Secondly, the nature of a person is to see other people's faults far sooner than his own. The king and his ministers would be able to recognize the shortcomings of their subjects and chastise them accordingly. This can only be accomplished if the king rules over them with a mighty hand, having the power to punish them if need be. If he lacks this authority then his rule is worthless.

Bnei Yisrael decided that they wanted a king. Unfortunately, the way they went about it was wrong. "So now appoint for us a king to judge us" (I *Shmuel* 8:5). From the words "for us," the commentators learn that their intention was that the king should be as one of them, an equal, willing to do the bidding of his subjects — in other words, just doing what is popular. That is why the next verse describes Shmuel's dissatisfaction at the request. The text then records how Hashem said that Shmuel should, in fact, do the bidding of the people and appoint a king, as the mitzvah in the Torah states, "but be sure to warn them and tell them about the protocol of the king who will reign over them." Hashem was telling Shmuel to convey to the people that the king would be appointed, not according to their request, but rather as the Torah's law required, that the king guide the people to Torah and mitzvos.

Warlords and Preachers

Rav Eliezer Shuelevitz[19] explains another difference between a Jewish and gentile king. The role of the gentile king is to lead the people in battle. The Jewish people, on the other hand, are to trust in Hashem. The role of the king is to teach the people that if they follow in the Torah's way, Hashem will guide events so that they will emerge victorious.

With this in mind, we can understand the verses in a different light. The Torah says that upon entering the land, the people will request a king "like all the nations that are around me" (*Devarim* 17:14); they will desire one whose role will be to lead them in battle. Scripture then retorts, "You shall surely set over yourself a king whom Hashem your God shall choose," indicating that only the choice of Hashem shall be appointed. This explains why we are instructed that the king must not be from a foreign nation. If his sole purpose were military, then a gentile king would be acceptable. Since the appointment is to adjure the people, strengthening Torah and mitzvos, only one who would lead the people along such a path is acceptable. The verse indicates that if the intent of the people is for the sake of Heaven, the appointment will be blessed and productive. If the only intention of the request is for someone to lead them in war, which is not the intention of Hashem in providing us a king, more harm than good will come out of it.

I'm Honored

The Gemara (*Kesuvos* 17a) derives from the verse "You shall surely set over yourselves a king" (*Devarim* 17:15), that if a king is willing to forgo the honor due to him he is not allowed to, while a scholar is permitted to do so. What is the reason for this discrepancy? Rav Chaim of Volozhin[20] explains that if a king forgoes the honor due to him, he loses his stature as king. This is because technically, any Jew could become a king, but only the chosen one is the actual king, as a result of people honoring him as befitting a king. Thus, if he forgoes this he is just equal to anyone else. A scholar, however, who chooses to forgo the honor people give him may do so, since he still possesses the wisdom that sets him apart from ordinary people.

In the *Sefer Hamakneh*[21] we find a different answer to this question. The reason a king is forbidden to forgo the honor due to him is because the kingship is not his, but remains under the authority of Heaven. What is not yours cannot be given away. On the other hand, a non-Jewish king can forgo his honor because it is not in the possession of Heaven; it was fully handed over to him.

With this idea, we can understand the difference between the *berachah* we recite on seeing a Jewish king and the *berachah* we recite upon seeing a gentile king. On seeing a Jewish king we recite, "Who imparts of His honor to those who fear Him"; the honor is only as a result of what Hashem has imparted to him, but it is still under Heaven's jurisdiction. The Jewish king has to use this honor to increase observance of Torah and mitzvos. Regarding a gentile king, we say, "Who gives of His honor to His creatures"; the honor is not Hashem's anymore and the king can be forgiving of it.

Credit Theory

What demands does the Torah place on the king? The verse tells us that he has to write two *sifrei Torah* which should always remain with him, and he should read from one of them every day, "so that his heart not become haughty over his brethren and not turn from the commandments right or left" (*Devarim* 17:20). What is the connection between the beginning of the verse that talks about not becoming haughty, and the warning about disregarding the commandments of Hashem?

The Dubno Maggid[22] answers with a *mashal*. Once, a merchant was returning from the market with a horse-drawn wagon stacked high with his valuable acquisitions. Suddenly, a small man-led cart with just a few items on it drew up next to him. "How dare you with your pathetic cart travel alongside me as if you are my equal?" snapped the wealthy merchant. The smaller merchant replied, "True, you are well known as a big trader in the market; however, you could be proud if all you bought was paid for in cash, but we both know that both of us could not advance enough ready cash and had to buy on credit. I didn't buy much, and what I did buy came out to little, while you bought great quantities of expensive merchandise. Therefore, your debt to your creditors is far greater than mine. Although you are richer than I am, the burden of debt you carry is far greater."

So too, Hashem is telling the kings that although their position is exalted and possessions many, the result is that they are in even greater debt to Hashem. Therefore, they are given a special warning that their power and wealth should not get the better of them, which would cause them to deviate from the path of the Torah.

This Is Your Life

The verse says about the king's copy of the Torah, "it shall be with him and he shall read from it all the days of his life, so that he will learn to fear Hashem …to observe all the words of this Torah" (*Devarim* 17:19). The commentators explain that the verse is not simply telling us about the king's obligation to read from it every day, but that by reading from it he should chart his life's course and let it guide him through decisions. He has to read in it "all the days of his life," meaning through all the events of his life.

During Rav Yaakov Kamenetsky's[23] early years in North America he lived in Toronto. In those days Toronto had a very small Jewish community. Someone was walking with him on Shavuos, after they had just read *Megillas Rus*, when Rav Yaakov remarked, "I'm no better than Elimelech. He left Eretz Yisrael because he was worried about his livelihood, going from a place where there were Jews to a place where there weren't any, to the fields of Moav. He was willing to sacrifice the education of his children to make a better living." He then continued "Why am I here despite the fact that my children are not in the best environment? Because of *parnasah*, and that's wrong. That was why Elimelech was punished. I have to move to a more Jewish environment." On that day he resolved to move to New York, where he became Rosh Yeshivas Torah Vodaath. A true king had read in the Torah how to plan his life.

Mothers and Mother Birds

T
he Torah gives the commandment that upon discovering
a nest, one must send away the mother bird before taking
its young or its eggs, "so that it will be good for you and
will prolong your days" (*Devarim* 22:7). The Midrash states that
there are some mitzvos for which the reward is honor, and others for which the reward is wealth. The Midrash continues that
for this particular mitzvah, one is promised that if one doesn't
have children prior to performing it, he will be granted them afterwards as a reward. This is alluded to in the beginning of the
above verse: "you shall surely send away the mother and take
the young for you." Although the basic understanding is that after sending away the mother, one can keep the young, the verse
can also mean that one who performs the mitzvah, will "take"
for himself the young, i.e., be rewarded with young.

How can the Midrash say that this is what the verse refers to,
when we find the verse explicitly talks about long life being the
reward for this mitzvah's fulfillment? The Ksav Sofer[24] answers
that in fact there is no contradiction. The two rewards are really
the same thing. It is inferred from the Gemara (*Nedarim* 64b)
that a person who leaves children behind him is considered as if

he hasn't died. Through his children, his memory will last throughout the generations. This is the intent of the Midrash. If you don't have children, Hashem will give them to you, and through them the verse's promise will be fulfilled. The "prolonged days" will be through descendants.

There is only one other place in the Torah where these rewards — that it will be "good for you" and you will have length of days — are promised. This is in the portion of the Torah dealing with the mitzvah of honoring one's parents. Let us examine three different approaches to answering the question of why they carry the same reward.

Rav Yaakov Weinberg[25] explains the common factor between these two mitzvos. Both require recognition of *mesirus nefesh* (self-sacrifice). The Torah tells us to honor our parents because of the great self-sacrifice that parents undergo for their children. By promising "length of days," people will come to appreciate this. On the other hand, if someone tries to take the young of a mother, the mother will remain with its offspring rather than fly away, in order to save them, even at great cost to itself. This is the maternal instinct in full force — a mother willing to sacrifice her own freedom in order to protect her young. Taking the young in front of the mother bird is taking advantage of the maternal instinct and of the *mesirus nefesh* it naturally exhibits for its young. By sending it away, one shows appreciation for the *mesirus nefesh* that even a bird has, which is why one is also entitled to length of days. Through these two mitzvos, the Torah is giving great recognition to the sacrifices, trials and tribulations that a parent undergoes.

The Mishnah (*Berachos* 33b) says that if one says about the mitzvah of sending away the mother bird that "Hashem is merciful on the bird," he is to be silenced. According to one opinion, this is because really it is a decree of Hashem with no other reason. The Vilna Gaon[26] explains that there are two mitzvos where long life is promised, to show that perfection is achieved in a person only if he uses two opposite character traits, such as mercy and cruelty. If a person is using only one trait, it does not prove that he is righteous; it only demonstrates that this is his nature. If one serves Hashem with two opposite traits then it can be attested to that he is righteous. Therefore, Hashem gave the mitzvah of honoring parents. This manifests itself especially when they are elderly and one has to have mercy on them.

Then there is the mitzvah of sending away the mother bird. The Yerushalmi says that sometimes, in its sadness at being sent away, the mother bird will drown itself in water. Certainly this is very cruel. Therefore, the reward for one's keeping both mitzvos is length of days, to show us that since he is using two opposite character traits, his service of Hashem is complete. This is also seen in the verse "To execute vengeance upon the nations...that will be the splendor of all His devout ones" (*Tehillim* 149:7-9). Even though His people are righteous by being merciful, it is praiseworthy that they will use the opposite trait when necessary and take revenge on their enemies.

It's So Easy

The Midrash relates that the mitzvah which is the "easiest of the easy," sending away the mother bird, and the "hardest of the hard," honoring parents, carry the same reward. This shows that we have no idea which mitzvos carry great or small rewards, so we should treat them all with utmost dedication, regardless of the effort required performing them.

Why is the sending away of the mother bird called the easiest of the easy and honoring parents the hardest of the hard? The Shemen Hatov cites a Ramban who explains that the reason behind the mitzvah of sending away the mother bird is to train us to have mercy. The Ramban stresses that the mitzvah is not necessarily just because Hashem has mercy on animals, but to teach us that we must be compassionate. If one is compassionate to a bird, one will be compassionate to humans as well. Now we can understand why this mitzvah is described as so easy, as it is in harmony with human nature. It is only natural to take pity on a poor mother bird and not let it suffer by seeing its young taken from before its very eyes.

It follows that honoring parents is described as so hard because it goes against human emotions. The mitzvah to honor parents is based on *hakaras hatov* (showing gratitude). Showing gratitude in a sincere way is one of the hardest things to do. Perhaps the psychology behind this is that by thanking someone for something, he is showing that he is dependent on that person. This offends the human ego, which likes to believe that it is independent of other people's favors. This is even more apparent with parents, as our very existence is dependent on them. It is hard to face up to someone and tell him that one owes him his entire existence. That is why honoring parents is described as the hardest of the hard, because it goes against human emotions, while sending away the mother bird runs in tandem with them.

If You Want Your Fill

There is another commandment in this week's *parashah* which promises long life — that of having honest weights and measures (with the mitzvos of sending away the mother bird and honoring parents the Torah promises that "it shall be good for you," in addition to promising long life).

Why is "length of days" an appropriate reward for this commandment? The Olas Chodesh[27] cites a *midrash* that says that Hashem only punishes a person once "his measure is filled." Since this person measured incomplete amounts, so too,

Hashem measures out a shorter measure for him than he would otherwise have received. Even if his measure is not full, he will be punished. On the other hand, if he measures out to others the full amount, so too, Hashem will deal with him in that way.

One Leads to Another

From the sequence of mitzvos in our *parashah* we derive many lessons. Following the mitzvah of sending away the mother bird, we find the mitzvah of placing a fence around one's roof. On the surface there doesn't seem to be any connection. Rashi, however, comments that we see from this the idea that *mitzvah gorreres mitzvah* (one commandment draws another commandment after it). If one fulfills the mitzvah of sending away the mother, he will merit building a new house, and he will be able to fulfill the commandment to place a protective fence on the roof. If one performs that, he will merit a field and vineyard, and will be able to fulfill the commandment not to sow *kilayim*. If he fulfills that mitzvah, he will merit nice clothes, about which he is commanded not to wear *shatnez*.

The Shem MiShmuel quotes the Gemara (*Kiddushin* 39a), which says that there is no reward in this world for a mitzvah. He explains that it doesn't follow that one should receive a materialistic reward for a spiritual act. However, this applies only to a reward that is an end in itself. Reward that is a means for fulfilling other mitzvos can be given even in this world. This is because the reward is only a medium to fulfilling other mitzvos, as *mitzvah gorreres mitzvah*. So too, by building a protective fence, a person will merit to begin a whole chain of events which will not only benefit him in this world, but also will enable him to gain even more merit for the World to Come. This is also what we request during the *aseres yemei teshuvah* when we say, "Remember us for life...for Your sake, O living God." We request life not as a reward in itself, but in order to serve the Divine will, fulfilling other mitzvos.

Not from the "Top Ten Investments Guide"

We find another example where the sequence of mitzvos is significant. Following the portion dealing with correct weights and measures, we find the commandment to destroy Amalek. Rashi says that the two passages are next to each other because if people have dishonest weights and measures, Amalek will attack them. In *parashas Beshalach* we find the attack of Amalek on Yisrael, which is preceded by *bnei Yisrael* asking, "Is God in our midst or not?" (*Shemos* 17:7). We see from this sequence that a lack of faith in God causes Amalek to attack. Which one actually brings Amalek, dishonest weights or a lack of faith? Rav Moshe Feinstein[28] explains that the two causes are really one. Failure to keep correct weights and measures results from a lack in faith in God. *Chazal* say that a person's livelihood is fixed on Rosh Hashanah, and nothing he can do will change this fact. Therefore, he has nothing to gain by cheating with weights and measures, as the money he thought he gained, he will lose through some other endeavor. In addition to that he will be punished. It is precisely a lack of faith in Hashem that causes one to cheat, which subsequently causes Amalek to attack.

PARASHAS KI SAVO

Fruit Baskets

T he mitzvah of *bikkurim* involves bringing the first fruits of
the new crop to Jerusalem in a basket, where the owner
would hand them over to the *kohen* and recite a special
declaration, after which he would prostrate himself before
Hashem. It is noted in the Mishnah (*Bikkurim* 3:3) that a joyous
ceremony would accompany the people bringing their fruits.
The elders of the towns they would pass on the way to Jerusalem
would come out to greet them saying praises and verses from
Tehillim. On reaching the gates of Jerusalem even more praises
were showered upon them.

There were many other times during the year when people
brought offerings up to the Beis Hamikdash, but why with this
mitzvah was there such ceremony? Furthermore, the Midrash at
the beginning of *Sefer Bereishis* brings down various opinions on
what the word *bereishis* is an acronym for. One opinion is that it
means *bishvil reishis*, for the sake of Yisrael, who are called
reishis. Another opinion says that it means that Hashem created
the world for the sake of *bikkurim*, which are also called *reishis*
(the first ones), as they are the first fruits. Why is *bikkurim* considered such a special mitzvah that the Midrash suggests that

the whole world could have been created for its sake?

The Alshich explains that there is a fundamental principle that is apparent upon fulfilling this mitzvah. The difficulty of farming is that its outcome is very uncertain. One has to deal with abnormal weather conditions, droughts and pests before one gets a complete crop. When one is successful, it is very tempting to be overcome with his success and believe "The strength and might of my hands made me this wealth" (*Devarim* 8:17). *Bikkurim* reminds a person that it is Hashem's land, as the verse says, "when you come into the land that Hashem your God gives you" (*Devarim* 26:1), noting that the land is from Hashem. The verse then reminds us that all the produce is from Hashem: "you shall take of the first of every fruit… that Hashem your God gives you" (ibid., 2), again stressing that He is the Source of all blessing. It is only through God's hand that a person receives sustenance, and a person has to realize and appreciate this. Because this is so fundamental to the Torah and life as a Torah Jew, the mitzvah of *bikkurim* is given such special mention in the Midrash.

A Tale of Two Baskets

The rich would bring their produce in baskets of gold, they would be emptied, and subsequently they would be returned to their owners. By contrast, when the poor would come, the *kohen* would retain the basket with its produce inside. Why was it done this way? One would have thought the opposite. Surely since the rich can afford another basket they should lose theirs, while the poor should have theirs returned.

The reason for this is that the rich would bring produce of the best quality, in abundant quantities. Since the Beis Hamikdash had no use for these baskets, they were returned to their owners. The poor, who were of lesser means, could bring only small quantities of produce of inferior appearance, so their offering was less appealing to the eye. If it were emptied out in front of everyone, in the middle of the fanfare surrounding the proceedings, it would certainly cause them embarrassment and sadness at their situation. To prevent this, the basket was taken from them with the fruit still inside it, and they would subsequently be accorded the same honor given to everyone.

Another answer is that since the rich would bring their produce in vessels of such splendor, and everyone would see such a display of wealth, their hearts could become full of *gaavah*. Therefore, by returning the vessels, it is as if Hashem had rejected their golden vessels, which symbolized their arrogance of heart. The poor, who brought fruit in simple, modest wicker baskets, expressed a lowly, humble spirit, as well as doing it *betzinah*, by not showing everyone their fruit. This act is far dearer and pleasing to Hashem, so much so that He wishes to retain their baskets as well.

Raise Your Voice

Another major feature of the mitzvah is the declaration that the giver recites. It is an abbreviated history lesson. It starts by mentioning Lavan's murderous designs on Yaakov Avinu, how we went down to Egypt, and how Hashem in His might brought us out of slavery and into Eretz Yisrael. Rashi derives from the instruction to make this declaration — "And you shall call out" (*Devarim* 26:5) — that one raises his voice upon its recital. The *Sefer HaChinnuch* (mitzvah 606) explains that by reciting this declaration out loud, a person's thoughts will be awakened and his heart stirred to remember the kindness that Hashem has done to Him. When Hashem sees his appreciation, He will subsequently bless him even more.

Why does one raise his voice with such a declaration specifically with the mitzvah of *bikkurim*? Furthermore, the Gemara (*Berachos* 24b) says that one who raises his voice in prayer is of those with little faith, so why is it appropriate to do so here?

The Chanukas HaTorah cites Rashi, who explains that the reason for the prohibition against raising one's voice in prayer is that it appears that he feels he will only be heard by shouting, and is denying that Hashem knows the thoughts of all men. It follows that if he says in his prayer something that attests to the fact that Hashem understands the recesses of his heart and knows his thoughts, then he is no longer considered as one of small faith and is permitted to raise his voice.

Rashi explains that in the statement "An Aramean tried to destroy my father" (*Devarim* 26:5), one mentions that Lavan, at the time of harassing Yaakov, desired to kill him, but Hashem saved Yaakov. With the nations of the world, their thoughts are actually considered as actions, so Lavan's desire was considered as if he had actually done it. When one brings *bikkurim* and mentions this statement, he is testifying that Hashem knows one's thoughts and intentions, as proven with Lavan, and he is therefore allowed to raise his voice and yet not be considered one of small faith.

The Main Ingredients

The declaration continues, "and now, behold, I have brought the first fruit of the land..." (*Devarim* 26:10). The Midrash comments that "and now" means immediately, "behold" refers to the *simchah* that they should be brought with, and "I have brought" means of my own.

This *nidrash* begs an explanation. *Bikkurim* is one of the gifts donated to the *kohanim*, for their use. The portion following *bikkurim* deals with the removal of tithes, symbolizing that both types of gifts involve an aspect of charity, especially as the concluding verse on *bikkurim* says one should rejoice with the *levi* and convert, both of whom are in need. What is behind this cryptic Midrash?

Rav Yosef Nechemiah Kornizer[29] of Cracow explains that there are three aspects involved in giving charity: the actual giving of money, the timing of the giving, and that it be given with a good spirit and in *simchah*, as the verse says, "let your heart not feel bad when you give him" (*Devarim* 15:10). He continues that the main part of *tzedakah* is not the giving of the money, as in truth it is not his anyway, as the verse says, "Mine is the silver and Mine is the gold, the word of Hashem" (*Chaggai* 2:8). If one gives at an appropriate time when he can prevent the person's decline, and he does it with goodwill and a glad heart, he has fulfilled the main part of the mitzvah.

This is what the Midrash is referring to. When the verse says, "and now," which means immediately, it refers to giving at the time that the poor person needs it. When the verse says, "behold," it refers to giving with *simchah* and with goodwill. It is these two characteristics — which are described when the verse continues, "I have brought" — which originate from the giver, that constitute the main part of *tzedakah*, and not merely the money, which anyway originates from Hashem.

With this Midrash in mind, we can understand a statement in the Gemara (*Kiddushin* 39b) which says that there is no reward in this world for a mitzvah. The Ateret Paz says that there are two things for which a person can receive reward in this world: for his zealousness and effort in performing a mitzvah, and for his joy in carrying it out. This is what the Midrash alludes to. "And now," meaning immediately, refers to a person's zealousness in doing mitzvos. "And behold" refers to them being done with joy. "I have brought" refers to the fact that it is these aspects, which are of his own doing, for which he will receive reward in this world.

The Only Response

O ne of the more puzzling parts of Rosh Hashanah is that upon returning home from shul, we eat specific foods, such as apple dipped in honey, so that we should have a sweet year, or the head of a fish so that we should only be at the head and not at the tail, to name but two. (Someone told me that their tradition is to have lettuce and raisins with celery, as they pray, "Let us have a raise in salary.") Why is it that after praying in the most sublime way, we return home and rely on these signs for our needs?

To answer this question we have to answer another question. Why are we told that on Rosh Hashanah three women — Sarah, Rachel and Chanah — were remembered? The Shemen Hatov[30] says that people come on Rosh Hashanah with a list of physical requests: health, wealth, children, and so forth. However, this is missing the point of the day. Looking through the liturgy, one notices hardly any references to these requests. The main theme of the day is proclaiming Hashem as King over us. He is the King, and we are His servants. Dealing with more earthly pursuits is inappropriate when claiming His Majesty. However, since it is still a *yom tov*, we must indulge in some physical pursuits as well.

With a full meal ahead of us, we are able to pursue our other interests, our material well-being. We allude to them only subtly, however; we say that we know that our purpose is to serve Hashem, but we hint that we can serve Him only if He gives us sustenance, children, success, and so on.

Now we can also understand why we are told these three women were remembered on Rosh Hashanah: because they all were concerned for someone else's needs. Sarah was remembered following the incident where Avraham prayed for Avimelech's cure. Since he prayed for someone else's needs, his wife was answered. Hashem remembered Rachel because she was concerned only about the embarrassment of her sister. Similarly, Chanah was answered because she asked for a child solely for the purpose of dedicating him to Hashem (that son was Shmuel). Indeed, this is the hard part of Rosh Hashanah, putting things into perspective. In our pursuit of being servants of Hashem, the requests for our needs must be in the context of whether they will help us achieve this goal.

A Yom Kippur Mystery

The Shemen Hatov continues with a story that illustrates this point. One Yom Kippur in Belz the congregation finished *minchah* early and took a break before beginning *Ne'ilah*. Everyone left their *streimels* by their seats until they would return. Just before the final prayer was to begin, one of the chassidim returned and was astonished to discover his *streimel* was gone. Someone had stolen a *streimel* on Yom Kippur! The Rebbe, unaware of the events, began the prayers.

After the fast the Rebbe, having noticed the surprise on his followers' faces, asked one of his chassidim about its cause. Upon being told of the incident he instructed everyone to break their fasts. Later, however he asked to see a certain chassid.

When he arrived, the Rebbe said to him, "You stole the *streimel*," which the accused firmly denied. However, the Rebbe was persistent until finally the chassid broke down and confessed.

The next day in Belz everyone spoke about the miraculous deed of the Rebbe, and about his having Divine inspiration. The Rebbe explained how he knew. "Before Yom Kippur everyone gives me a paper with the things that they would like me to daven for. One asks for health, another for children, all types of requests. This chassid asked only for *parnasah*. Since that is the only thing on his mind on Yom Kippur, then he is certainly capable of stealing a *streimel*."

Although our other requests are important, we must put them into perspective. They should be the means with which to serve Hashem, and His Kingship should be established over the entire world.

A Higher Purpose

We find a similar idea in our *parashah*. The Torah tells us, "See, I have placed before you today life and good" (*Devarim* 30:15). The Kli Yakar tells us that the verse is teaching us that if one desires life one should do good in the eyes of Hashem. If so, surely the verse should have stated the word "good" before the word "life," and not the other way around. He answers with a tremendous principle, that one should not do good so that he will be rewarded with physical rewards, but should seek life as a means to serving his Creator even more. This is what David Hamelech says: "Who is the man who desires life, who loves days to see good?" (*Tehillim* 34:13). He seeks life in order to do that which is good and straight before Hashem. This is also seen in the concluding verse of the *parashah*: "to love Hashem, your God, to listen to His voice and to cleave to Him, for He is your life and the length of your days" (*Devarim* 30:20). Hashem gives us life so that we will "listen to His voice and...cleave to Him."

You Can't Take Anything For Granted

Rav Moshe Feinstein[31] asks on the above verse, What is the significance of the word "today"? He explains that on any given day a person can choose between two paths that are in front of him. If until now he was going on a corrupt path, now he has to choose the just path. If, on the other hand, until now he was on the correct path, he cannot rely on his previous resolution and assume that he will automatically stay on this path. Rather, every day he has to know that there are two ways in front of him and every moment he has to strengthen himself and choose the way of righteousness and justice.

Parashas Nitzavim is very appropriately read just before Rosh Hashanah. There is a fascinating portion in the *parashah*: "For this commandment...it is not hidden from you and it is not distant. It is not in the heavens for you to say, 'Who can ascend to the heavens for us and take it?'... Nor is it across the sea for you to say, 'Who can cross to the other side of the sea and take it for us?'...Rather, the matter is very near to you, in your mouth and in your heart to perform it" (*Devarim* 30:11-14). According to many commentators, the mitzvah referred to here is that of *teshuvah*. Rav Chaim of Volozhin[32] explains that when someone sins, he is causing a spiritual blemish, which manifests itself in the heavens. Strictly speaking, in order to rectify the sin, he should have to travel up there to the place of the ruination in order to correct his actions. Instead, the verse says, "It is not in the heavens"; you don't have to travel up there, for in this world *teshuvah* is effective. Furthermore, the next verse continues, "Nor is it across the sea." This is explained by a *gemara* (*Kiddushin* 40b), that says that in order to discourage one from sinning one should view himself, and the whole world, as if it is half meritorious and half guilty, and that one extra sin will tilt the balance. Therefore, his sin will, *rachmana litzlan*, cause punishments "across the sea," in places far from the event of the sin. By telling us that it is not across the sea, it means that one doesn't have to go over there to the place of the punishment in order to correct the matter. Rather, "the matter is very near to you"; one can do *teshuvah* wherever he is.

Three Ways

Dayan Yechezkel Abramsky[33] says that there are three levels of *teshuvah*. The lowest is when one is confronted by the *middas hadin*, and sets about doing *teshuvah* as he realizes that his punishments are the result of his sins. This is described in the Torah as "when all these things come upon you...then you will take it upon your heart...and you will return to Hashem" (*Devarim* 30:1-2). The intermediary level is when one sees punishments coming upon other people and is awakened to *teshuvah*, as it says, "Hashem...will place these curses upon your enemies...you shall return" (*Devarim* 30:7-8). The highest level is when one comes to a realization of his own accord, without any Heavenly reminders. This is what our verse says: "when you shall return to Hashem, your God, ...with all your heart and all your soul" (*Devarim* 30:7). When one returns through an inner realization, without any outer motivation, one achieves the highest level of *teshuvah*.

What Time?

Let us conclude with the following verse in our *parashah*: "The hidden things are for Hashem, our God, but the revealed things are for us and for our children forever, to carry out the words of this Torah" (*Devarim* 29:28). The Ksav Sofer writes that there are two points in time that Mashiach could come. One is a hidden time, which only Hashem knows of. No prophet, not even Moshe, knew it. The second is the more well-known opportunity, on any given day, if "you listen to His voice" (*Devarim* 30:2). The former is alluded to with the words "the hidden things"; the redemption which is concealed from man, "are for Hashem our God." "But the revealed things," the scenario which man can bring about, "are for us and for our children," since any generation can make themselves worthy "to carry out the words of this Torah." Through Torah and *teshuvah*, the redemption can come immediately.

PARASHAS VAYEILECH

Bringing "Up" the Children

One of the final mitzvos in the Torah is that of *hakhel*. During the times of the Beis Hamikdash, on Sukkos following the *shemittah* year, there was a great ceremony when the entire Jewish people would ascend to Yerushalayim to hear the king read from the Torah scroll. It is an interesting fact that only the males above thirteen years were required to ascend to Yerushlayim for festivals, whereas for *hakhel* the entire population would ascend, including women and children. The *Gemara* (*Chagigah* 3a) says that the men would come to learn, and the women to listen, and the children would come so that those bringing them would receive reward.

The commentators ask, If there was a purpose in the children coming, then the Gemara shouldn't have to try and find a reason for it, and if there is no purpose at all in their coming, then why should the adults receive reward for bringing them? The Nachalas Yaakov says that certainly there is a reason for this mitzvah, but like other mitzvos, its reason is hidden. The question of the Gemara is why were the parents specifically commanded to bring the children, since they would be going anyway; the children would certainly not be left at home unattended. The Gemara is telling us that bringing the children would in fact be considered a mitzvah which the parents would receive reward for, and it was not simply that they came along because the parents were going anyway.

What Do You Expect?

Rav Nosson Adler[34] comments that surely having the children around would disturb the parents, who wouldn't be able to hear the reading properly. With all the noise they would wish that the children were at home. Therefore, the verse is informing us that the reward for educating the children by bringing them to the Temple supersedes that of actually listening to the reading. He then cites an unbelievable principle which must be handled with caution. One is better off sacrificing some of his own *shleimus* in order to educate his children in the spirit of Torah. This reminds me of what my *mashgiach* once told us, that when one has young children, one cannot sit at the table on Friday night being a *"rosh yeshivah,"* saying *divrei Torah* continuously, and expect them to be intrigued. Rather, one has to "educate the child according to his way," presenting Torah within his grasp, making it interesting and informative.

An Unforgettable Experience

The Malbim writes that the mitzvah required such a great gathering in order to make a tremendous impression upon everyone, but in particular on the children. This is seen in the verses "Gather together the people, the men, the women and the small children...and their children who do not know, they shall hear and they shall learn to fear Hashem your God all the days" (*Devarim* 31:12-13). When it says "children who do not know," it is referring to the reason for them being brought along. Since they are too young to understand, and don't concentrate on what the Torah reading is about, their minds will be more receptive to the events around them. Since they are so young, the impression will last them a lifetime. When the verse continues, "they shall hear," it means that despite not being able to understand the words, they will still feel the importance of hearing words of Torah. By seeing the great crowd gathered specifically for that purpose, and standing to attention at its words, as if nothing else in the world matters, they will understand the importance of Torah. The verse continues, "They shall learn," to tell us that by seeing the king in his splendor, reading from the Torah, they will see the importance of learning, since if the king does it, it must be important. When the verse says, "to fear," it refers to the fact that the children — having participated in such a great assembly, each person standing in fear and trembling before Hashem, Who "dwells" in that place — will continue to cultivate *yiras Shamayim* (fear of Heaven). In addition, seeing the king will add to their fear of Heaven. Since he is anointed from all the tribes, and everyone has tremendous respect and fear of him, the children will then translate this fear of the king into fear of Heaven. They will remember how small they felt in front of the king and will realize how much more they should fear Hashem, Who is infinitely greater than the most powerful of earthly kings.

Stop!

Rav Hutner[35] offers an explanation based on the Rambam in *Hilchos Chagigah* (3:3) which lists the order of passages that the king was to read. He starts with the beginning of *Devarim* and continues to the end of the first paragraph of Shema, and he then skips to the second paragraph of Shema. This sequence of reciting and skipping continues until the verse "besides the covenant He entered into with them at Chorev," after which the

Rambam states the word *u'posek*, "and he stops." Why does he have to state that he stops? Surely the king would read only those passages which have been mentioned. What extra information is the Rambam telling us by the word "stop"? Another question is why do we find the Rambam calls the day *yom hakhel*, an expression not found anywhere in the Gemara?

Rav Hutner answers by explaining to us what the nature of *hakhel* is. It is supposed to be a reenactment of *bnei Yisrael* standing at Har Sinai in order to receive the Torah. This is seen as the Rambam further describes (3:6-7) that "one has to turn his heart and listen attentively, to listen in fear and to see with great trembling, like the day you stood at Sinai...and view oneself as if he now was commanded...and he heard from Hashem's mouth." This is why the Rambam states the word *u'posek*, which instructed the king to stop following the words "the covenant He entered into with them at Chorev." By stopping there and going no further, the people would take that message away with them, causing them to remember the actual standing at Sinai. It is like saying, "last impressions count." If the king would read beyond this, the effect would be ruined.

Now we can also understand why the Rambam refers to it as *yom hakhel*. If one takes away the vowels one gets *yom hakahal*, which is a reference to the gathering at Sinai. This also explains why we bring along the children, and why there is reward for bringing them. Since at Sinai they were also brought, in this reenactment they should also be present, and because the children make it complete, as it was then, with the entire nation present, the adults should be rewarded for bringing them.

One More...

Having said all this, we are left with the following difficulty. The *hakhel* ceremony took place on the Sukkos immediately following the *shemittah* year. During that year the farmers were released from the pursuit of a livelihood and would spend the whole year learning Torah. If the purpose was to reenact Sinai and emphasize the centrality of Torah, surely this was not needed at this particular juncture, but should have occurred at some other time when the people needed strengthening. We learn from here that if something is important enough to someone, he cannot get enough of it. We are taught that despite having toiled for an entire year, dedicated only to Torah, we should still desire more — another *shiur*, another *daf Gemara*, another chapter from the Mishnah. Since Torah is so central to our identity as Jews, we must never tire of learning more and exerting ourselves that bit extra.

Take Them with You

I would like to conclude with something from this week's special haftarah, where the prophet exhorts the people to repentance: "Return, O Yisrael, to Hashem…Take words with you and return to Hashem" (*Hoshea* 14:3). The Chofetz Chaim[36] comments that over the *Yamim Nora'im* many people cry, confess and regret their sins of the past year, resolving never to repeat them again. However, as soon as they have left shul, they cannot even remember what they accepted upon themselves during the prayers. This is what the prophet is referring to when he says, "Take words with you and return to Hashem," that one should take those words which he spoke of, and not just leave them in shul. If they accompany him throughout his endeavors, and he actively works on improving himself, then he will merit Divine salvation, as the haftarah continues, "for He is of abundant mercy" (*Yoel* 2:13).

Atone with a Song

The main part of *parashas Haazinu* is written in the form of a *shirah* (song), as is evident from its poetic language, and the way it is written in the *sefer Torah*, two columns side by side. In fact, the whole of the Torah is described as a song, as it says regarding the commandment to write a *sefer Torah*, "and now write for yourselves this song..." (*Devarim* 31:19).

Why is it that the Torah is called a song? One answer stems from the difference between music and all other fields of human endeavor. If you tell a mathematician a deep, complicated mathematical proof, he may get great pleasure out of it. Show it to the other 99 percent of us and it at best may raise a few eyebrows here and there, but usually it will lower eyelids. In contrast, when a fine piece of music is played, everyone will get something out of it. A great musician will appreciate the finer points of the piece, while the musically uninitiated will at least somewhat appreciate the quality.

So too, with Torah. A *talmid chacham* who has learned a verse hundreds of times will still get great satisfaction delving more deeply into it, appreciating its infinite wisdom. A young child, on the other hand, will also appreciate the same verse, albeit on a different level. The Torah is therefore referred to as a song, since everyone can appreciate Torah, irrespective of their level.

Falling from the Sky

The second verse of our *parashah* states, "May my teaching drip like the rain; may my utterance flow like the dew" (*Devarim* 32:2). Rashi comments that dew is mentioned because everyone is happy when dew falls. It would not have been sufficient to compare it to rain alone; although rain is usually good, it is sometimes an annoyance, such as to travelers.

The Ksav Sofer asks, Why is it necessary to compare Torah to rain which is not always good for people, and only subsequently compare it to dew? Why doesn't the Torah mention dew alone? He answers that there is a fundamental difference between rain and dew. While rain falls from above, it originates from the land and seas below. On the other hand, dew originates only from the sky. The Torah which people learn also has two sources. An example of one of these sources of Torah knowledge is when a person says, "I delved and I found" (*Megillah* 6b), referring to one's own efforts bearing fruit. The other source of Torah knowledge is through *siyatta d'Shmaya* (help from Heaven).

Rain and dew are symbolic of these two ways of acquiring Torah. Just as rain originates from the ground and then falls from heaven, so too, one who puts much effort into his Torah study will be granted help from Heaven. However, his Divine assistance will be in proportion to the effort he puts in. On the other hand, dew falls only from above, not originating down here. This refers to one's being given Heavenly assistance which is not commensurate with his effort to reach heights in his learning. We aspire to attain Torah through both sources. We strive to put in all the effort, and pray that Hashem opens up our eyes to learn His Torah more deeply.

There is another explanation for the comparison of Torah to rain. Just as with rain, its effects are not noticed at the time it falls, but only at a later date, similarly with Torah, its effects and results are seen only at a later time. When one looks at one's progress on a day-to-day basis, he will not notice any change. It is only after a month or a *zman* of learning that one will notice an appreciable change.

Lawyers Don't Forget

Many of the other themes in the *parashah* are particularly appropriate for the week of Yom Kippur. The verse says, "You ignored the Rock Who gave birth to you, and forgot God Who brought you forth" (*Devarim* 32:18). The Shaar Bas Rabbim explains that "the Rock" refers to Hashem, Who created within man the ability to forget. This was for man's benefit, as otherwise he would live in constant anguish at events that had befallen him in the past, never being able to put anything behind him. However, the words "You forgot God Who brought you forth" refer to the fact that *bnei Yisrael* used the ability to forget for a corrupted purpose, to forget Hashem and move away from Him.

The Dubno Maggid[37] explains this idea with a parable. Once someone was arrested and taken to court under false charges. The prosecution had somehow concocted all sorts of false evidence against the man and seemed certain to win the case. In the accused's despair, his lawyer advised him that he had one last hope. If he would pretend to be insane he might somehow be released and not charged. Surely enough, he followed the lawyer's advice and was subsequently acquitted. When the lawyer came to him to collect his fees, he found his client acting insane and talking nonsense. The lawyer said to him, "You can't fool me. I was the one who told you to act like that. You mustn't use against me the very same ploy that saved you."

Time Is...

We find in our *parashah* another idea which is very pertinent to Yom Kippur. The verse says, "Is it to Hashem that you pay this, O people who are foolish and not wise?" (*Devarim* 32:6). The Vilna Gaon has a principle regarding the concept of *din vecheshbon*. *Din* is the strict letter of the law, of which a person is held accountable for his sins. *Cheshbon* refers to the fact that one is held accountable for the mitzvos he could have performed in the time during which he was sinning. When the verse says, "O people who are foolish," it refers to the sins committed. Following that, the words "not wise" refer to the fact that had they been wise they would have calculated how much they stood to lose by not doing mitzvos in that time, having instead chosen to sin.

The verse then continues, "Is He not your Father, your Acquirer?" telling us that from the point of view of Hashem being a Father, and our being His children, we should follow His instructions. Furthermore, as He is "your Acquirer," the Master of all, one must have fear of transgressing His instruction. The Meshech Chochmah points out the same idea when Hashem informs Moshe of his forthcoming death: "because you trespassed against Me...because you did not sanctify Me" (*Devarim* 32:51). The trespass refers to *din*, to the actual sin committed, namely that Moshe struck the rock. That "you did not sanctify Me" is the *cheshbon* part of Moshe's sin, as Moshe had been in a position to sanctify Hashem's Name but didn't.

Get Rid of Them All

The *Avinu Malkeinu* prayer is one of the features of these days of awe. Why is it that first we pray, "exterminate every foe and adversary from upon us," and then we say, "seal the mouths of our adversaries and accusers"? Surely if we have prayed for the removal of the accusers, why is it still necessary to pray for them to be silenced?

The Chofetz Chaim[38] explains that with most sins ordinary accusers are created. If they come before Hashem's throne to prosecute, Hashem in His mercy can remove them from His presence. However, with accusing angels emanating from improper speech, it is impossible to remove them, since they were created through speech, and these angels accuse verbally; even without any other presence or form in front of Hashem, their voices will be heard. The Chofetz Chaim compares this to a king who wants to acquit someone in a judgment, but since the accuser calls out in public for him to be punished, the king is forced to at least be seen doing justice. This is evident in the prayer. Even if our first request, "exterminate every foe and adversary from upon us," is answered, we still need extra mercy to have the mouths of the other type of adversary closed.

You Can't Be Serious

Let us conclude with the following story[39] that is relevant to Yom Kippur. Once there was a *din Torah* involving an amount of money that was being disputed. It was suggested that until a verdict could be reached, the money be deposited in the hands of a third party. The litigants went to Rav Moshe Feinstein, who ruled in favor of one of the parties. The victor went to the person holding the money to collect his due. Upon being asked for the money, the man holding it replied, "Rav Moshe made a mistake." The victor could hardly believe his ears. He went back to Rav Moshe to inform him that the man was not willing to hand anything over. Rav Moshe then gave him a letter to take to the man, but he would not change his mind, and he repeated his claim that there was a mistake in the verdict.

At first the victor had been too embarrassed to tell Rav Moshe the reason for the man's refusal to hand over the money, but this time, upon seeing the man's stubbornness, he told him what the problem was. Rav Moshe called up the third party and was told that his ruling was void, as it had been made at night, which is forbidden. However, Rav Moshe replied that he had ruled that this was allowed nowadays because of the advent of electricity. The third party told him, "Well, I don't agree!" Finally after several painful months passed the money was released.

A few years later, there was a knock on the door of Rav Moshe. It was the third party. "I would like to get *semichah* from the Rav," he said. Rav Moshe took him in and tested him on various aspects of halachah and could not fault his knowledge. He began writing the *semichah* certificate, while the face of his gabbai turned pale at the title being given to a man who had caused such distress. After his exit the gabbai could not contain himself any longer. "How could you give him *semichah*?" he asked.

Rav Moshe replied, "Since between then and now a Yom Kippur has passed, before which we say *Tefillas Zakah* (the prayer in which we express our forgiveness to anyone who may have wronged us), I had already forgiven him. Can you really say it without meaning it?"

The Point of Rejoicing

Why is it that Simchas Torah, when we rejoice over the Torah, is not celebrated together with Shavuos, when the Torah was given, but only separately, several months later? The Dubno Maggid[40] answers with a parable. Once there was a king who had all the earthly possessions a ruler could possibly want. He lacked only one thing: children. He consulted the best doctors of the day but to no avail. One day, someone told him of a mysterious Jew who lived in the forest, who would pray for various causes and was usually answered. Realizing nothing else was working anyway, he decided to give it a try, and he set out to meet him.

After a long and tiresome journey, the king finally got to meet the man. The elderly Jew softly recited a few prayers, and informed the king that he would be blessed with a daughter. However, there was only one condition: if any man were to see her before she would marry, she would immediately die. Preparations were made for her to be raised on a remote island where she would be cared for entirely by her mother the queen and her attendants.

Following her birth the baby was raised surrounded only by females. The king remained in his palace, receiving occasional reports on her progress. As time went by, she became of marriageable age and the king announced that any eligible person with royal status should present himself as a candidate for her hand in marriage.

On the appointed day, many people came to the palace to meet the king, and presumed that the princess would be there as well. When they were given the news that they couldn't meet her, one by one they all slipped out, worrying something was wrong with her. Only one candidate, whose father was a good friend of the king's, stayed, not wishing to further humiliate his host, and actually agreed to marry her, despite not having met her beforehand.

The wedding was very strange as no male, not even the bridegroom, was present during the first part of the ceremony. Following the ceremony, the prince found to his delight that she was as beautiful a woman as he could have hoped for. Subsequently, he became worried that perhaps she was not as intelligent as he was, but as the weeks went by he discovered that even if he would have met her before, he could not have chosen better. Following the honeymoon the prince went to his father-in-law and told him what his reservations had been, but that they were all unfounded, and he requested a special public celebration in honor of his marriage, as the first could not have done justice to his joy over his bride.

So too, the Torah was offered to the other nations but they all refused, each with their excuses. When Yisrael was offered the Torah, they gratefully accepted it as a loyal servant, declaring "we will do and we will listen" (*Shemos* 24:7). Subsequently, *bnei Yisrael* had to find out the real nature and content of the Torah, learning all its laws and details to truly accept it and appreciate it. Therefore, on Shavuos, Yisrael was not ready to rejoice with the Torah; it was only after a few months of delving into it that they could truly appreciate it. Thus, Simchas Torah is the time to rejoice and give thanks that we received the Torah.

A Leading Question

We also find this idea alluded to in the *parashah*. The verse says, "Hashem came forth from Sinai and He shone forth to them from Seir; He appeared from Mount Paran" (*Devarim* 33:2). The Midrash says that Hashem went to the children of Esav and offered the Torah to them, and they asked what is in it, to which Hashem informed them of the prohibition against murder. They replied that this was a characteristic they had inherited from their ancestor and, with all due respect, could therefore not accept the Torah.

Rav Raphael Hakohen of Hamburg[41] comments that on the surface it seems that it may have been unfair that when the children of Esav were being offered the Torah, Hashem chose to mention these particular points so that they would have to refuse. He suggests that we have to understand the nation's response. By asking, "What is in it?" they were trivializing it. Hashem understood that at best they would keep only the written law, but they certainly wouldn't keep the oral law, and if the two are separated, neither will in fact be kept. Therefore, He immediately presented them with the most difficult commandment for them, knowing that they would refuse. On the other hand, Yisrael responded "all that Hashem has spoken, we will do and we will listen." This includes even the oral law, which Hashem taught Moshe at Sinai. Therefore, on this basis Hashem gave Yisrael the Torah.

We Also Wanted To

On the above verse, Rashi comments that when it says, "He

shone forth to them from Seir," it is referring to how Hashem first offered Torah to *bnei Esav*. The words "He appeared from Mount Paran" refer to how He offered it to the children of Yishmael, who gave a similar refusal. Rebbi Akiva Eiger[42] asks, How is it that we find gentiles who decided to convert to Judaism, and yet we find apostates who wished to desert their religion for another? He answers using our *midrash*, that at the time of the giving of the Torah, Hashem offered it to all the nations and they all refused. However, within those nations, there were individuals who wished to accept it, but they remained silent out of fear. These were the souls of the converts who in the course of time eventually did join with Yisrael. On the other hand, within Yisrael there were individuals who didn't want to accept the Torah, but they were ashamed or fearful, so they joined in and said, "We will do and we will listen." However, years later these souls would depart from their faith and tragically convert or assimilate.

Let Us Begin

The Gemara (*Sukkah* 42a) says that when a child is able to speak, he should be taught the verse, *Torah tzivah lanu Moshe morashah kehillas Yaakov*, "The Torah that Moshe commanded us is the heritage of the congregation of Yaakov" (*Devarim* 33:4). The Tosefes Berachah asks, Why is it that this verse in particular is chosen? Surely there are many other verses that would also be suitable for them to be taught first (such as "And this is the teaching which Moshe placed before *bnei Yisrael*" [*Devarim* 4:44], which would also teach them to accept its authority). He answers that with all the other verses, it could mistakenly be understood that only adults who understand what they are learning would have the obligation to learn Torah, while children are exempt from being taught until they are old enough to understand. Therefore, this verse was chosen because it calls the Torah a "heritage," i.e., something that is inherited. Just like with an inheritance, the rule is that even children partake along with the adults, so too, with Torah study, the young are obligated to be taught and to learn just like the elders, and the Gemara tells us that the responsibility for this is placed on the father.

The Gemara (*Megillah* 10b) says that a great miracle was performed with the ark in the Mishkan. If one would measure from one wall of the holy of holies to the other, and then measure from one wall until the ark and then from the opposite wall to the ark, and add the two together, he would find that this sum was exactly the same as the first amount. Miraculously the ark took up no physical space.

What does this miracle symbolize? The commentators say that there were three items in the Mishkan that had crowns around their edges: the ark, the table and the incense altar. These represented three crowns — the crowns of Torah, kingship and priesthood. The ark represented the crown of Torah because of the tablets it contained. The table represented kingship because a table symbolizes status and wealth. The incense altar symbolized the crown of priesthood because it was the priests who would perform the Divine service.

The Rambam (*Hilchos Talmud Torah* 3:1) says that the crown of priesthood was taken by Aharon and his descendants. The crown of kingship was taken by David. However, the crown of Torah is ready to be taken by any Jew, as it says, "The Torah that Moshe commanded us is the heritage of the congregation of Yaakov" (*Devarim* 33:4). What emerges from this is that while two of the crowns exclude anyone else from possessing it, the crown of Torah is available to anyone. This is symbolized by the objects in the Mishkan. The table and incense altar both occupied space; nothing else could enter that space at the same time. The ark, however, took up no space; there was no limit to the number of arks that could enter that space. Similarly, there is no limit to the number of people who can wear the crown of Torah.

In the Event of War...

The verse says, "Rejoice, Zevulun, in your departure, and Yissachar in your tents" (*Devarim* 33:18). The Netziv[43] writes that when *klal Yisrael* would go out to war, in addition to the soldiers, they would designate men who were to remain on the edge of the battlefield and occupy themselves in Torah and *tefillah*. We find this during the war against Midian, where the Midrash relates that they took twelve thousand men for this purpose. So too, with Yehoshua, before going out to the war of Ai. The verse relates that he "remained in the midst of the valley (*emek*)" (*Yehoshua* 8:13). The Gemara (*Megillah* 4a) comments with a play on the words, and says that it means he remained *umkeh*, i.e., in the midst, or the depths of halachah, in his learning, before going out to war.

This is what the verse describes: "Rejoice, Zevulun, in your departure," referring to those who go out to war, because you have "Yissachar in your tents." What kind of battle strategy is this? The answer is that we believe that Hashem guides wars and that it is His will that ultimately counts. The Torah is a protective force against our enemies. Since Yissachar was found in the tents of Torah by the battlefield, Zevulun could be confident and trusting of victory. May we be blessed with the fulfillment of that which we request at the end of the *Shemoneh Esrei*: "Grant us our share in Your Torah"; that we are able to delve deeper into the light of Hashem's Torah.

Notes

Bereishis

1. *Michtav Me'Eliyahu*, vol. 2, p.19.
2. *Tiferes Yonasan.*
3. *Perush HaGra al HaTorah.*
4. *Haemek Davar.*
5. *Chofetz Chaim al HaTorah.*
6. *Peninim Mishulchan Gavoah.*
7. *The Parsha Anthology*, Rav Rubin.
8. Author of *Hadra shel Torah.*
9. *Oznaim LaTorah.*
10. Quoted by Chida.
11. *Ohel Torah.*
12. Transcribed from *shiurim* by Rav Yissachar Frand.
13. By Rav Mordechai Kodosh.
14. Introduction to *Shaalos U'Teshuvos, Emek Halachah.*
15. *The Parsha Anthology.*
16. Ibid.
17. Quoted by Rav Frand.
18. *The Parsha Anthology.*
19. *Chiddushei Rebbi Shlomo.*
20. *The Parsha Anthology.*
21. Ibid.
22. *Nesivos Shalom.*

23. *Divrei Shaul.*

24. *The Parsha Anthology.*

25. *Torah Ladaas.*

26. *Chiddushei HaGriz al HaTorah.*

27. Quoted by Rav Frand.

28. *Kisvei Hasaba MiKelm Vetalmidav,* vol. 2, chap. 12.

29. *Oznaim LaTorah.*

30. *Peninim Mishulchan Gavoah.*

31. Quoted by Reb Chaim Halpern.

32. *Peninim Mishulchan Gavoah.*

33. Ibid.

34. Sifrei Rebbi Nosson Adler.

35. By Rav Matis Blum.

36. *Chochmah U'Mussar.*

37. *The Parsha Anthology.*

38. *Chofetz Chaim al HaTorah, Maasei Lamelech.*

39. Heard from Rav Bernstein.

40. *Chochmah U'Mussar.*

41. *Kovetz Maamarim.*

42. *The Parsha Anthology.*

43. *Torah Ladaas.*

44. *Shaalos U'Teshuvos HaRashba,* vol. 1, no. 581.

45. Quoted by Rav Frand.

46. *Hadra shel Torah.*

47. *Peninim Mishulchan HaGra.*

48. Stories from *The Parsha Anthology.*

49. *Lev Eliyahu.*

50. Stories from *The Parsha Anthology.*

51. Ibid.

52. *Chofetz Chaim al HaTorah.*

53. *Zachor L'Miriam,* chap. 18.

54. *Talalei Oros.*

55. *Oznaim LaTorah* to *Bereishis* 45:15.

56. *Ohr Yahal.*

57. *Talalei Oros.*

58. Ibid.

59. Rav Avraham Mordechai Alter of Chicago.

60. *Oznaim LaTorah.*

61. *Talalei Oros.*

62. *Hadra shel Torah.*

63. *Chofetz Chaim al HaTorah* to *parashas Vayeira, Maasei Lamelech.*

64. *Daas Chochmah U'Mussar,* vol. 1.

Shemos

1. Maharil Diskin.

2. *Chiddushei HaRim al HaTorah.*

3. Transcribed from *shiurim* by Rav Frand.

4. Story from Rav Frand.

5. *Chofetz Chaim al HaTorah, Maasei Lamelech.*

6. *Chofetz Chaim al HaTorah.*

7. *The Parsha Anthology.*

8. Ibid.

9. Stories from *The Parsha Anthology.*

10. Ibid.

11. *Haemek Davar.*

12. *Kemotzei Shallal Rav.*

13. *Shailos U'Teshuvos, Zayis Raanan, chelek 2, likkutei chiddushei Torah.*

14. *Torah Ladaas.*

15. As quoted by Rav Frand.

16. Related by Yonoson Rosenblum.

17. *Peninim Mishulchan HaGra.*

18. *Biurei Rabbeinu Chaim MiVolozhin.*

19. *Darchei Mussar.*

20. *Chofetz Chaim al HaTorah.*

21. Heard from Rav Zafrani of Shaarei Torah, New York

22. *Shailos U'Teshuvos, Zayis Raanan, chelek 2, likkutei chiddushei Torah.*

23. *Otzar Hamashalim* by Zeev Greenwald.

24. *Oznaim LaTorah.*

25. Inspiration and Insight, ArtScroll Publishers.

26. *Hadra shel Torah.*

27. *Aparion.*

28. *The Parsha Anthology.*

29. *Peninim Mishulchan Gavoah.*

30. *Peninim Mishulchan Gavoah.*

31. *The Parsha Anthology.*

32. To *parashas Terumah.*

33. *The Parsha Anthology.*

34. *Darash Moshe.*

35. *Toras Moshe.*

36. *Hadra shel Torah.*

37. *Chochmah U'Mussar,* to *parashas Va'era.*

38. *Sifrei Rebbi Nosson Adler.*

39. *The Parsha Anthology.*

40. *Sichos Mussar, chelek 2,* essay 23.

41. Idea from Rav Frand.

42. *Peninim Mishulchan Gavoah.*

43. *Otzar Hamashalim.*

44. *The Dubno Maggid and His Parables.*

45. *Nimukei Ridbaz.*

46. Story from *The Parsha Anthology.*

47. *Kemotzei Shallal Rav.*

48. *Toras Moshe.*

49. Rav Frand.

50. *Peninim Mishulchan Gavoah.*

51. *Sefer* on Purim.

52. *Chofetz Chaim al Shabbos U'Moadim.*

53. *Daas Kedoshim, derash* 3.
54. *Peninim Mishulchan Gavoah.*
55. *Hadra shel Torah.*
56. In his commentary to *Chumash.*

Vayikra

1. *Peninim Mishulchan Gavoah.*
2. *Peninim Mishulchan Gavoah.*
3. *Shemonah Perakim.*
4. *Otzar Hamashalim.*
5. *Hilchos De'os* 1:4.
6. *Torah Ladaas.*
7. Pesach Krohn.
8. *Michtav Me'Eliyahu,* vol. 1, *Kuntres Hachessed.*
9. *The Parsha Anthology.*
10. *Emes LeYaakov.*
11. *Torah Ladaas.*
12. *The Parsha Anthology.*
13. Ibid.
14. *Peninim Mishulchan Gavoah.*
15. As in *Peninim Mishulchan Gavoah.*
16. *Peninim Mishulchan Gavoah.*
17. *Peninim Mishulchan Gavoah.*
18. *Peninim Mishulchan Gavoah.*
19. *Nitzotzei Ohr Hameir.*
20. *Ohel Torah.*
21. *Sichos Mussar, chelek* 2, essay 31.
22. *Peninim Mishulchan Gavoah.*
23. Introduction to *Sefer Chofetz Chaim.*
24. *The Parsha Anthology.*
25. *Chofetz Chaim al HaTorah.*
26. *Oznaim LaTorah.*

27. *Daas Kedoshim, derash* 1.

28. As in *The Parsha Anthology.*

29. *The Parsha Anthology.*

30. *Tiferes Yonasan.*

31. *Peninim Mishulchan Gavoah.*

32. *Torah Ladaas.*

33. *The Parsha Anthology.*

34. Ibid.

35. *Tiferes Yonasan.*

36. As in *Torah Ladaas.*

37. *Nitzotzei Ohr Hameir.*

38. *Chiddushei Moran Riz Halevi.*

39. *Chasam Sofer al HaTorah.*

40. *Torah Ladaas.*

41. *Peninim Mishulchan Gavoah.*

42. *Peninim Mishulchan Gavoah.*

43. *Mishnas Rebbi Aharon,* vol.1, p.45.

Bemidbar

1. Cited by Rav Frand.

2. *Emes LeYaakov.*

3. *Darash Moshe.*

4. *Torah Ladaas.*

5. Heard from Rav Alter of Chicago.

6. *Torah Ladaas.*

7. *Me'am Loez.*

8. *Yeshuos Malcho.*

9. *Talalei Oros.*

10. *Torah Ladaas.*

11. *Peninim Mishulchan Gavoah.*

12. *Talalei Oros.*

13. Heard from Rav Frand.

14. *Daas Chochmah U'Mussar.*

15. *Ohr Yechezkel,* vol. 4.

16. *Torah Ladaas.*

17. *Ohel Torah.*

18. *Peninim Mishulchan Gavoah.*

19. Ibid.

20. Ibid.

21. *Ye'aros Devash,* vol. 2, *derash* 8.

22. Heard from Rav Yosef Kaplan of Yeshivas Bais Yisroel.

23. *Talalei Oros.*

24. *Darash Moshe.*

25. *Me'am Loez.*

26. Heard in the name of Rav Aharon Kotler.

27. *Peninim Mishulchan HaGra* to *parashas Shofetim.*

28. *Chofetz Chaim al HaTorah, Maasei Lamelech.*

29. *Torah Ladaas.*

30. Stories from Rav Alter.

31. *Peninim Mishulchan Gavoah.*

32. *Haemek Davar.*

33. *Toras Moshe.*

34. *The Dubno Maggid and His Parables,* Feldheim Publishers.

35. *Peninim Mishulchan Gavoah.*

36. Ibid.

37. Ibid.

Devarim

1. Heard from Rav Mendel Weinbach.

2. *Peninim Mishulchan Gavoah.*

3. *Peninim Mishulchan HaGra.*

4. *Peninim Mishulchan Gavoah.*

5. *Peninim Mishulchan HaGra.*

6. *Torah Ladaas.*

7. Ibid.

8. *Kovetz Maamarim.*

9. *Aparion.*

10. *The Dubno Maggid and His Parables.*

11. *Talalei Oros.*

12. *Rebbi Akiva Eiger al HaTorah.*

13. *Torah Ladaas.*

14. *Talalei Oros.*

15. *Mishnas Rebbi Aharon*, vol.1, p. 246.

16. *Chochmah U'Mussar, chelek* 2.

17. *Peninim Mishulchan Gavoah.*

18. Ibid.

19. Ibid.

20. Ibid.

21. *Hamakneh* to *Kiddushin* 32b.

22. *The Dubno Maggid and His Parables.*

23. Heard from Rav Frand.

24. As explained in *Torah Ladaas.*

25. Heard from Rav Frand.

26. *Peninim Mishulchan HaGra.*

27. *Torah Ladaas.*

28. *Darash Moshe.*

29. *Talalei Oros.*

30. Rav Frand.

31. *Darash Moshe.*

32. *Biurei Rabbeinu Chaim MiVolozhin.*

33. *Peninim Mishulchan Gavoah.*

34. *Sifrei Rebbi Nosson Adler.*

35. *Peninim Mishulchan Gavoah.*

36. *Chofetz Chaim al Yamim Nora'im.*

37. *Mishlei Yaakov.*

38. *Torah Ladaas.*

39. Heard from Rav Alter of Chicago.

40. *The Dubno Maggid and His Parables.*
41. *Daas Kedoshim, derash 12.*
42. *Rebbi Akiva Eiger al HaTorah.*
43. *Haemek Davar.*